SCHNOZZOLA

Also by Gene Fowler

TRUMPET IN THE DUST

SHOE THE WILD MARE

THE GREAT MOUTHPIECE

TIMBER LINE

FATHER GOOSE

SALUTE TO YESTERDAY

THE GREAT MAGOO
(*A Play in Collaboration with Ben Hecht*)

ILLUSION IN JAVA

THE JERVIS BAY GOES DOWN
(*Poem*)

GOOD NIGHT, SWEET PRINCE

A SOLO IN TOM-TOMS

BEAU JAMES

SCHNOZZOLA

The Story of Jimmy Durante

GENE FOWLER

The Viking Press · New York

1951

Part of this book appeared serially in *Collier's*.

SET IN JANSON AND BARNUM TYPES AND
PRINTED IN U.S.A.
BY AMERICAN BOOK–KNICKERBOCKER PRESS

To

MR. BERNARD ("TOOTS") SHOR

Contents

Left: **Jimmy at the age of three.** *Below:* **Bartolomeo Durante, Jimmy's father, in his barbershop. The family lived in the same building.**

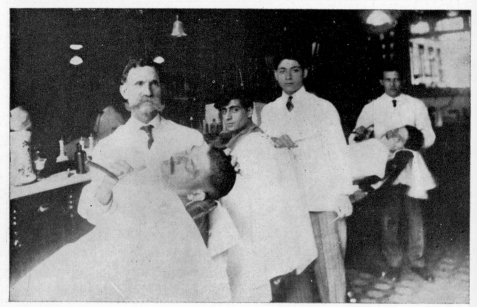

Lou Clayton, Jimmy, and Eddie Jackson at the beginning of their long partnership.

In one of his early roles.

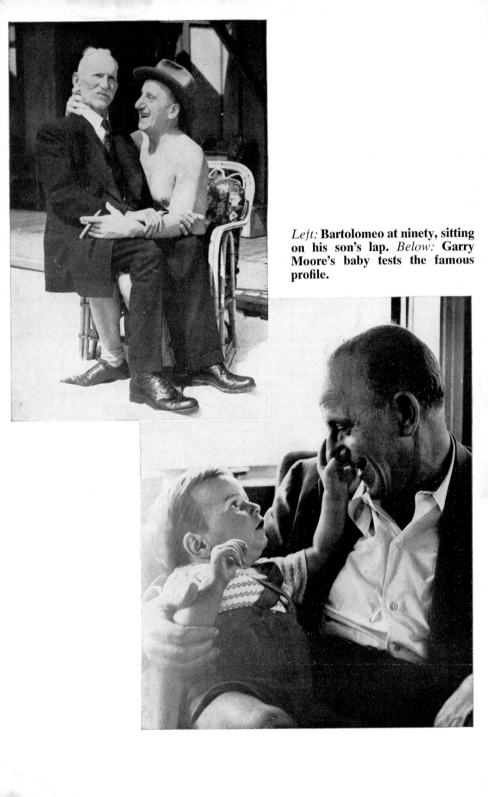

Left: **Bartolomeo at ninety, sitting on his son's lap.** *Below:* **Garry Moore's baby tests the famous profile.**

Right: Studying a script at his Beverly Hills home. Below: With his script and recording files.

Durante having tea at home after having read "Emily Postum."
(CREDIT DAN KELEHER)

Two public faces and a private one.

"Jimmy, the Well-Dressed Man."

The Durante brand of cheesecake. (CREDIT KEYSTONE PICTURES INC.)

With Don Ameche in a scene from "Cyrano de Bergerac." Jimmy never thought he would see the day when his nose had to be built up for a part.

One of Bill Baird's puppets interrupts Jimmy's act.
(CREDIT KEYSTONE PICTURES INC.)

Jimmy and Marjorie Little.

The maestro in one of his famous scenes with Helen Traubel.
(CREDIT KEYSTONE PICTURES INC.)

The last picture of Lou Clayton with Jimmy, taken on a Universal Studios lot.

As a character in Durante's Inferno. (CREDIT JOHNNY FLOREA)

Eddie, Jimmy, and Lou with Gene, their favorite author.

SCHNOZZOLA

"I don't want nobody to
put me on a pedasill."

From the sayings of
MR. JAMES DURANTE

Preview of a Nose

IN THE days of the Great Sleigh Ride, which is to say the hurly-burly 1920s, a little man with a big nose became the clown laureate of Broadway. His name was Jimmy Durante. Half hooligan and half saint, his knockabout ways and razzmataz songs exactly suited the age that gave him his early fame. There was a peculiar shine to this man, a grotesque tenderness that reached into the hearts of everyone, and the love of him has lasted through the years.

The world of the theater is a fickle one; our stage favorites fall almost as regularly as do the premiers of France. Comedians, however, fare somewhat better than others. Minstrels of the first rank seem comparatively immune to age and circumstance. When a clown excels in his profession, and his private life stays beyond blame, he engages public affection that outlasts applause.

Such a man is James Francis Durante, the Schnozzola, son of smiling old Bartolomeo Durante, the barber of Salerno.

At fifty-eight Durante has entered upon his most promising role, that of a television star. No entertainer of our time has surpassed his record in so many branches of showmanship. During the past thirty-eight years Jimmy Durante successively has been a night-club entertainer of the first class, vaudeville headliner, musical-stage principal, motion-picture actor, and radio comedian. He now has come explosively to the television screens to bring into our homes the violent though wholesome radiance of his personality at a time when good cheer seems but an old poet's remembrance and terror rides the world.

During these years Jimmy Durante has jitterbugged with Fame without seeming to know her for what she is or is not. So naïve is he, so lacking in self-esteem, that, were he a failure, the curators of the Inferiority Complex might display the Schnozzola as their classic specimen. "Sometimes," says this word-mangler, "I rake my brains to find out why people pay me all that money."

An essential goodness underlies both the weakness and the strength of the Durante character. When victimized by plain-as-day parasites of Broadway and Hollywood—and this happens with amazing frequency—the Schnozzola not only fails to confess his errors of judgment but becomes angry if someone puts in a word against the offenders. Perhaps months after Jim has been soundly rooked he will blurt out, "You know, you was dead right about that guy." But so faulty is his memory that he seldom can recall the name of the malefactor. Consequently members of his troupe are left in the dark as to the identity of the swindler or ingrate their pal has in mind.

"There are more good people than bad ones in the world," the Schnozzola says. "I don't mind if a gentleman scratches a match on the furniture, so long as he is careful to go with the grain."

Lately the Schnozzola has been wearing horn-rimmed spectacles, but he says, "I think I'll quit putting on my glasses, because everybody looks so beautiful the other way."

He rarely carries much money; if he did, it would go within the hour. When he takes a walk the Schnozz never attempts to avoid a panhandler. He will be the first to speak, cordially always, and sometimes borrows cash from companions to meet the "bite."

His generosity, together with his huge income tax, means that Durante, who made almost half a million dollars in 1950, had not a nickel left of it for his savings account. The tax code permits him to deduct fifteen per cent of his earnings for organized charities, but he actually gives away more than forty per cent. Says Jim, "I only wish I was Rockinfellow."

If his own goodness blinds him to the faults of others, causes him to misplace his trust, to waste money and energy upon shameless moochers, that same virtue has protected him against the taint of his early environment and the temptations of latter-day prosperity. At seventeen he played the piano at places frequented by gangsters, thieves, prostitutes, and murderers, but little of their wickedness rubbed off on the strangely insulated man, although the lingo of the underworld became part of his way of speech.

As "Ragtime Jimmy" he pounded the piano in Coney Island dives. His mother feared that her boy might become a drunkard, and his brothers that he would turn out to be a procurer. But he remained one of the most temperate of men, and has continued into his fifty-ninth year to regard all women as great ladies.

From the Coney Island honky-tonks he went to the cafés of Harlem, didn't know a gangster from a vestryman, and then, in the wild twenties, emerged in the midtown night spots as the mightiest clown since Grimaldi.

The assumption that Durante is a modern Grimaldi rests upon evidence drawn from the memoirs of that early nineteenth-century star of Sadlers Wells. A year after Joseph Grimaldi's death in 1837, Charles Dickens, under the *nom de plume* of "Boz," edited these memoirs and acclaimed "Little Joe" a genius of merriment.

Like Grimaldi, Durante is of Italian parentage. Grimaldi's father was a dentist and a dancing master, and Durante's a barber. The physical characteristics of Grimaldi were similar in many ways to those of the Schnozzola, even as to size. Durante stands five feet seven inches and weighs one hundred and fifty-seven pounds, with Grimaldi an inch or so and a few pounds this side of the Durante marks on rule and scale.

Grimaldi had extremely strong legs. When his shanks became enfeebled, he forever put aside the cap and bells. Durante's legs endure enormous strain. He walks with the straddling appearance of a king penguin. The man seems tireless, sure-footed, and has a strong rhythm to his stride. He keeps his legs in condition by means of systematic exercise and massage.

Without sound legs a clown becomes static. Grimaces, gestures, posturings lose their projective quality when the comedian totters upon an infirm foundation. The late W. C. Fields found out this was so, and sturdy Red Skelton takes care of his legs first and his scripts second. Durante, upon awakening each day (which he says he "starts out with a song," but actually with a prayer) stays on his back, thrusts, flexes, stretches, twists his legs, threshing the air for perhaps five minutes. Then he calls out in his sandpaper voice for hot water, prune juice, and a vitamin pill. Breakfast follows half an hour later, say, about noon.

Jimmy may read as few as two or three of his many letters and telegrams at breakfast time. Most of them he puts aside until the first of the next month. He tears up some of his correspondence absent-mindedly and frequently loses or destroys paychecks, which causes his bankers a lot of worry.

To enlarge upon the comparison of Grimaldi to Durante—great clowns born more than a century apart—each was inclined toward a moderate way of living. Grimaldi was abstemious, as is Durante, neither one ever having been intoxicated. A glass of ale with a biscuit was Grimaldi's casual refreshment. Several years ago Durante would sip an Old Fashioned to be polite, but for some time now has not tasted so much as a glass of wine.

In Durante's Beverly Hills house—a comfortable though inconspicuous residence for a Hollywood personality—a clothes closet off his den is stocked with liquor. If a guest is a moderate drinker, Durante will set out a bottle; but if Jim finds a lush in the house, he will not unlock the door to the liquor supply. For a man otherwise so generous it might seem that Jimmy is downright stingy with his whisky, as well as with his food.

He entertains at restaurants on a come-one-come-all basis and allows no one else to pick up the check; but in his home, except for several quarts of milk, soft drinks, and boxes of candy—which he cares for only when the sweets are very cold—the Durante refrigerator has the aspect of Mother Hubbard's cupboard.

Durante, as was Grimaldi, is generous, sometimes absurdly so, shortsighted in business if it touches personal loyalties, forgives to a degree that—again like Grimaldi—he has been the victim of robbers whom he could have identified to the police but would not. These traits cause a never-ending turmoil in Jim's affairs. When he tries belatedly to resolve matters, he behaves as though he were colliding with himself. The frenzied frustrations he portrays in his comical roles are but a parody of his own confusions in everyday life.

Still further comparisons of Durante to Grimaldi offer themselves. Each clown is identified with his very own song. Durante's trademark, "Inka Dinka Do," seems downright silly in title and sounds quite dull when sung by anyone other than the galvanic Jim. Similarly, one hundred and twenty years ago, Grimaldi sang "Tippety-wichitt," which suggests nothing that makes sense; but from Charles Dickens' account it proved enormously popular.

Dickens tells us that Grimaldi had "a gigantic mouth," and artist George Cruikshank's drawings bear out this description. The public of today cannot think of Durante without thinking at the same time of what critic Whitney Bolton called the cathedral of a nose that has brought Jimmy the nickname "Schnozzola."

Grimaldi's cavernous mouth caused him distress as a boy. He suffered the kind of heartache that comes to almost every sensitive child born with a real or fancied malformation. Durante's outsize nose also kept him wretched in mind for a long time.

To divert attention from his nose Jimmy has allowed his voice, a vast one to begin with, to become even more raucous than nature intended. Upon overhearing his back-yard conferences, passers-by mistakenly believe that he is preparing to slay his guests. His hurricane voice would seem that of a strongly self-confident person. Actually he is too retiring to ask simple favors or to move of his own volition into preferred positions customarily demanded by egotistical creatures of public fancy.

The story of his triumph over his ugly duckling complex, how he "snapped out of it," may bring good cheer to anyone handicapped by the vagaries of nature. Just recently he discussed his nose problem and how it had made of him "a shrinkin' violence."

"And those pimples too," he said. "And those little eyes." He flapped his arms against his thighs as he recalled those troubled days. "Every time I went down the street I'd hear, 'Lookit, the big-nose kid!' And when anybody'd stare, I'd just sneak off. Even if they said nothin', nothin' at all, I'd shrivel up and think they was sayin', 'What an ugly kid! What a monster!' And then I'd go home and cry. All through life, even when I am makin' a fortune on account of the big beak, and while I am out there on the stage laughin' and kiddin' about the nose, at no time was I ever happy about it. It was a catastrastroke!"

Not long ago Durante received a letter from a boy: "I've got a big nose, Mr. Durante. Everybody laughed at my nose. But then I saw you, Mr. Durante, in a movie. And gee! When you kept laughing about your nose, it made me feel good all over. And the other fellows call me 'Schnozz,' and I'm awful proud." Durante sat silently at the breakfast table for a while, then he called out happily to his housekeeper, Maggie Arnold, "A big load has just fallen off'n me, Maggie, like an awful curse!"

Of the frustration that cast a shadow across his childhood and lasted into middle age Durante has said, "I was hurt so deep that I made up my mind never to hurt anybody else, no matter what. I never make jokes about anybody's big ears, their stutterin', or about them being off their nut. Once I said something on the radio about people in Oklahoma not wearing shoes, a thoughtless joke. And an editor down there wrote in his paper—not mad, but just patient and kind to me—and he said lots of people in Oklahoma listened to me, and that I came into their homes each week like a welcome friend, and that maybe I'd like to know they do wear shoes, and are real nice people, just like the rest of us Americans. Well, the editor was so right; and I'll never do it again."

The key word to Durante's character, one might say, is simplicity. Simple in his religious faith, simple in his way of living, which is that of a plain American citizen, the man never changes. He has no inclination to be artificial or "smart." "If I learned how to pronounce the big words, sixty of my pals would be out of work next day, includin' myself."

In April 1951 the Schnozzola won the annual George Foster Peabody award, the most prized honor among television performers. The judges proclaimed his work the best entertainment in the field of televised comedy.

Historians of the stage have made us familiar with the names of its great actors—from David Garrick, to Edwin Booth, to, more recently, John Barrymore. However, a few men of lesser theatrical genius than those immortals stay on in the minds and affections of a mercurial public. These men have had so much love for mankind in their own natures that they could project it with electric immediacy across circus rings or stage aprons, and they have become "institutions."

Joseph Jefferson was one of these outstanding dispensers of personality, Will Rogers another. And now we have with us Jimmy Durante, the Schnozzola, whose only enemy is the King's English.

I

The Little Shaver and the Old

JIMMY DURANTE's father, Bartolomeo, lived to be ninety-three years old. He spent those years making friends.

The last twenty-one years of his life Bartolomeo became a neighborhood legend. When his wife Rosa died of a brain clot in 1921, the widower came down from his Bronx house to live out his years with his daughter, Lilian Romano. She and her husband Genaro and their three sons, Michael, Robert, and Julie, lived in a six-room frame house in the Ridgewood section of Brooklyn. Jimmy had bought the house when, shortly before his mother's death, she had expressed a desire to leave the Bronx. Genaro had contributed his share toward the purchase. Then Mrs. Durante became too ill to be moved.

Son-in-law Genaro had an inflated view of his own importance, and one day he left for Italy without too much thought of his family's welfare. Jimmy supported his sister and her young sons even before he began to make "big money."

In good times as well as bad, the younger Durante saw to it that his father had "something for the pocket." The spry old man with the white hair and the long white mustache, worn in the style of his youthful time in the Italian army, this blue-eyed old gentleman would tip his hat to the men as well as the women whom he chanced to meet during his daily strolls. A stranger or not, he would offer you a present or a coin.

When Jimmy began to make his thousands in the night clubs— beginning in 1923—he gave his father as much as fifty dollars at a time. The smiling old gentleman passed out these bills severally to the first persons he met on the street. Jim devised a more sensible plan; he made Lilian the banker, and she doled out pocket-money to her father each morning in quarters and dimes.

Shopgirls at the neighborhood five-and-ten-cent store became very fond of the old man and marveled at his clear, fair complexion. He usually was the first customer at the store of a morning. He would select handkerchiefs for the ladies whom he might meet that day, candy for the children, pencils and inexpensive wallets for the men. Although he never learned to speak much English, he understood the little jokes of the shopgirls. He would pinch their cheeks, wink, and indicate that he still was full of fire.

If Bartolomeo liked you—and the odds were long that he would—the retired barber would shave you or cut your hair, free.

Early in his Ridgewood days the sweet old fellow sought to do something for the priests of the Church of Our Lady of the Miraculous Medal. After confession one day he asked the Reverend Father Offel if he might cut the clergyman's hair. He had brought his tools of trade with him. Before Bartolomeo had dinner at the rectory he barbered the parish priest and his assistants, and he continued to perform that service until the time of his death.

During the elder Durante's visit to Hollywood in 1935 he barbered the priests at the Cathedral Chapel in his son's parish. One time, while calling on his son at the Metro-Goldwyn-Mayer Studios, the old gentleman chanced to come upon Johnny Weissmuller of the *Tarzan* films. He startled that long-haired actor—who had no idea who the old man was—with broken-English recommendations and sign-language gestures that he submit to a haircut. Bartolomeo offered to do the job gratis.

Mr. Durante had learned the barber's trade in Salerno, a town thirty miles southwest of Naples, Italy, the place of his birth in 1849. Before he left for America in his twenties, he had to sign up with a contractor's agent as a day laborer. In New York, Bartolomeo joined a construction crew on the Third Avenue El. Later on he became a nightwatchman.

"Pop told me," Jimmy recalls, "that in all the nights he stood guard on the El nobody ever stole a girder off'n him."

Mr. Durante boarded in Brooklyn with a Mr. and Mrs. Lentino, fellow immigrants from Salerno. One evening Mrs. Lentino said, "Mr. Durante, I got a beautiful sister in Italy. You send Rosa—that's her name, my sister—the ticket. If you don't like her—but you will—Mr. Lentino will give you the money back; and if you like Rosa, you get married. Yes?"

Mr. Lentino offered to advance the money for Rosa's fare, but the suitor said no. "When I'm able to pay, I'll send. I want no debts."

After a long correspondence with Bartolomeo, Rosa arrived in New York on the October day of 1886 when the Statue of Liberty was being unveiled on Bedloe's Island. She became Bartolomeo's wife soon afterward. They had four children, in this sequence: Michael, Albert, Lilian, and Jimmy.

Mrs. Durante made it possible for her husband to open a barber-shop in Brooklyn, and three of their four children were born in that borough. After the birth of Lilian in 1891 the Durantes moved to Lower Manhattan, where Bartolomeo took over a barbershop at 112 Cherry Street.

The family resided in three ground-floor rooms at the rear of the shop. The family entrance was at 90 Catherine Street, just around the corner from the Durante barbering place. The East River lay two short squares to the southeast, and the fringe of Chinatown a hundred yards or so to the north.

One heard the cries of pushcart peddlers from early morning until night, and the lion-voiced whistles of tugs and cargo vessels alongside the South Street waterfront.

Jimmy Durante was born at the Catherine Street address February 10, 1893, a short time before Grover Cleveland began his second administration as President, a year that was to bring the great financial panic. An Italian midwife delivered the fourth child of the Durantes. He was baptized at St. James Catholic Church on Oliver Street, near the birthplace of Alfred E. Smith.

During Jim's childhood the family moved upstairs to a larger apartment. "I remember cryin' my eyes out the night after we moved," Durante has said. "I was left alone. Next day my mother sent me to the butcher's, and he give me some firecrackers. The next day was the Fourth of July. The Fourth meant a big bonfire, street fightin' and shootin' guns, and big parades. Men rode up on horses to my dad's to get him to donate a shavin' cup, and if you'd be a customer to the shop he'd put your name on. Then they'd go to the saloons and get bottles of whisky, and take a ferryboat to Staten Island for target contests in the groves.

"Well, these firecrackers the butcher give me," Durante continued, "I lit a big one and it wouldn't go off. So I blow on it, and bing! My brother took me to the hospital. It was a miracle I didn't go blind."

Of the celebrations in the streets on election night, Jimmy remembers the crowds near Catherine Slip and the bonfires sometimes two stories high. Jim's father would hide his barber pole in the cellar until after the election was over.

On Saturdays Michael and Albert helped in the shop by lathering customers for the master barber. When Jim was old enough he did some lathering too, for his father intended to make him an apprentice.

When Jimmy was about ten the family moved to No. 1 Catherine Slip, where they had steam heat for the first time. Jim sold newspapers after school. He had the loudest newsboy's voice ever heard in City Hall Park. Mayor Seth Low used to send out for a paper whenever Durante's cries shook City Hall.

When Jim reached the eighth grade—as far as he got in school—his parents decided that he should take piano lessons. The boy wanted to be a ragtime piano player, but his parents thought he should learn classical music. Bartolomeo engaged Professor Fiori, a small Italian with a big black mustache and an air of authority. The professor gave his students such compositions as "Poet and Peasant," and "La Paloma."

"We used to have concerts," Durante says. "You played two hands, four hands, and wore a Buster Brown collar, and had to sit with a little girl. Holy good night! How many blue notes I hit!"

Jim's brother Albert had a job as a bookbinder's apprentice, and his other brother Michael worked for a photo-engraving firm. But the boys of the neighborhood had few ambitions other than to be policemen or firemen. Albert quit the bookbinding business, passed the examination for the police force, and remained a policeman the rest of his life. Albert, a six-footer, had a nose even longer than Jim's. Michael also quit to become a policeman but soon went back to his trade. Jim, after considering a policeman's career, chose to stay at the piano. He had no thought of becoming a theatrical figure.

Jimmy associated with "tough young characters." Among them, however, there was a "right" boy named Joey McLaughlin.

"He was a kid that would inspire you," Jim says. "He'd say, 'Go on, Jim, do this, or do that.' And with the gals of the neighborhood, he used to be a little bit of a favorite with all of them. And me, they'd be around me while I was playin' piano, you know, but they used to wind up with Joey, makin' a fuss over him and forgettin' me. It was my collosial nose and a lot of other things that made 'em winch."

One of the larger boys of the district used to torment Durante about his nose. Friend Joey said one day, "Jimmy, if he ever pipes up again, go after him." Durante fought the bully for two and a half hours and received a broken nose, a mishap that did not improve the appearance of the Schnozz.

Across the street from the Durante barbershop a politician named George Horne owned a saloon frequented by sportsmen and prize fighters. Florey Barnett, a well-known referee, drank there daily. "Jimmy," said Barnett one day, "we got a fighter from Brooklyn, and we'd like you to try out with him." The sixteen-year-old Durante was not eager to take on this veteran mauler, known as "the Kraut." But several of Jimmy's cronies were present, and Jimmy, who often did things out of pride, said, "All right."

Saloonkeeper Horne staged the Durante-Kraut bout in the sports hall above the barroom. Durante, under the *nom de guerre* of "Kid Salerno," paused on his way inside the ropes to have a word with a friend of his father's. "If you fight that tough mug tonight," said the friend, "I'll hit you right in the nose."

"I don't want to," explained Kid Salerno, "but I promised."

When the Kraut entered the ring Jim saw a scarred burly who must have been in every battle since Waterloo. A ringsider called out, "Go get him!" and, ever alert to audience reaction, Durante turned to identify the spectator. The Kraut hit Jim flush on the chin. It was Kid Salerno's last fight.

At the concert halls on Cherry Street there were dances once a week. Jim played the piano at these places for a fee of seventy-five cents a night.

When Jim went to Professor Fiori's, his mother would give him a dollar for the music lesson. On his way Durante often would meet Joey McLaughlin and other boys. They would go to a coffee place to play an Italian game of cards called "Sweep" or "Scoop." The loser bought black Italian coffee and round cakes.

Durante had but little skill at cards, then or at any other time. He would lose his dollar and go home and sit down at the piano to make a bluff at practicing. Next day Professor Fiori would come to the Durante house to complain, "I no see your boy. Where wasa the boy?"

The teacher spoke little English, so Durante was safe in protesting, "He wants me to come *twict* a week so's he can make more money out of us."

The professor fell in love with a woman much younger than himself and composed passionate letters in Italian, which he had Jim rewrite in so-called English. Durante also translated the girl's replies, reading them aloud to the professor.

The girl would send footnotes to Jimmy, and in one of them said that her suitor's December was too great a contrast to her own Maytime. The professor chanced to suspect Jim's translation of this particular postscript. "What she say there?"

"She says," Jim answered, "I'm makin' up my mind to give in this December."

The professor shrugged. "There's nothing left to do but wait."

"The girl finally met me," Jimmy recalls. "She took one look and dropped me out of her afflictions."

Jimmy quit school to take a job as driver of a one-horse coal wagon. There was a big umbrella over the driver's seat. When he came home covered with coal dust his father exclaimed, "I want you to be a player of piano; but now look at you!"

Jim quit his coal-wagon job after three days. He then went to work at a wholesale hardware store on Chambers Street. Across a narrow court there was a candy factory. The hardware-store men used to flirt with the girls across the way until their employer put up window blinds.

Durante now earned seven dollars and fifty cents a week. He had charge of the stockroom and also served as one of the several errand boys. The week before Christmas the boys appointed Jim their spokesman to ask for a raise in pay and shorter hours. They shook hands, and Durante went in to see the boss. He fell back when the great man barked out, "Leave the office!"

The next Saturday Jimmy found a slip of blue paper in his pay envelope, and on it the information: "Your services no longer are required."

Jim assembled his followers. "What's the next plan?" One fellow said, "Well, I need the job." Another said, "My mother is sick." A third one explained, "I can't quit. I been here three years." The foreman came on scene, and Jim's friends promptly sauntered off, as if they were strangers. That was his last experience as a labor leader.

The family life of the Durantes was warm and wholesome. They used to have parties on Sundays. Jim's brothers played the mandolin and guitar, and one of his cousins the piano.

Durante's parents often called his attention to the artistic tastes of his cousin. "Now look, Jimmy, why don't you be good like he is, and play classics?" Years afterward, when Jim was making a great deal of money by means of his own type of piano-playing, his cousin, still a devotee of the classics, never could find a paying job. This mystified Mr. and Mrs. Durante, who had no liking for ragtime music.

Jimmy's brother Michael was working at the American Banknote Company on Broad Street and he obtained a place there for Jimmy as glass-washer and errand boy. Jimmy used to make his bosses laugh with political speeches, such as, "Ladies and gentlemen, as I was saying, the hypocrisy of the thing is beyond control."

In the summer of 1910 Michael became ill, lost his job, and Jimmy also was discharged. The doctor suggested, "Jimmy, there's a job open at Diamond Tony's in Coney Island. Why don't you take it?"

One April day Jimmy, wearing a cap and a turtle-neck sweater—his favorite garb—went to Coney Island, to Diamond Tony's, a beer hall off Surf Avenue and Fifteenth Street, near the ocean. He went to work there at a salary of twenty-five dollars a week. He delivered his first week's pay to his mother. "Oh, Mom!" he exulted, "I'm makin' more than the barbershop!"

The next afternoon the wealthy piano player got into his father's barbershop chair. "Haircut and shave please, Mr. Durante." The old gentleman smiled, trimmed his son's hair, then gave him his first shave. Bartolomeo continued to do this service until Jim went to far-off Hollywood.

"If I'd been taking care of this boy after he got to be a Hollywood fellow," the old gentleman long afterward confided to an old crony, "he'd never lost the hair."

The Coney Island Romance

DURANTE BEGAN his Coney Island career in April of 1910, at a time when the new Mayor William J. Gaynor promised to chase all iniquity from that "nickel paradise." The Island by now was a peninsula, for a tidal creek that long ago had separated it from Brooklyn had been filled in. It was a place where New York gangsters of assorted talents took the sea air each summer season.

From Decoration Day until the autumn Mardi Gras, millions of New Yorkers visited Coney Island. Picnickers and bathers peopled the six miles of Atlantic beach on hot summer days and patronized the two great amusement centers, Fred Thompson's "Luna Park" and George Tilyou's "Steeplechase."

Into this Poor Man's Eden young Jimmy Durante came to play piano. At that time cafés such as he worked in had no orchestras, and it was not legal for patrons to dance in beer halls. A piano stood on a little platform. A musician played for the various singers, most of them males of effeminate bent. After a vocal solo, or a chorus by singing waiters, the pianist filled in with instrumental numbers until time for the artists to perform again.

Song-pluggers called each night to demonstrate ditties newly born in Tin Pan Alley. A plugger usually played the piano himself or had his own accompanist. This meant a recess for the house musician, some fifteen minutes or so for a sandwich or a flirtation.

On the street where Jimmy first worked stood eight or nine frame houses. Police reports of things that occurred inside these traps were enough to curl the hair of a cigar-store Indian. Three of these seedy seraglios belonged to Diamond Tony.

When business was slow on weathery nights, Durante loafed inside the café, read the *Police Gazette,* or played at dice or Hearts with the waiters. Diamond Tony, however, stayed outside in all sorts of weather, on the lookout for suckers. If prospects strolled his way, Tony would dash inside, clap his hands, and shout, "Come on, you!" At this signal the musician would spring to his instrument, to play furiously until the strollers either came into the place or passed it by.

Until Mayor Gaynor's successor, John Purroy Mitchel, actually purged the Island in 1914 of its larger vices, prostitutes walked of nights along Surf Avenue. It was the practice to take a pick-up to one of the cafés and then to a room above it or to some nearby house of assignation.

Several waiters at Diamond Tony's had women "in harness," as the saying was, or "on the turf," and took most of their earnings. The men entertainers, there as elsewhere on this sinful shore, as a rule had but a passive interest in the ladies, bleached or dyed their hair, and answered to the names of actresses such as Edna May, Leslie Carter, or Sarah Bernhardt. When customers arrived the waiters would sing, "Come on, there's company in the parlor. Come on down! Come on down! Come on down!"

Jimmy went to work at eight o'clock each night, seven nights a week, and stayed until six the next morning, playing piano, as he always phrased it.

The women of the streets were kind to Jimmy Durante. Their affection for him seems to have been free of the least intent to tamper with his morals. The uncritical young fellow regarded as ladies the sorry sisterhood who regularly suffered beatings or reprimands by the men who lived off them.

Concerning them, Durante says, "Some of those gals used to sit beside my piano every night at Coney, and they was really crazy about me in a way; they really was. They used to come over to me with all their troubles.

" 'Jimmy, could you loan me five dollars? I didn't make enough tonight. And I'm scared to go back to my man.'

"I'd say, 'Let me talk to him, will you?'

" 'Oh, Jimmy, no! Please don't! You don't understand.'

"So I'd draw five dollars from the boss, and the gals would always pay it back. One wouldn't have made a dime. Maybe she hadn't eaten, or wanted a loan to go out and get somethin' to eat, so she'd have the stren'th to make the money, and then she'd bring it back and give it to you. And down there, there used to be the most beautiful gal in the world, I thought. She used to sit next to the piano and have her drink.

"I don't know where she come from," Jimmy continues. "Suppose we say her name was Gladie. She was twenty or maybe nineteen, and she was beautiful, a brunette, and considered the prettiest gal on that walk. At the time she first sat down near me she had just broken up with her boy friend—a piano player too. And she used to come into the place once in a while with this guy, before they broke up, and this guy would buy wine. Boy! Buy wine at six dollars a quart, and you was a big shot when you came in there and bought wine. You know the big sportin' men in them days used to come in there and say, 'Twenty beers.' But a guy that would come in and buy wine, Holy Moe! Gladie used to sit there with her man, proud as a peacock. She used to wear them big hats, with the Bird of Paradise, and rooz on her cheeks. Oh, a gal that didn't have the big hat, a hustler, was a minor leaguer."

When Durante's mother found out where he was working she was shocked. "I come home early one mornin' and find my brothers waitin' up for me," Jimmy recalls. "And they give me the talkin' of my life. They say, 'What's the matter with you?'

" 'Why,' I says to my brothers. 'I got to make some money for the house.'

" 'You're goin' to the dogs, kid,' my brother Albert says. And Mike, he puts in, 'What do you want to be, a souse? A pimp, workin' in a dive? That's the way you're gonna wind up.' "

Jimmy insisted that he was all right at Coney. "I don't drink. I don't chase."

Durante says, "You'd picture a piano player in them days as a bum because all you could see there in a jernt was beer or whisky on the piano. But getting back to Gladie: she sat at the piano there and looked sometimes at my ring with the little yellow stone, not a big stone, but a nice stone that belonged to my mother. I never wanted to wear diamonds. But anyway my mother says, 'Wear it, Jimmy.' I don't know, it must have been worth a couple hundred, bought on time, like everything else we had. Gladie liked little melodies, and I used to play them for her. I really liked her. She was a hell of a lovely gal, and one night she says, 'Jimmy, can I borrow your ring?' "

Gladie did not come back the next night, and Jimmy did not know what to tell his mother. He did not want to say that he had lost the ring. Each night Jimmy would sit looking at the door at Diamond Tony's waiting for Gladie, and worrying.

On the fifth day Jim's mother asked, "Where's the ring?"

His brothers echoed, "Yeah, what did you do? Already you're learning to hock things."

"I loaned it to somebody," said Jimmy uneasily. "They'll give it back tonight. Don't worry."

In about two weeks back came Gladie with the ring. "And what do you think happened?" says Jim. "She hocked it to pay for a certain kind of operation."

She now had quarreled with her man and wondered if Jimmy would lend her a few dollars, which he did. He asked if he might take her home some time. She said she'd think it over.

"I was just a kid," Jimmy says. "What the hell? I'd fell in love with her. I'd thought I was in love before, but this was different. I'd go to the corner drugstore and wait there for a phone, for we had no phone at the shop. Once in a long while there would be a call, but more often there wouldn't, and I really went crazy. And then one night she came into Diamond Tony's and my heart all lit up, and I played some songs she always asked after, but when I turned and looked at her she said, 'I don't want to see you no more, Jimmy. I've gone back with my man. And I don't want ever to see you no more.' "

Jimmy lived in a tempest of yearning. Gladie no longer came to Diamond Tony's. Finally Jim went to her house and waited until she came home. "When I tried to speak to her she said in a pretty harsh way, 'Don't ever come around here no more.' "

"I don't know if it was really love," Durante comments. "It was just a new world to me. You know, in a café with the lights and the singin' and the drinkin', it was a new life. I came from grade school to this kind of a thing. After the season ended, now what do I do? I am hangin' around the drugstore where she used to call, waitin' for the phone to ring, and she'd never call. Then I get a job at the Chatham Club in New York's Chinatown. This is only about five blocks from where I lived. I says to myself, 'This is a tonier jernt, and maybe Gladie will come up here,' because she did travel around."

From eight o'clock at night until after six o'clock each morning Durante worked the rowdy Chatham Club, which was considered the "best place" in this slum district, but that was a sinister boast. It was here that Irving Berlin once worked. Among the many other cafés in the neighborhood were Nigger Mike's, and Jimmy Kelly's Mandarin across the street, and Callahan's on the corner of Pell

Street and the Bowery. Gangland's overlords and their molls found recreation there, and held underworld conferences in the back rooms.

The storied Chuck Connors brought sightseers to the Chinatown maze in the early mornings to show them opium layouts, where Chinese and sallow bums pretended to smoke the drug. "At three o'clock in the morning down there in Chinatown," Jimmy recalls, "it was like Broadway and Forty-second Street. I made more money at the Chatham Club than I've made in any jernt until I went in with my partners Eddie Jackson and Lou Clayton. The entertainers used to split two or three hundred a week on tips."

Durante's torch was still flaming high for his vanished princess. "I was workin' and waitin' for a sight of Gladie, and, as sure as fate, one mornin', who comes in as beautiful as ever? Must have been about four in the mornin'. Gladie was with her sweetheart, a new one, and they got on the floor to dance. The Chatham used to close the doors at one o'clock, pull the tables aside, and dance all night. There was no dancin' allowed in cafés in them days, but they danced at the Chatham irregardless.

"Well, my heart jumped when Gladie came in. I played one of the melodies she always liked. But she just turned her head away, without even a hello or a how-do-you-do. Gee! It broke my heart. I'd smile and look at her, but every time her head would go the other way."

Mayor Mitchel's closing-hour law greatly annoyed the proprietor of the Chatham, Mr. Shivers, who announced that he was going to run his place the way he wanted. The police came in one night to see that he closed on time. Jimmy, halfway downstairs to the barroom, heard Mr. Shivers saying to the police, "If you're going to break up the jernt, I'll break it up myself." Whereupon he threw a seltzer bottle through one mirror and then began to break all the other mirrors.

A pickpocket mob used to hang out at the Chatham Club until seven o'clock each morning, an hour when they left for "work" among the crowds on the subway. One of these pickpockets, "the Slicker," was an immaculate dresser, and, says Jimmy with his usual generosity of spirit, "a fine guy."

"There happened to be nobody upstairs one night," Jimmy recalls. "It was pretty early, about half-past eight, and there was a fellow downstairs at the bar who I'd become very chummy with, a fellow named Charlie Daw. I went downstairs to kid around with this Charlie for a while, and at the end of the bar there was a phone, and the Slicker was talkin' on the phone to his sweetheart, and he says, 'Listen'—and you know how some things stick out in your memory and you remember the dialogue—and this fellow the Slicker says, 'Listen, I gotta see you tonight. What! You got a date? I *gotta* see you tonight. If you don't see me, I'm gonna shoot myself right in the head. You don't believe it? You don't believe it! You don't, huh!' And now he's hysterical. So help me, I see him pull a gun right out of his pocket and shoot himself right in the head, topple over—but he lived. He is in the hospital, I think, for a year. The bullet goes right over his brain, I guess. And it makes me think of the torch I am carryin' for Gladie. And it makes me afraid to be in love."

As to Charlie Daw, that gentleman used to smoke opium. "And he was a hell of a good-lookin' young guy, so I watched him one night as he got on his hip. He was tryin' to coax me to take a smoke. No! No! And to this day I don't even take an asperum or no other kind of a broom ride. I watch this Charlie Daw, and he drowses off and says with a smile, 'I'll take six dozen of them blue roses, Annie.'"

Jimmy, still heartbroken about Gladie, stopped working at the Chatham. He called upon a girl friend of hers to ask if she would say a good word for him. "This girl was named Julie, and I asked her, 'Julie, can't you get her to call me? Gee, I'd like to see her.'

"And Julie says, 'Just forget about her. She's going steady with another fellow now.' Then I says, 'I don't want nothin'. I just want to see Gladie. I just want to talk to her. What the hell did I do to her?'

"And Julie says, 'Jimmy, every time you used to play piano for her, it only roused her thoughts of the other guy. Forget her, forget her. You're only a kid now.'"

Jimmy went back to Coney Island the next summer to work at Kerry Walsh's, a place across the street from Diamond Tony's. There he met a singing waiter with big brown eyes and a good voice, a boy named Eddie Cantor. Eddie and Jim became friends at once.

Of this time Jim says, "Eddie and me had lots of fun, the two of us. We seemed to match. If a guy would ask for a song, and we didn't know the song, we'd make one up on the spot. If a guy wanted 'The Hills of Kentucky,' which I didn't know or ever heard of, I'd fake a melody and Eddie would sing, 'The Hills of Kentucky are far, far away, and when you're from them hills, you're away from them hills, yes, away from them hills of Kentucky.' So the guy who'd asked for the song and slipped us a couple of bucks for it, would object, 'What the hell did you sing to me?' Then Eddie would say, 'Why, "The Hills of Kentucky." ' Then the guy would say, 'What? That ain't the words.' And Eddie would say, innocent like, 'Are there *two* of them? Well, gee, I'll ask the piano player does he know the other one.' And then we'd go on from there, and we'd make a regular routine out of it, and Eddie would say to the man, 'Oh,' he'd say, 'you must mean *this* one.' And he'd sing the title right in the guy's kisser and turn to make double talk like he's singin' some lyrics, and I'd follow him on the piano: 'Old Kentucky in the hills, which we love so dear . . .' And the guy would yell his brains out, 'Stop it! That's not it either.' He'd say, 'What are you guys? Wise guys?' Eddie, with his big brown eyes, would shed real tears and sob. 'No,' he'd cry, 'and if you want the money back, we'll give you the money back!' But as he says this he's walkin' away from the guy. The money is in his shoe already, and the guy wants his money back; but Eddie walks away too fast. What a guy, that Eddie! He's tops."

Eddie and Jimmy were pals after hours too. According to Jimmy, Cantor was very ambitious and something of a philosopher. This was the last café he worked in, and he urged Durante to go on the vaudeville stage with him, but Jimmy replied that he didn't want to go away from his piano, ever.

"Jimmy," Cantor predicted, "believe me, you're going places, but not as a piano player."

"What else can I do?" said Durante.

Once Eddie said, "I know you want to be a piano player, but piano playing is going to get you nothing. You'll be a piano player till you're a hundred years old. You gotta look further than that. People like you a whole lot. So why don't you get up on the floor and say something to the people? Make remarks while you're playing the piano?"

To this Jimmy answered, "Gee, Eddie, I wouldn't do that. I'd be afraid people would laugh at me."

Toward the end of Durante's third season at Coney Island he

gradually began to forget about Gladie. Years afterward, when he was appearing as a headliner with the vaudeville act of Clayton, Jackson, and Durante at the Palace Theatre, a frail old woman stopped the Schnozzola outside the stage door.

"Hello, Jimmy."

"Aw gee! Hello!"

"How's your mother? How's your brothers? Your sister?"

"Fine," Jimmy replied, thinking it was someone from his old neighborhood. "Except my mother passed away."

"I'm sorry, Jimmy." Then, "You know who this is?"

"Sure. You're from the neighborhood."

"I'm Gladie."

Jimmy found this hard to believe but said cordially, "Gladie! Gladie!" He then repeated it as a question, "Gladie?"

She smiled a little. "Yeah." Then she went on, "Jimmy, the reason I came is I need forty dollars for my teeth." And she began to weep. "Maybe I'd of been your wife now if I hadn't done that."

"Done what?" Jimmy patted her on the shoulder. "You didn't do anything, Gladie. Wait a minute! How do you know you'd have been my wife? The world moves around. What do we know?" Then he said sympathetically, "What have you been doin' with yourself?"

"Oh, Jim, it's been pretty rough."

Jim gave her the money to have her teeth fixed. Whenever Jimmy played New York, Gladie would call on him at least once a week for refinancing. One time, when Jim was appearing in the musical comedy *Red, Hot and Blue!* he found Gladie waiting at the stage door. "Jimmy, I need seventy dollars." She went on to explain, "The fellow I'm living with now, while he was in jail I hocked his clothes, and I gotta get them out. He's coming out of the Tombs tomorrow morning."

Durante once received a letter from Gladie in which she said that she was about to undergo an operation. The letter read in part: "I got nobody, Jimmy. And God forbid that something happens to me while I'm under the operation. I feel so alone. I don't want to get pathetic, but I don't want to go under the operation feeling alone. Would you send me some money for the operation?"

It seems that she also had written to Eddie Jackson, Jim's fellow entertainer, and asked him for a fifty. Eddie had told Jim of this touch.

Jimmy called Gladie long distance. She said, "Well, Jim! It's you. Gee! I'm glad."

"Now about this operation," said Jim. "How much did you say you need?"

"A hundred."

"You jumped the price," Jimmy objected. "You said to Eddie you needed only fifty."

But he told her he would send her a check not only for the fifty she had asked of Jackson but also the hundred she had requested of him. And she said, "God bless you, Jimmy!"

In recounting his youthful sufferings over Gladie, and how matters have changed with the years, Jimmy says, "Ain't it fantastic?" And for once he didn't mangle a big word.

III

The Alamo

RAGTIME JIMMY had played the piano in perhaps twenty places —none of them monasteries—when in 1915 the police closed the rowdiest of them all, Maxine's, in Brooklyn.

"Maxine's was so tough," Jimmy once said, "that if you took off your hat you was a sissy."

Durante was twenty-one years old. During his Brooklyn and Coney Island engagements he had become acquainted with turf touts of the Gravesend and Sheepshead Bay race tracks. He kept tipsters' sheets and the daily racing section of the *New York Morning Telegraph* on his piano and studied the form charts of the ponies as he pounded the keys.

Jim never was a successful gambler. Whenever he won a small bet he would broadcast his good luck with the gusto of one who had come into a sudden inheritance. Even in later years he seldom "bet big." His desire to have a winner, however, caused him to wager on four or five horses in a race—a system not advocated by the late Pittsburgh Phil, the most famous of all "scientific" bettors.

During his early night-club days Durante complained because neighborhood bookmakers paid off at prices considerably less than odds quoted at the track. Once a waiter decided to play a prank on Jim and informed him that he knew "a guy who'd pay the limit." Jimmy made a note of the telephone number and called it next day, not realizing that he was talking to District Attorney Edward Swann's office in the Criminal Courts Building. The dignified Mr. Swann had been campaigning against gamblers since the Black Sox baseball scandal, in which Citizen Arnold Rothstein put in the fix for the 1919 World's Series.

Durante placed several bets—or thought he had—then added, "If I win, please send the money to the café."

Jimmy's horses, as usual, lost. One of District Attorney Swann's plain-clothesmen assigned to the anti-gambling detail called at the café. Durante, mistaking him for the bookmaker, thought he had come to collect and began to count out the money. The man accused him of attempting to bribe an officer, then let him off the hook with, "On account of your brother, an up-and-up cop, I'm not going to pinch you this time. But we expect you to tell us the names of all your bookies."

"Does Macy's tell Gimbel's?" was Durante's reply to this stool-pigeon invitation.

After the police closed Maxine's in the winter of 1915 Durante began to get wrinkles in his belly, as the saying goes. New York pavements seemed unusually hard and cold to the feet of the job-seeker; men everywhere were worried, for the German Kaiser had Europe by the beard.

The unemployed musician was walking down Broadway one cold day when a friend informed him that a job might be had at the Alamo, a cabaret in Harlem. This downstairs hutch did a noisy business on West One Hundred and Twenty-fifth Street between Seventh and Eighth Avenues. It had a bar in one room and seated about two hundred persons at battered tables in another dimly lit room. The only fresh air to be had was what the customers brought in on their clothes. There was a bandstand upon which a piano player and four other instrumentalists, and various singers and dancers, performed.

"I landed the job at the Alamo," Jim says, "and I got forty-five dollars a week and tips for playing from eight o'clock at night till I was subconscious."

After Jimmy had been at the Alamo for six weeks Agent Al Davis persuaded the proprietor, Mr. Sakerson, to put Durante in charge of the so-called "big numbers." Sakerson was "the silent type," Durante says, and used to sit at a table at the rear of the unholy room, his fingers spread over his eyes. The employees believed that he was peeking at them to see who was cheating, and how much. Perhaps he sat so quietly because of a heart ailment, which sometimes sent him to a cot in a small office near the washroom.

By now it was legal to dance in cabarets, and Durante and his five-piece band were very popular with the fox-trotting ladies and gentlemen. Many customers at the Alamo were well behaved, but the big spenders were the rougher citizens who lived by their wits or by their blackjacks and firearms.

One gang leader, Big Joe Tennyson, admired the way Jimmy

Durante played the "Meadowbrook Fox Trot." It is unlikely that Mr. Tennyson was a descendant of the late poet; he lacked that delicacy of feature shown in portraits of the Victorian bard. Big Joe had worked at an iron foundry that made fire hydrants, was built on similar lines, and was just as rugged.

There was a Mrs. Tennyson, a frail little woman to whom Big Joe was passionately devoted. To celebrate the christening of their baby. Mr. Tennyson rented a piano and commanded Durante to get off the Alamo piano stool and appear at the Tennyson apartment in the Bronx. When neighbors complained to the apartment-house superintendent of the all-night brawling, Mr. Tennyson broke three of the superintendent's ribs, and also the Tennyson lease.

At the Alamo, Durante conducted piano-playing contests and weekly balloon dances. Whenever Jim got up from the piano stool to make a speech during a dance, Sakerson warned him, "Make it short! Not long!" If Jim tried to say something funny to the dancers or drinkers, the proprietor would put the clamp on him.

One evening three masked holdup men came in while Jimmy was at the piano. They flourished pistols, ordered the customers and waiters to stand against the wall, then told pianist Durante and the band to keep on playing, but loud.

"One thing they teach you in the night-club business," Jimmy says. "No matter what fights or holdups or fires or anything comes up, the band is to stay there to the end, playin' louder and louder. It's a bad piece of etiquette to leave."

Durante observed that one bandit, the largest of the three, was holding a snub-nose pistol against the ribs of the proprietor. Also, Jim recognized the voice of this masked man as that of Big Joe Tennyson.

"Strewin' etiquette to the winds," Durante says, "I leaves the bandstand. Mr. Sakerson is standing as cool as a watermelon, but I am fearin' for his bum ticker."

"Now look, partner," Durante said to the big man behind the gun, "my boss here, he has a leaky pump. Lay off!"

"Now get back to that piano, Big Nose," the bandit said through his mask, "before we shoot you right between the eyes!"

"Yes, sir." The perspiring Jim obeyed. "Would you like anythin' special?"

"Start playin', or you'll get somethin' special between the eyes!"

Durante rejoined his orchestra and played a repertoire of fox trots while the bandits took money, watches, rings, and stickpins from the guests and waiters.

At work next night Jim was called to the telephone. The speaker identified himself as the holdup man who had browbeaten Durante the night before. "In case you pegged me las' night—" the fellow began.

"Aw no, partner," Jim interrupted with a hearty lie, knowing well that it was Big Joe Tennyson. "I never seen you in my life, Never!"

"That's good, pal. Sorry I shoved you around, but you gotta learn not to get out of line. You're okay, Big Nose, and I'll be around soon to hear you play piano."

"Please do," Jim said cordially, "and bring the missus."

Durante went to the proprietor's office, where the poor fellow was lying down, his heart still jumping from last night's experience.

"What do you want?" Sakerson asked wearily.

"The stickup leader just phoned to apologize. Wasn't that swell of him?"

"Are you kidding?"

"No, and he says he'll be back."

"Oh, my God! No!"

"Only socially," Durante hastened to reassure him. "He likes to hear me play piano."

The boss turned over on his side, groaning. "Go away! Please go away. I just can't figure you out."

One early morning, when Jimmy was leaving the Alamo, two tough "admirers" of his, Footsie Vinny, who specialized in kicking out the dentures of his victims, and Archie Montis, an excellent pete man, or safeblower, accosted him with, "You're comin' with us."

"I gotta get home," Jimmy said. "My mother's had a stroke."

"Quit stallin'," said Footsie, and seized Jimmy's overcoat. "We're goin' lookin' for somebody."

"You said it," remarked Montis. "And we mean to find this certain bimbo and shoot him right in the head."

"Look, partner," Durante said to Footsie, "on the level, my ma is sick. Can I have my coat back?"

"Come on," said Footsie.

The protesting Durante accompanied them to a saloon, at the

doorway of which they were joined by a very thin but also very tough gentleman, Hacker Spinnet. He had tuberculosis and coughed a lot, hence the name Hacker.

"He ain't showed." Spinnet coughed sadly. "Musta heard you was lookin' for evens"—meaning that the prospective victim was the object of revenge.

Somewhat disappointed, the three thugs and Durante went into the saloon, where Footsie ordered drinks for everyone.

Montis asked the bartender, "Has Jig Foley been in this premises tonight?"

"No," said the bartender. "Who's it that inquires?"

It suited Mr. Montis's sense of humor to reply, "If he shows up, just tell him Jimmy Durante was in here lookin' for him." Then he added slowly, "And tell him likewise that Durante'll be back, *with a gun!*"

The terrified Jimmy slipped out of the place and went on home. Next day he learned that the saloon had been held up. He remembered that his name had been given to the bartender, and that he had last seen his overcoat draped across the bar. For some days he expected a call from the police and had a mind to grow a mustache and wear spectacles. When no one arrested him for this crime Jim asked one of his nefarious friends, the Topeka Kid, a counterfeiter, "Why do you guys always chose me for a pal?"

"Jimmy," Topeka replied, "you're the only real beauty we got in our lives. The swell tunes an' everything."

The Alamo management acquired a place on Coney Island known as the College Arms. So Jim worked winters at the Alamo and summers at the College Arms. Eventually Sakerson took over another Coney Island café on Surf Avenue, the College Inn, and closed the College Arms.

In 1915 Jim met Eddie Jackson, a high-silk-hat cakewalker and baritone. Jackson had a vaudeville partner, Eddie Murray. They appeared at Jim's invitation one night at the Alamo but failed to make the grade. It was Durante's first experience at firing performers, for him an ordeal.

"I'm sorry, fellows," he told Jackson and Murray, "but the boss just won't let you come back any more."

Eddie Jackson, born in Brooklyn of Jewish parents, was about three years younger than Durante. His father was a huckster. The family surname was so difficult to spell that an immigration officer had changed it to "Jacobs." When son Eddie became a professional, he took the name Jackson.

Eddie managed to get through the eighth grade in Public School 55 only after the principal, Professor Lapham, made a deal with him. He agreed to allow Eddie to graduate if he would learn and recite "Casey's Revenge," a sequel to "Casey at the Bat."

Jackson admired the singing of the Negro theatrical team of Williams and Walker. Bert Williams was regarded as the greatest Negro comedian of all time.

Eddie Jackson was the youngest of three brothers and two sisters. As a boy he worked after school hours, first in a confectionery store, and a year or so after his graduation in a bookbindery in the Bush Terminal Building, Brooklyn. His foreman was a young Italian named Al Capone.

Although Capone earned eighteen dollars a week and Eddie but eight, the foreman sometimes had to borrow a quarter from Jackson for the noonday box-lunch. Capone was a horse player, and not always a lucky one. Eddie at this time was "doubling" as a singing waiter on week-end nights in Canarsie, and from his tips could afford to lend money to the future gang leader. In the bookbindery days, Jackson says, Capone was a tall, slim man, and, adds Jackson, law-abiding.

There was a strike of the bookbinders, and Jackson did not return to work there, but Capone never forgot Eddie or the quarter loans. In later years, when Capone, as overlord of Chicago's gangland (traveling incognito as Al Brown), visited New York night clubs where Jackson sang, the Big Fellow would toss hundred-dollar bills at Eddie. Scarface Capone would smile and say, "He's a good boy. We used to be pals."

While Durante was at the College Inn in the summer of 1917 he again met Eddie Jackson. Jackson had split with his partner Murray and now was teamed with Miss Dot Taylor, blues singer and exponent of the shimmy, a dance craze of the time. Jackson and Taylor were appearing at Solar's Garden.

Durante like the act and booked it through Al Davis for the Alamo that winter. The team split, however, and Miss Taylor went elsewhere. Jackson went to work at the Alamo.

"Those were great days," Eddie Jackson recalls, "and the competition was terrific. We had no microphones anywhere, and you had to score every time in those noisy joints. That old school of singers had timing. Like Jolson and Sophie Tucker. They could put over songs. Jimmy always picked out my songs for me. He has an uncanny instinct for the right ones, and he is a great accompanist. He has a genius for tempo, never too fast or too slow. He keeps heating you up, and when you go on the floor with that man, you're in. He never tries to steal the show, always shares the glory, which he has plenty of. I don't read music, and Jimmy teaches the melody to me. He works awful hard, and he's serious about it."

Eddie Jackson was a nervous young man, something of a hypochondriac, and took pills whether he needed them or not. He carried a little green bottle with him at all times—smelling salts. Soon after his split with Dot Taylor he had a nervous breakdown and shook and perspired easily. Each morning after work Jim would take Eddie on long walks to soothe his nerves. One time, when they were playing the College Inn, Jim went with Eddie to his Brooklyn home. He found a great many pills and patent medicines in a bathroom cabinet and threw them out the window. Eddie's health improved temporarily.

Dixieland jazz bands were the rage in 1917. Jimmy sent down to New Orleans for a jazz combination, a five-piece band. He had a drummer by the name of Johnny Stein and a truly great clarinet player, Archie Baquet. Jimmy sometimes stood at the piano, to play with one hand for the shimmy dances and "irritate" the drummer with remarks. This was his first effort to be a comedian.

"Our band was a riot," Jimmy says. "On the level. From all over the country they used to come to hear our band. We called the combination 'Jimmy Durante's New Orleans Jazz Band,' my first big billin'."

Early in 1918 a young lady named Maud Jeanne Olson, a girl from the Middle West, wandered into the Alamo at about eight o'clock one evening. She was seeking employment as a singer. She had been sent by Al Davis to try out at the Ritz, a night club not far from the Alamo, and she had mistaken the Alamo for the Ritz.

She walked into Jimmy Durante's life to stay for as long as she lived.

I V

The Brown Taffeta Dress

M^AUD^ JEANNE OLSON was born in Toledo, Ohio, of Swedish, Scottish, and French-Canadian ancestry. During her childhood the family moved to Detroit. After her parents were divorced, she was brought up by her grandmother. Subsequently her mother remarried. Jeanne maintained good relationships with both sides of her family and with her only brother throughout her life.

She had a lyric soprano voice and sang in Midwestern vaudeville houses under the name of Maudie Jeanne. Early in 1918 she went to New York to seek a place in the show world and obtained a singing and dancing part in a Shubert production, but she sprained her ankle at dress rehearsal. The unemployed girl chanced to meet a sympathetic restaurant owner and booking agent, Sigmund Werner, a jovial Hungarian who supplied musical talent for Broadway restaurants such as Churchill's, Reisenweber's, the Kaiserhoff, and for hotels in Atlantic City. It was he who had given Rudolph Valentino his first job as a dancer. Until then Valentino had been a porter at Bustanoby's Restaurant.

At the Werner restaurant on Thirty-ninth Street Maudie Jeanne got a job singing. When she lost her voice temporarily because of a cold she became the cashier, but she showed no skill as a balancer of figures. Whenever she was short in her accounts, Mr. Werner conspired with a friend to find out just how much, and one of them would surreptitiously drop that amount in the till.

Almost every night Mr. Werner would escort Jeanne to her rooming house on Fifty-sixth Street, for he did not want an innocent girl from the Midwest to be molested. On Sundays she was a welcome guest at the Werner home. Mr. Werner's daughter Jenice remembers Jeanne as a pretty but somewhat thin young woman, with large light-brown eyes, reddish-brown hair, tiny hands and feet, and a shapely mouth. "She had the most beautiful eyelashes you ever saw, and a very sweet way of speaking. She played the piano and sang well, and was a naturally intelligent person."

32

Jeanne Olson was in her late twenties when she sought a job at the Alamo. It disturbed Durante to learn that Maudie Jeanne was a soprano—Jimmy never liked to have lyric sopranos in his shows. "Sopranos and violins always seemed a little bit sissy. We wanted noise, brasses and drums and piano."

When he accompanied Jeanne during the Alamo tryout, she asked, "Whoever told you *you* could play the piano?"

It was then that he coined the saying, "Them's the conditions that pervail."

Of their first days together Jim says, "She didn't make me mad when she panned my piano playin'. I had to laugh. When we finished work we used to go have a little bite to eat, and I'd drop her off at the door of her roomin' house, and I was really crazy about her."

One afternoon Jim asked Jeanne to go to the Hippodrome Theatre with him. Oddly enough Jimmy never had seen a play or a big musical show. He had attended burlesque shows, vaudeville, and amateur nights, but never a "regular" show. The Hippodrome was famed for its spectacles. Jimmy had asked Jeanne to meet him at the corner of Forty-third Street and Sixth Avenue. She kept the appointment, to find him wearing a cap and a turtle-neck sweater.

Jeanne seemed embarrassed. "Are you going to the show with me?"

"Why, sure," Jim replied. "Who else?"

"In that sweater and a cap?"

She turned away as he exclaimed, "Daniel Boom wore a cap!"

About this spat the Schnozzola recalls, "For the life of me I couldn't understand it. I had got tickets in the orchestra too. I tore 'em up and walked away. So after that, anytime I met her, I had a necktie on, and I never wore a cap again, which I found out to be the right thing to do when you go out, not to wear a cap or a sweater.

"Down in that neighborhood where I was born in," Durante says, "believe it or not, some people went through their whole life without ever leavin' the neighborhood, and never seein' a show. I don't think my own mother, Lord have mercy on her soul, ever left any neighborhood once she moved into it. They had their motion pictures around there, the nickelodeons, and the little dances in the neighborhood. On the East Side, the Democratic Social Club had a dance, the St. James Church had a dance: that was their form of entertainment."

Durante, New Yorker though he was, did not see a stage show until after he married; it was the Broadway musical play *Rio Rita.* "Oh, how great it was, that show!" he says. "All my life had been lived in Harlem and Coney Island and Lower Manhattan, never on the Avenue except to walk on it."

By "Avenue" Durante meant Broadway. The gentlemen of the Prohibition night clubs frequently referred to Broadway as such.

In a burlesque show near the Alamo there was a leggy performer named Toodles Z. Lemay, a lady who drank a seidel of gin at one sitting. Any man, woman, or giant who could drink a seidel of Harlem gin at one session, and still recognize the undertaker in time to avoid interment, was more rugged than Jack Dempsey or Richard the Lion-hearted.

Mademoiselle Lemay did not drink the seidel of gin in one gulp— and who could? She would sit at the Alamo after the last of her three nightly performances as a strip-teaser, sip at the gin, gargle it, and smile like a wax doll. She was very sweet on Jimmy Durante, and he had a yen for her.

Jeanne observed this flirtation of Sir James and Lady Toodles and did not like it at all. Toodles had a loud voice, in contrast to Jeanne's quiet way of speech, and when Mademoiselle Lemay and the rasping Durante conversed it sounded like the mating season of sea lions.

One night Durante returned to the bandstand after a tête-à-tête with Toodles, and Jeanne asked, "Who's your friend? From the Vanderbilts?"

"Naw," Jim replied, "just a little gal who is a good customer."

"What's she drinking there? Water?" Then, "You going out with her tonight?"

"Oh, I take her home onct in a while."

When Jimmy tried to catch Jeanne and kiss her she said, "What are you, a two-timer?"

Jim insisted that he liked Jeanne better than he did Toodles and tried to explain that he was just going out with the burlesque queen for laughs. Jeanne told him that she didn't care what he did.

Jim threatened, "You know, I can fire you."

"Then why don't you?"

"Aw," and he smiled, "I guess I'll let you stay another week."

Jimmy used to take Jeanne to a place on Lenox Avenue for coffee cakes. Eddie Jackson and other members of the troupe would go along. Jackson now was married.

"We would be sittin' ten at a table and havin' coffee, cakes, and scrambled eggs," Durante recollects, "so I'd say, 'Now, Eddie, I'm goin' out with Jeanne alone tonight, but I don't want nobody to know it but you.' Then I'd say, 'Eddie, wave your hand when I get to the cashier's desk and everyone will think I'm goin' home alone. Jeanne will come outside later to meet me on the sly.'"

"So I'd walk up to the desk and I'd tell the boss that the fellow that's goin' to wave his hand, it's a signal that he's goin' to pay the check. So Eddie would wave his hand, and when he came out, he'd get stuck. And after a few times of that, Eddie never waved his hand no more, even to this day, in a restaurant."

The boys at the Alamo played poker and dice after hours. "Fellows," Jimmy told them, "I'm rentin' a room near here. I'll take a cut of the game, and you will have a nice place to gamble."

It so happened that Jeanne moved to the apartment house in which Jimmy had rented a room for the game.

"When we started gamblin' up there," Jim says, "there was a little violin player who worked with us in the afternoon. That was when we started havin' afternoon dances at the Alamo. When he was holdin' something good, a muscle would tweak or twitch in his wrist. So whenever that happened we'd say, 'Pass.' When it came to him to declare he'd say, 'I open! I open!' So we'd all watch his wrist, and if you bet a quarter and he raised it and the muscle would go up, everybody would drop out, and sometimes he would have aces back-to-back. We called him 'the Twitch.'

"Finally he came to me one day and said, 'Why is it I can't win?' 'Well, you've gotta get the cards to win,' I said. 'I get the cards,' the Twitch shouted. 'I get 'em! I get 'em! But everybody drops out! But whenever I bluff they call me. And they ain't got nothin'. Nothin'.'"

Although Jim's was not a jealous disposition he felt green pangs whenever Jeanne flirted with other men. She did this to get even with Durante for paying attention to the lady seidel champion.

"There was an airplane flyer living at the apartment house where Jeanne lived," Jim recalls, "and where I ran the card game. This fellow would take her out for coffee, you know, take her out for breakfast, and, well, I could see 'em from the window, and the card game was never on my mind, because every minute I'd go to the window to see when she's comin' back with that cloud-chaser, and when I'd come back to the card table the guys would say, 'What's the matter with you?' and I'd say, 'I gotta look if it's rainin'!' Even on a hot day. And then when I'd see Jeanne again I'd make like as if I ain't disturbed about it, so I'd just ask her questions, like, 'Where was you? Did you enjoy yourself?' And then when she'd toss her head I'd say against my will, 'I like him. He's a nice fellow.' So she'd say at len'th, 'Yes, I had a lovely time. Grand time.' She'd build it up and up and then she'd say, 'Good night.' And I'd say, 'What's your hurry?' And she'd torment me with, 'Well, you're busy with your game—your *business*.' And I'd say I'd wind up my business and give it back to the guys. Then she'd ask, 'By the way, how's your seidel-of-gin girl friend?' Then I'd say I was only try-ing to be courteous to Miss Lemay, and Jeanne, she'd snort and say, 'Well, you can't play both ends in the middle.' Oh, gee! I sure was in love with Jeanne!"

In the winter of 1920 Jeanne complained of severe pains in her side. "Papa used to go with her from doctor to doctor," Miss Werner recalls, "and then her mother came East for the summer and later on she was operated on. Her mother Mary at that time was married to a Mr. Joseph Blenman. Jeanne liked her mother real well, and liked her father. She had a brother, Earl Olson, who had been gassed during the World War. There wasn't must differ-ence in their ages."

During Jeanne's stay at Flower Hospital the Werners met Jimmy for the first time. On New Year's Eve, Mrs. Werner lent the girl a fur coat to wear when she left the hospital to convalesce at their home. "If I ever live to have a coat like this," Jeanne said, "I'll be happy."

"You'll have a million of 'em," Durante said.

On New Year's Day Jimmy telephoned Mrs. Werner that his mother had just died. Mrs. Durante had been ill for some time, and this had been aggravated by the death of her son Michael. Jimmy had spent long hours at her bedside. Now he wondered if he might call on Jeanne after the funeral. The fact that Durante asked per-mission to visit Jeanne made an "impression" on the family.

Concerning Jeanne's feelings for Durante, Jenice Werner recalls, "Jeanne said he walked like a chimpanzee. She used to fall in be-hind him and imitate him, but he did not know this until years afterward. She was mad about him."

Upon her recovery Jeanne went to Detroit to visit her family. "While Jeanne was gone those weeks," Durante says, "we started correspondin' on close terms, and I would call her 'Toots' and she would call me 'Tootis.' And that's what we called each other all the time. She was a smart girl. Aw, what a smart girl! And a great inspiration for me."

After Jeanne returned from the Detroit visit Durante proposed to her. "And," he promised, "this here Miss Toodles Lemay is a thing of the past."

Jimmy Durante and Jeanne Olson were married June 19, 1921, at St. Malachy's Catholic Church on West Forty-ninth Street. Durante was twenty-eight years old, and Jeanne a year and several months older than he. For her wedding Jeanne bought a brown taffeta dress at a sale at Bloomingdale's. She spent the night before the ceremony at the Werners', sitting up late to alter the wedding gown.

"It was a flowered dress," Jenice Werner recalls, "and Jeanne had a large picture hat, brown, and brown shoes to go with it. Jimmy's favorite color is brown, and I think it's because Jeanne wore brown the day they were married. I remember that she sewed this dress first with her left hand and then with her right. She was ambidexterous, and we laughed because she sewed so quickly and so well. We laughed about other things, like certain words she would hesitate over. She had a bit of a French accent too, because her grandma, Mrs. Peel, was a French-Canadian."

The Alamo waiters, the singers, musicians, and Mr. Sakerson accompanied the newlyweds to the wedding party at South Beach, east of Dongan Hills on Staten Island. Bartolomeo Durante, of course, and the Romanos went along. The old ex-barber was fond of his daughter-in-law, and she of him. He gave her a rose to wear at the celebration, held in a roadhouse owned by distant relatives of the Durantes. There were ball games on the beach, Italian dishes, soups, and red wine for dinner, and then music and dancing. The next night Jimmy returned to work at the Alamo—alone.

Jimmy had astonished Jeanne by saying, "I don't want you to work any more." As to this decision Durante says, "Of course, I figured twenty-four hours together would spoil the marriage. And in most cases I think it is the truth. If a party is twenty-four hours together with each other, well, naturally I'd get on her nerves and she'd get on my nerves. And I've got an awful bad habit: instead of tellin' the truth so as not to harm nobody, I tell them little lies; you know, like not tellin' Jeanne I'm playin' cards with the boys. So I tell Jeanne I worry about her health if she works, when all the time I just don't want her to work because I'm old-fashioned. And it was a big mistake to kill off a talent like Jeanne's, as things later turned out."

Soon after their marriage the Durantes began housekeeping in a furnished room on Twenty-third Street. Later on they rented a room in a house on Ninety-fifth Street, where they shared the kitchen and bathroom with a doctor. Jeanne tired quickly of that arrangement, so Jimmy went on Sunday afternoons with his Memphis Five (as his band now was known) to Brooklyn, to earn seven dollars extra, which the Durantes put aside for rent on an apartment on West Fifty-second Street. Jeanne let rooms there because the rent was a hundred and twenty-five dollars a month, too much for Durante to pay.

Their first roomer was Jack Roth, Jimmy's new drummer, and his wife. The Roths just recently had been married. Another roomer was a poet, a stout gentleman of sixty. Mr. Bloomish wrote verses that no one would publish, so he published them himself. One of them went something like this:

> *East Wind blows from the South,*
> *South Wind blows from the West,*
> *And nobody knows where the East Wind goes*
> *When the West Wind blows from the North.*
> *Oh, the East Wind blows from the South . . .*

Jim set this to music. "I wouldn't call him a poet like Kipping or Burns, or any of them guys who I don't know at all, but he was a great gentleman, even if he was slow to pay the rent."

In the summertime when Durante and Jackson appeared at the College Inn at Coney Island, Jimmy felt the need of fresh air after working hours. He would hire a hansom cab and take drives with Jackson each morning. An old cabby, Joe Marat, kept on the lookout for Durante and his singing pal.

One morning, when Marat was full of beer, Durante gave him two cigar-store coupons instead of dollar bills. That evening Marat called at the Inn.

"Why," said Durante, "I must of made a mistake in the dark."

"Don't pay him," Jackson advised. "The man has a left-handed horse. Remember what you said last night?"

Marat said that his horse definitely was not left-handed. Durante insisted that it was. During this colloquy Jackson went to the horse's head harness, unsnapped, then criss-crossed the reins at the bit.

"Mr. Marat," said Jimmy, "I'll prove to you that your horse is a southpaw."

"You're provin' nothin' of the kind," said Marat.

"Come on, Eddie!" Durante cried as he got onto the cushions, and the cabby onto the driver's seat overhead. Marat flicked the ribbons, and his veteran nag began to violate every rule in the book of chariots.

"What'd I tell yah?" shouted Jimmy from below deck. "Your horse has blowed his cork!"

Jeanne Durante urged Jim to ask for more money at the Alamo. He was timid about this but finally asked for, and got, fifty-seven dollars. Soon afterward Jeanne advised Jim to quit the place.

"But what'll I do?" Durante asked.

"You've got to take a big step, because you have talent, and you're too big for that place up there."

In October of 1921 Durante quit the Alamo. He applied at Rector's and at Reisenweber's, and then went to work for two weeks in Brooklyn, in a café underneath the Orpheum Theatre. He tried out for two or three jobs on Broadway but missed. He returned to the Alamo, but Jeanne induced him to quit once again. Eventually he obtained a job at the Nightingale, a café at Forty-eighth Street and Broadway, where he became leader of a six-piece band.

Jim had misgivings about a Broadway debut. It was a street of mighty legends and mighty names, and he did not feel up to breaking into "the big circle." Besides, he had to wear a tuxedo, his first one, and he did not know how to loop a bow tie. Jeanne said she would tie it for him, but he had no desire to travel to and from work in a tuxedo. So a member of the Nightingale orchestra would stand behind Durante each evening to fix his bow tie.

A flirtation at this time threatened the peace and quiet of the Durante home. "I'm down at the Nightingale," Jimmy recalls. "They're not all a lot of angels, including me. There's a little gal down there by the name of Rose. You know, sometimes, whether you mean anythin' by it, it's just a flirtation, nothin' serious in it, but sometimes that's the root of things. This little gal down there, I am foolin' around with a little bit, and Jeanne happens to find out about it. Brother!

"Well, we used to get a lot of tips down there in the Nightingale. After work I'd be flirtin' with this little gal, and I'd be late home, and I'd say I am workin' extra down at my old pal Jimmy Kelly's place on Sullivan Street. The tips that I used to get from the Nightingale, I'd say this is the money I am getting from Kelly's. Another one of them little lies. After a couple of weeks Jeanne finds out the truth, and she is very much put out and I don't blame her. Believe me, she was a sincere girl. She was very, very sincere. I told her, 'Jeanne, there's nothin' to it, believe me, there's nothin' to it.'

"Anyway, I quit seeing the gal any more. And Jeanne is one strict gal, and she wants me home after I have finished work. That is one of the main things. She is alone all night, and she insists that I come home, and I think it is no more than right; and anyone will tell you, from then on after I finish work I used to go home every night."

By "every night" he meant every morning, for when Jim arrived home it was Jeanne's breakfast time. She became a lonesome bride.

"I should have let her go back to work as a singer," Jim says, "but how am I to know the future?"

V

Of Broadway and Bass Fishing

BROADWAY, the longest street in the world, goes like a daddy longlegs northward from the Battery, to carry its name even to Albany, one hundred and fifty miles away. Notwithstanding its length, the fame of Prohibition-time Broadway rested mainly upon one Mazda mile extending uptown from Forty-second Street, with side reaches from Sixth Avenue on the East to Eighth Avenue on the West. That was the Great White Way of the twenties, shabby and tin-horn in the daytime but a Babylonian mirage at night, with hanging gardens of electrical bombast. Everyone had a future on Broadway, or so it seemed, although the future lay behind most travelers on this road of gypsy guarantees.

Mindful of Eddie Cantor's opinion of mere piano players and urged by Jeanne Durante to better himself, Jimmy pointed his nose toward a Broadway career; he did not know exactly what kind. It did not occur to him that he might become an actor, a comedian. Rather he felt that he should try to write songs.

He made friends with a popular songwriter, Chris Smith. Smith had scored with several hits—among them, "You're in the Right Church but in the Wrong Pew," "Ballin' the Jack," and "He's a Cousin of Mine." A baker by trade in his native Charleston, South Carolina, Smith used to play the guitar while keeping an eye on the dough-pans.

Durante and Smith wrote "Daddy, Your Mamma Is Lonesome for You." Jeanne went with her husband to the offices of a music company, where Durante's first demonstration failed; he had the voice for a bowling alley. Jimmy asked Jeanne to sing the song for the Triangle Music Company and sold it outright for a hundred dollars.

Durante and Smith then wrote "I've Got My Habits On," a near-hit. For this Durante received almost fifteen hundred dollars in royalties, his first real money. Jeanne and he now could afford a holiday in California. Mrs. Durante's mother and stepfather, the

Blenmans, had bought a camp on the shore of Clear Lake in North-
ern California, and invited the Durantes to be their guests.

"It's thirty-six miles long, the lake is," Jimmy says. "The finest
bass fishin' in the country, and the best catfish. In the summer
there's no breeze up there, and they have millions and millions of
gnats, and we used red lights. The minute the white light is there,
the gnats come by the millions. They breed in the weeds around
the lake. The Blenmans had fifteen acres of camp grounds, fruit
trees, but they didn't do much about the trees. They just had the
camp there. And we fished. And we loved it."

From that summer in 1921 until the death of Mrs. Durante in
1943 Jimmy and Jeanne spent several pleasant seasons there. "I
haven't had much of a chance since I lost Jeanne," Jim says. "I
haven't been up there except once on a hasty visit, because I've had
my radio show in the summer, and I am busy makin' pictures, and
fulfillin' night-club engagements, and now television."

Durante last visited Clear Lake in 1946. Of the changes there he
says, "Well, it's busier. It's lost the quaintness that it had twenty or
twenty-five years back. We knew everybody. And we all used to
go out fishin', to see who'd catch the most fish. Now it's a little bit
commercial, and Mr. Carpenter, who owns the general store up
there, he is a great pal of mine, and he's still there, and while I am
away he keeps me informed about the little cottage that we had
down at the beach, away from the bigger house, so we'd have a
place to fish off there, you know, and where Jeanne and I were so
happy in the summers."

Durante now has caretakers at the cottage, for he cannot find
time to go to Clear Lake these days, and sentiment prevents his selling this place.

"We were just about two blocks from the beach, right on the
road, the main road. Jeanne bought the little house down there
from her savin's later, so we could be alone and have a place with
a rowboat and our little speedboat. Jeanne loved to fish, and her
mother was the greatest fisherman up there. It was a different life
entirely from Broadway. I'd get up in the mornin', say about eight
o'clock, have breakfast, go right out with my boat with some soda
pop and milk and some little cakes, attach the motor on the boat—
outboard motor. It's hard to fish with a speedboat because you
gotta get into the little holes, and you dassn't run your motor. You

get your motor the way you want to go and you row. Some of the fishermen up there had carpet in the boats."

Durante, who had learned to fish after a fashion off the East River docks, became an enthusiastic angler at Clear Lake, and greatly enjoys the sport both in fresh water and the deep sea.

"The bass is one of the finest fish we have," he says of his Clear Lake expeditions, "and one of the fightin'est fish we have. And the funny thing, you pull this fish out of the water, and you hate to keep 'em—that's how beautiful they are. Fresh and beautiful. Gee! Like diamonds. It was like diggin' for a diamond. And believe me, after I'd catch them, if I'd catch two or three, four- or five-pound bass, and I'd catch any more, I'd throw them back in, not to let 'em go to waste. Because we got no freezers up there, and your ice gives out, and then you gotta get down the next day to the village and get ice. Sometimes we'd cook the fish over a campfire, and they was beautiful. When they piped gas in there we got a gas stove and it was pretty modren. But we still had kerosene lamps.

"Jeanne loved that kind of life. We tried never to miss a summer the first ten years; that is, until we moved out to California, and then we'd go every chance we'd have. Funny thing, the nearer you get to a place the less you go to it.

"She liked to visit her folks. Jeanne liked plain folks, and not celebrities, and she didn't care too much for the people I met on the Avenue, but they didn't seem so rough to me, and nobody does if they are decent. The greatest memories in my life are up in Clear Lake, up at that lake with Jeanne. We lived in old clothes. I used to have an old pair of pants on and an old hat, and I think that's where I got the idea for the song 'Jimmy, the Well-dressed Man.' "

When asked if, at Clear Lake, he missed Broadway, Durante replied earnestly, "No! No! It was beautiful up there, because it represented something to us personally. And I liked it a lot. But my heart is in New York. I love the tunnel of New York." (Mr. Malaprop meant "tumult," but, come to think of it, New York does seem a tunnel at times when the pennies run out and one is alone.)

He says of the Big Town, "I love the crowd. I love the tempo of New York. It's really somethin' that no other city in the world has. What is it? Well, it keeps your mind workin'. The difference out here in California, and there in New York—I'm talkin' about Los Angeles and not San Francisco in the north—well, out here, I don't think it's the tropics, but it's somethin' like the tropics, they tell me, and you go along in a shiftless manner. Your brain don't want to function, and I guess you get lazy. But in New York you're on your toes. You're up against a kind of storm of thinkin' and doin', and your mind works, and you're on the go all the time. You're not lookin' to get out in the sun because there ain't no sun. It's like a big band playin' all the time. Like a big band. That's the way I'd describe New York. And you want to get out and get in it.

"It's like openin' a show. The crowds are comin' in, and you're ready. You're out there walkin' up and down behind the curtain. Then you're in the wings. You walk up and down the wings. Then you go in the dressin' room. You go from the make-up table to the coat hangers and chew on a cigar. You're doin' nothin', but you're ready to go on, and you're fidgety, and you're ready. Like a horse race. And the overture plays. And now you're keyed up, and you throw away your cigar, and go on. And that's the way you always are, and that's the way New York is. It's like the band is playin' all the time."

Jim and Jeanne spent three months at Clear Lake the first time and returned to New York three weeks before the season opened in September at the Nightingale. They had spent everything on their vacation trip, so Jim went one Saturday to see agent Al Davis in the Gaiety Building. While he was talking to Al a telephone call brought a request for a three-piece band to play in Freeport, Long Island.

Al turned to Durante. "Jimmy, want to take it?"

"What's it pay?"

"Ten dollars a man."

"Well," said Jimmy, "what's the combination he wants?"

"Anything you want to bring! Banjo, violin, saxophone."

While this conversation was going on a great banjo player, Strummer McLeod, a popular man on the Avenue, walked in. The Strummer owned a banjo with five strings.

Durante said, "McLeod, you want to go to Freeport tonight?"

They went down to the street to recruit a violin player. They stood in front of the Gaiety Building, where "talent" looking for jobs always gathered in the afternoons.

A boy with a violin case under his arm soon appeared on the scene, and Jimmy asked, "You workin'?"

"No," said the young fellow.

"Wanta work tonight in Freeport?"

"Sure."

Jimmy told McLeod that he was to get ten, then turned to the violinist. "I'm the leader. It ain't much of a job for you. You'll just be killing time most of the while, so you get six. That means fourteen dollars for the leader."

The kid apparently was very happy about this arrangement. "Six? Sure, I'll grab it."

"Wait a minute," Durante said. "Just to play safe, would you knock out a little tune for us?"

The young fellow brought out his violin. As a crowd gathered Jimmy said, "Come on into the hallway, partner."

The people standing around were tossing a few nickels and dimes on the sidewalk. The leader picked up these coins with hoarse thank yous but finished the audition in the privacy of the foyer.

The three artists reached Freeport that evening and found that they were to play in a back room of a saloon. They had had no rehearsals, had brought no sheet music, and didn't seem able to get together except on four tunes: "Somebody Stole My Gal," "Ida, Sweet as Apple Cider," "The Dark Town Strutters' Ball," and "Some of These Days."

The boss came over after having given them the eye for a time. "Don't you know any more numbers?"

"They're all requests," Jimmy lied.

At midnight the musicians quit. But no early Sunday trains to New York left Freeport until seven o'clock. The boss said they could sleep in a room upstairs.

When Jim asked for their money the boss said, "Oh, it's locked up now. I'll give it to you first thing in the morning."

The room assigned to the musicians had but one double bed, so the boss put up a cot and Jim gave it to the young violinist.

Durante did not awaken until ten o'clock Sunday morning. He roused the Strummer to inform him that the violinist had disappeared.

"Well, he must be downstairs getting his breakfast," the Strummer said.

"Let's hurry down before he eats too much," said Jimmy.

Downstairs Durante asked the boss two quick questions: "Where's the kid? Can we have our money?"

The boss seemed pained at the latter request. "What was that you just said?"

"The money for the trio," Durante replied. "Thirty seeds."

"Oh! So you want to collect twict?"

"What do you mean, twict?"

"The violin player early this morning tells me he's the leader," the boss said. "So I gives him the money, and he makes the seven o'clock rattler."

"Oh, what the hell!" Durante protested. "You know I am the leader."

"Whoever heard of a piano-player leader?" the boss snorted. "It's the violin that stands up, ain't it?"

Durante surrendered. "It's proposperous! But if you'll just stake us to the fare back to town, we'll call it square." To the Strummer he said, "Things like this makes a fellow more cautious."

Jim resumed work at the Nightingale late in September of 1921. One of the waiters there, Frank Nolan, also owned a little speak-easy down the street.

One evening Nolan's hole-in-the-wall was held up by Jimmy's old friend Big Joe Tennyson. Nolan made what is called a terrible beef about this catastrastroke. He went to certain guys and reported Big Joe's lack of consideration.

Tennyson regarded this as a breach of good manners and, accompanied by three of his underworld serfs, dropped in at the Nightingale. The callers were nasty-tempered fellows, expert in the use of "Tammany mittens," as the boys say when speaking of brass knuckles, and they wanted very much to part Mr. Nolan's hair.

"Nolan's not here," Durante said. "And you're killing the night's business." He begged the muscle men to leave at once, and please to spare the bric-a-brac. He pointed out that the customers were "taking an Arthur Duffy," or running for the door without pausing at the cloakroom for their hats.

Tennyson held out two one-hundred-dollar notes. "Here, Jimmy, is two bills; ring it up. I love you. You was to my christenin'. Want to see that kid tonight?"

Emphatically Durante replied, "No, and you keep the two hundred."

Tennyson beckoned to his plug-uglies, repeated again and again that he loved Jimmy, then started out of the place, saying, "Don't worry. I'll never do nothing up here, Jim. Un'nerstand? But if I ever meet that big Dago (Mr. Nolan was an Italian) on the street, I'll shoot him right in the head!"

In the summer of 1922 Jimmy got a job at Green Lake, a resort in the Catskills. Jeanne wanted to stay there with him, but he insisted that she go West to visit her mother. Jeanne shed tears over the separation, and Durante grew irritable. "You know, Toots, we're not millionaires. We gotta pay for that house."

The Durantes had bought a small place in Flushing, Long Island. Jimmy had been making a hundred and ten dollars a week, but this was reduced to a hundred when his trumpet player demanded a ten-dollar raise. Jimmy had to pay the hike out of his own pocket. Two pals, Eddie Jackson and another warbler, Lovesong Harris, chipped in from their tips to make up the difference in Jimmy's pay.

While in California, Jeanne and her stepfather made a down payment on a small house in Pasadena. Jeanne dreamed of a time when Jimmy would leave Broadway and settle down out West. She had a premonition that her husband one day would be taken away from her, not by another woman but by success. This first separation gave her a foretaste of the unhappiness and loneliness that soon would beset her. She wanted Jimmy to succeed, urged him on to procure better positions, but paradoxically feared the very success she envisioned for her man.

She was away from Jimmy for three months, which she spent partly at Clear Lake and partly at Pasadena. Jeanne worked on the Pasadena house, planted a garden, and supervised the building of a garage. She wrote Jimmy that she was crying her eyes out for him.

After January 16, 1920, when the Volstead Act became effective, speakeasies sprouted up all over the five boroughs. In the autumn of 1922 there were several thousand places that served illegal liquor behind locked doors. Many of the Manhattan speaks were clip-joints and traps, but the Broadway sector presented some thirty night clubs where society drinkers sat with reasonable safety among racketeers, thugs, mobsters, and bootleg kings. There were floor shows, pretty girls—and some not so pretty—music, and hilarity.

Texas Guinan, Harry Richman, Helen Morgan, Evelyn Nesbit, and many others had clubs listed under their names. The money of beer barons and gamblers, more often than not, financed the larger night clubs or was available for attorneys' fees to resist padlock proceedings. Big spenders might be seen at the Crillon, the Embassy, the Lido, the Forty-fifth Street Yacht Club, the Little Club, the Casanova, and scores of other bootleg havens where café society had its genesis.

At the Nightingale, waiter Frank Nolan proposed that he and Durante establish a night club. Jimmy did not like the idea. He neglected, however, to make that fact plain. And this is Durante's abiding fault, which he admits readily. He lets the other fellow believe that he is for something when, in reality, he is against it, or, at best, unsure of his own intentions. His desire to be friendly and agreeable frequently causes him to nod his head, smile, or clap a favor-seeker on the back although he has no interest whatsoever in the scheme advanced. Afterward he seems to forget all about such matters, puts off making decisions, and, when cornered at last, becomes confused. Once he does make up his reluctant mind, however, he moves with stubborn purpose and cannot be sidetracked. To everyone's amazement he then shows his "strong" side and settles things with loud pronouncements.

Nolan, mistaking Jim's hemming and hawing for acquiescence, went on the make, to use an expression of the time, and obtained some money from two of the city's bootleg liquor barons. He then went shopping for a likely site. He found a room over a garage on West Fifty-eighth Street, east of Broadway and next to the United States Rubber Company's building. The place was about twenty feet wide, a hundred deep, and had the appearance and the odor of a damp cave. There was no exit at the rear except for a rusty iron ladder. A steep and narrow stairway, used as the front entrance, was a hazardous means of descent for heavy drinkers or fugitives from a ruckus.

When Nolan reported that he was "ready to go," Durante said, "Frank, why don't you take it alone?"

Nolan grew angry. "I get the place! I put a deposit down! Do you want me to lose my money?"

"I don't care what yah do," was Jimmy's belated decision. "I don't want to go in. In the first place I got no money, and in the second, I wouldn't go in anyway, unless you took Jackson and Harris with yah."

"Why do we need them?" Nolan objected.

"I want Jackson with me."

"Well, why Harris then?"

"Because," Jim said, "they're like partners now. Let's take 'em in, and then you got your entertainment."

"Okay then."

Jeanne, home from California, objected to the night-club project. "You'll only get messed up in Prohibition, Jimmy. Please don't touch any of the money we've saved up."

Of this incident Durante says, "I didn't sleep. And where to get the money? Then down comes Frank Zaccarini, a big liquor operator, one night, and he says, 'Jimmy, I got a whole floor at the Pennsylvania Hotel. Come over to see me.' And I did, and he loans me seven hundred dollars. But I am uneasy."

Jimmy got together eight hundred dollars in all, then announced to Nolan, "I'm goin' in on one condition. Hot or cold, I want seventy-five a week. And if we don't do business, let's close up the place the first week I don't get my seventy-five."

By the time the partners had furnished their club with second-hand chairs, tables, and carpet, and had hung black curtains all around the walls and over the windows to muffle the band-playing and singing, they had nothing left to pay for an electric sign. But Durante insisted there be an electric sign. "Don't let's get like them sneakin' jernts," he said to Nolan, "with no numbers on the doors, and where they gyp all the guys, and when the guy comes back with a cop he can't prove what number he's been clipped at."

A signmaker named Brody was present at the Nightingale when word reached its proprietor over the Broadway grapevine that Durante was quitting. Brody overheard Perlman force a confession from Jimmy that he was planning to leave. Perlman denounced him as "a big-nosed ingrate" and predicted, "You'll not make a dime, so when you come crawling back, don't expect me to kiss you."

Brody volunteered to supply a sign, free of charge, for the new club. The signmaker did not know that Durante's last name ended with an "e," so the electric sign he donated read, "The Club Durant." It was generally referred to, however, as the Durant Club.

Jimmy Durante, the Cyrano of the cellars, now moved "upstairs" to lead his own band at his own place. He pounded his piano, became increasingly popular, but for the remainder of the winter season and on into spring his income seldom amounted to more than eighty or ninety dollars a week.

In the late autumn of 1923 a soft-shoe dancer, Lou Clayton, entered into Jimmy's career and his friendship.

V I

The Soft-Shoe Dancer

THREE PERSONS, above all the others in Jimmy Durante's color-ful career, had the deepest influence on him. First there was Barto-lomeo, his sweet-tempered father. The second was Jeanne, his loyal wife, who loved him possessively. The third was Lou Clayton, fiery-tempered worshiper of the Durante star. Of these three, Clay-ton became Jimmy's chief mainstay, his adviser, confidant, best friend, and sometimes severe disciplinarian. Broadway set down the love these men had one for the other as one of its outstanding miracles. There had been other great friendships, to be sure, but almost always the friends had quarreled and parted, as in the split-up of George M. Cohan and Sam Harris, two of the finest men ever to walk the storied Avenue.

Clayton had known a "tough life," and his give-and-take experi-ences were reflected in his personality. He was plain-spoken to the point of aggressiveness; but in all his dealings he was fundamen-tally just.

Clayton was born Louis Finklestein in East Brooklyn in 1887. (He chose the name Clayton when, as a vaudeville performer, he read a station sign while passing through the town of Clayton, Missouri.) His family, who were very poor, moved to Flushing, Long Island, when the boy was seven. Each afternoon he sold news-papers at a busy intersection where streetcars stopped to take on or let off passengers. It was a popular station with the newsboys, but Lou figured out a way to beat his competitors. He would start to run just as the motorman slowed down for the crossing and would leap onto the steps to sell papers before the others could get there. He was fleet of foot always and could hold his own in juvenile fistfights.

One rainy day Lou fell under the wheels of the streetcar. His right heel and the sole of that foot were torn loose as far as the big toe. The ends of the smaller toes on his left foot were all but sev-ered. At St. Catherine's Hospital surgeons took sixty-four stitches in his right foot and sewed back the ends of the toes on his mangled left foot. Gangrene developed, and the surgeons wanted to amputate his legs. The strong-minded little fellow, however, raised such a storm that the medical men decided not to operate.

During this painful time Lou's mother would go to the steps of nearby St. Catherine's Catholic Church to look up at the boy's window while she prayed for his recovery in her own Jewish Orthodox faith. While in the hospital—a period of nineteen months—Lou learned to say the Our Father and Hail Mary, and though in later years he never departed from his own beliefs, he had the greatest respect for the religions of others.

He left the hospital a cripple. He had to walk on the toes of his right foot, the heel being so tender that he could not touch it to the ground. The lame boy neglected school to go with other truants to hangouts on New York's East Side, gimping around, as he put it, and running errands. On his crippled foot he wore a specially made shoe with several layers of leather in the built-up heel.

Lou became a roustabout at a blacksmith's shop where firehorses were shod. He liked horses, rode the big animals bareback to and from the firehouse, and learned to sit the broad backs well.

The boy put to good use the skill of tying neat bow ties, which a Sister of Mercy had taught him to do out of bits of ribbon while he was in the hospital. Downtown gamblers gave him twenty-five cents each to tie their ties.

Lou had the gambling fever when he was but twelve years old. Whenever he had saved up a few dollars he would go in season to the Sheepshead Bay Race Track to bet with the bookies. There he became acquainted with hostlers and stableboys, pitched coins and played at dice with them. Eventually he got a job cleaning stalls in the early mornings, when thoroughbreds were being worked out and clocked. One horseman noticed that the crippled boy had a way with horses and suggested that he exercise one of them in the mornings. The kindly horseman had a special iron boot made for the right stirrup to accommodate Lou's lame foot.

The ambitious Lou became a good exercise boy but still kept his first job. In the stalls he made friends with a colored boy, Sunny Swinton, a lad somewhat older than he. After their morning's work was done Sunny would dance on the stable floor.

"In all my after life as a dancer and associate of great dancers," Lou Clayton said, "I never saw a boy of so much native talent in this respect. The upper part of his body was perfectly relaxed, and he never used his arms at all. He danced from the waist down and could do a roll just as easily as a drummer does with his sticks. He never lost his rhythm."

The crippled boy envied Sunny Swinton and tried to copy his steps. The polite Sunny paid no attention to Lou's lame foot. Month after month that foot became stronger. About every four weeks or so Lou was able to remove a layer of leather from his high heel. Will power and exercise overcame the lameness.

"I kept on dancing," Clayton recalled, "and finally I became pretty good. There was a big old theater, the Majestic in Brooklyn, where they had amateur dancing contests during intermissions of the plays on Saturday nights. The finalists qualified for rhythm while an old geezer player a guitar. Six colored boys were pitted against six white boys each week. The first prize was a twenty-dollar gold piece. The second prize a ten-dollar gold piece. The third prize a five."

One Saturday Lou proposed, "Let's be partners, Sunny, and try for them prizes tonight."

Sunny didn't think they would do very well but agreed to try. Charles T. Dazey's *In Old Kentucky* was the play at the Majestic. Clayton, long afterward, remembered with a smile that a three-horse race was run on treadmills on the stage, and that a horse named Queen Bess won the "race."

Lou and Sunny qualified for the amateur event. The white contestants were given the even numbers and the colored boys the odd numbers. This Saturday night Lou was Number 6 and Sunny Number 9. There were three judges, the first of whom sat in a box at one side of the stage to judge the "execution." A second judge sat on the opposite side to appraise the "style." A third judge stayed under the stage and out of sight to listen to the "rhythm." After a contest the judges would match their findings, using numbers instead of the names of contestants.

"I made two paper cones," Clayton remembered, "and put sand in them. I said to Sunny, 'Now we are all supposed to sit in a line behind the dancers till our numbers are called. You take one cone of sand, and I'll take the other. When I go into my break, you shoot a little sand under me, so I'll have something to scratch on. When you go into your dance, I'll do the same thing for you."

The sand enabled the dancers to make tremendous slides and slips.

Both Lou and Sunny received great applause. When the announcer boomed out Number 6 as the winner of first prize, the disappointed Sunny said to the official, "Look here, ain't you got that number upside down?"

The announcer told Sunny that as Number 9 he had won second prize. Outside the theater Sunny said, "Lou, you know I can dance better than you. I should of got first prize."

"What's the difference, Sunny? We got thirty dollars in all, so we'll split it right down the middle."

"Of course I worshiped him," Lou said of Sunny. "My dance, my style, and my rhythm all were his. He taught me all I knew. We later on got a job in a café, and then some vaudeville spots. One day we get a great break, an offer of a job in the Orpheum for twenty weeks in town and twenty weeks out of town. I am tickled to death at this. I tell Sunny I am signing us up for the big time. He says no. He has a girl he loves very much. He says, 'I know how to play the piano. You go on.' "

Subsequently Clayton became a headliner on the Orpheum Circuit at fifteen hundred dollars a week. One time, on a bet, he danced for three hours and ten minutes without a pause. He had endurance and guts.

By this time he had married a Brooklyn girl, Ida, a nonprofessional. Lou was quite a dandy, wore expensive clothes, custom-made boots, and spent much time in barbershops and at the haberdashers'. In 1919 he was playing the Orpheum in San Francisco, living in style at the St. Francis Hotel, and thinking about hiring a valet.

According to Clayton, he was walking down Market Street one evening after the matinee and turned into a bootblack place. As he got on the high stand and picked up a newspaper he observed that the fellow who was about to shine his shoes was a colored man with a peg leg. "After I get up on the stool and start to read racetrack selections for next day, I hear something vaguely familiar. My years of dancing made me sensitive to rhythmic sounds. The fellow shining my shoes is working the polishing rag in perfect rhythm. Not only that, but it's the rhythm of the old song, 'Virginia,' the one I danced to with soft shoes. I put aside my newspaper, and I look down and say, 'Hey, look up here a minute, partner.' "

The shoe-shiner made no response, so Clayton reached down

and pulled his chin up. It was his old friend and teacher, Sunny. Lou got down from the chair without waiting to have his other shoe shined and amazed the Greek proprietor by handing him a fin and saying, "Would you mind letting this gentleman go out with me for a while?"

Clayton took Sunny to his hotel room, opened his wardrobe trunk, and said, "Take your pick. I got all kinds of clothes."

"No, Lou," Sunny said. "I don't need a thing. I'm doing all right."

"Now look here, Sunny," Lou said, "you come with me all over the circuit, and I'll pay you double top price to keep my clothes in order, and you won't have a thing to worry about in the world."

"No, thanks," Sunny said. "I got my job in the afternoon in the shoeshine parlor and at night I play in a saloon. They can't see my peg leg behind the piano while I tap out some routines."

Sunny had passed the theater that day and seen Lou's picture in the foyer. And though Lou was shown in brown-face, the features seemed familiar. So he had gone to the matinee and wept all through the act.

"I just got to thinking," he told Clayton, "how you was a cripple the first time I met you. And here now you're the star and I'm the cripple. And I thought, all the time you was dancing up there on the stage, it really was me, because it was my style and my rhythm. And I was proud."

Clayton became one of the best soft-shoe dancers since the days of Minstrel George Primrose. Lou earned a fortune, but dissipated it by gambling, his greatest weakness.

One Sunday night in 1919, shortly after his return from the Orpheum tour, Clayton dropped in at the Folies Bergère, a cabaret over the Winter Garden at Fiftieth Street and Broadway, managed by the famous maître d'hôtel John Steinberg. Previously Steinberg had managed Reisenweber's until Prohibition went into effect.

He was the first café man in New York to institute a cover charge, twenty-five cents a plate. The purpose of this seemingly small added fee was to impress big spenders. Whenever a vain fellow called at Reisenweber's, John would say, so that the spender's guests might overhear, "No cover charge for Mr. So-and-so." Elated by this special attention, the big spender would buy more wine and order more expensive food than he had intended. And on the way out he would give psychologist Steinberg a fat five or a ten. Steinberg never accepted money from a guest on the way *in*. That would have made him seem greedily common. He also was the first to put up velvet ropes at the entrance of a New York café, a device that roused the determination of men and women who wanted most the things that seemed hardest to get.

On Sunday nights there were impromptu concerts at the Folies Bergère, put on by famous entertainers after their performances at their respective theaters. The night Clayton dropped in, Ukulele Ike Edwards was on the bill. Steinberg asked Clayton if he cared to dance for the customers. Lou was tired. He also had lost ten thousand dollars in a dice game earlier that evening. However, when Edwards began to play his ukulele and sing, Clayton's feet tapped out the lively rhythm. Then, of a sudden, he leaped up from the table, jumped across it head first, landed on his hands and then flipped to his feet, and danced to great applause.

Steinberg suggested that Lou and Ike form a vaudeville team, which they afterward did. Eventually they quarreled and separated after a fistfight in the dressing room.

Clayton had an extremely hot temper. He backed away from no one. He once fought a fister known as Kid Piper for three hours, in an old building on the site of what is now Madison Square Garden. The battlers wore skin-tight gloves in a duel which had come about after Kid Piper merely had suggested that Clayton's dice were loaded.

One autumn day in 1923 Clayton gambled all he had left of his season's earnings. His rent was due at the Hotel Alamac, where he was living with his wife Ida. Ida had a diamond ring worth perhaps two thousand dollars. Clayton asked her to lend him the ring "for a night or two" and went on to a "floating crap game." He borrowed two hundred dollars on the diamond from a "Shylock." Money-lenders at these games accommodated players who "had the shorts" for one- or two-day loans at ridiculously high rates of interest.

The secret meetings of dice players got the name of floating crap games because they moved from one hotel suite to another to escape police raids as well as holdups. A known player would go, say, to Lindy's on Broadway at Fiftieth Street, and a "steerer" would answer the whispered query, "Where's it at tonight?"

Clayton took the money borrowed on the ring and began a three-night tilt at a floating game. He ran his stake up to ninety-eight thousand dollars the second night. The third night he went broke.

One of his close friends, Benevolent Charlie, also lost heavily during this three-night session, dropping a hundred and fifty thousand dollars. But that did not worry Charlie too much. He was a multimillionaire operator in gambling and other businesses peculiar to that era of free spending.

The benevolent one received his nickname because of his good heart, his many charities, and his pleasant personality. It is said that he supported an orphanage anonymously and had financed the building of a church.

The two gentlemen of chance left the game at three o'clock that cold, cloudy morning to walk uptown. After a time Benevolent Charlie said, "What's the matter, Lou? You look so dejected and downhearted."

"Charlie, I got plenty busted. I haven't got the price of a newspaper."

"Don't worry about it," Benevolent Charlie said. "It's only money. Your life don't go with it. Let's drink a little wine somewheres and forget your sorrow. Let's go to a place where nobody knows us."

Gloomily they walked up Broadway. On the east side of Broadway and Fifty-eighth Street Clayton happened to see a little bit of a sign, and it said, "Club Durant." You had to have pretty good eyesight to see it, because it wasn't too big a sign, and he said to Benevolent Charlie, "Let's go over there. This must be a speakeasy."

Benevolent Charlie asked, "You know anybody in there?"

"No, you don't want to go any place where we know anybody."

As they got to the door the doorman said, "Hello, Clayton."

Benevolent Charlie rapped Lou behind the head. "I thought you was taking me where nobody knew us?"

"I don't know about people knowing you, Charlie, but if you took me out on the desert, I think the coyotes would come up and say, 'Hello, Clayton,' because I've been around a good many years. I was on this Avenue, Charlie, when it was a prairie, when they didn't have this kind of buildings, and they was farms along here."

"Well," said Charlie, "let's go in anyhow."

The doorman said the "word" at the locked door, and the two sleepy-eyed gentlemen walked up the ramshackle stairs. When they entered the room itself at the head of the stairs, you could have fired a cannon off, Clayton said, and it wouldn't even have hit a waiter, because there were no customers in the place.

Concerning this incident, Clayton observed, "Don't forget, this is the time in the morning when, as a rule, these places are jammed. It is now about four or four-thirty, and I walk in, and it seems as though Benevolent Charlie knows Jimmy Durante. I did not know Jimmy Durante, and I did not know Eddie Jackson, because I was a vaudevillian star, and I was in big shows on Broadway or on the road.

"We sit down at a table and order a couple of quarts of wine, Dry Monopole, and Jimmy leaves the piano and he comes over. I do know Jimmy's brother, who is on the police force, and he has a beat near the Forsythe Baths on the East Side. We all used to go to the baths, and swim and have a rubdown and stay in condition, because you never know from one minute to the next what is going to happen.

"While we are drinking our wine Jimmy comes over to Charlie to exchange salutations, just to say hello to Charlie, and Charlie exchanges salutations with him, and one word leads to another, and they start talking, and then Jimmy goes back to play the piano. Charlie says to me, after we drink a quart or two of wine, 'Sing me a song, Lou.' I says, 'What kind of a song would you like to hear?' 'Well,' he says, 'anything you'd sing would be all right with me.' "

Clayton thought for a moment, then asked, "How'd you like to hear a song by the name 'Willie the Weeper'?"

This was a song about an opium addict. Under the influence of a drug known as Chinese tobacco, or Wyoming ketchup, Willie had a dream, a very long dream, one that made him weep when he reviewed his misspent life.

"I never had a melodious voice—today what they would call crooners. Mine was one of those robust, one of those rough voices. I could carry a melody, but it wasn't any too sweet."

At the piano Clayton said to Durante, "Do you know 'Willie, the Weeper'?"

Durante looked up from the keyboard. "I don't have the pleasure; or maybe I do, but I forget just who the gentleman is."

"No, no," Clayton said, "it's a song. Do you, or do you not, know it?"

"If you'll hum a few bars of it," Durante replied, "I'll follow you. I'm pretty good at that."

There were numerous choruses to this melancholy ditty. When Clayton had finished the saga of Willie, Jimmy said that his guests should have caviar, and that everything would be on the house.

The Durant Club may have looked like a dump, and in many respects it was one, but Jimmy kept caviar and wine there for any bloods who might drop in.

At about six-thirty or seven in the morning Jimmy said to Clayton, "Lou, why don't you come in here with us?"

The swarthy and lean-jawed Clayton had what was known as a deadpan face. It showed no emotions unless he got very angry or else cared to smile. He was an earnest gambler and had to show a stoical façade when the bankroll was under attack.

Clayton cast an appraising glance at Jim. "How much money you making a week here?"

"Oh," Jimmy replied pridefully, "eighty, ninety, maybe a hundred dollars a week."

One can easily imagine how Clayton felt to hear this man telling him that he was making a maximum of one hundred dollars a week, when Lou had just lost ninety-eight thousand. He said to Jimmy, "I can't even give it any consideration at all."

"Sorry to hear that, partner," Durante said. "Didn't mean to insult you."

"Forget it," Clayton said. "And good morning."

Outside, Benevolent Charlie called a taxicab. He dropped Clayton off at the Alamac, saying, "Any time you need any money, Lou, five or ten thousand dollars, you can have it; but, remember Lou, don't take my money from me, or don't borrow my money from me, if you're going to use it to gamble with it, because I can gamble as fast as you can, and I know you're pretty fast. But if you want it for business, I wish you'd see me or call me. This week end I'm going down to Atlantic City. I'll be at the Ritz-Carlton, and I'll be back Monday. So if you want me during the duration of that time, while I'm away, just give me a call."

Next day, walking along Broadway, Clayton chanced to run into Durante. "Jim, just what did you mean by coming over last night and asking me to come into that café of yours?"

"Well," Durante replied, "I'll tell you, Lou. We've got a fellow by the name of Harry Harris. You know the people who are comin' to this place, they're not strait-laced fellows. They're fellows who are runnin' liquor mostly. And when a fellow comes in with a girl, this Lovesong Harris leans over and starts singin'—'The Oregon Trail Is Where I Found You,' or 'Melancholy Baby,' or one of them blues songs—and this Harris never looks at the fellow whatsoever. He keeps lookin' at the girl, and he keeps lookin' in the girl's eyes, or at her busts, the whole time. I'm scared one of them fellows some of these nights is goin' to get liquor in him, or flit or somethin', and he'll shoot this fellow Harris right between his two eyes. Rather than have some inflection befoul us, I'd just as leave get him out of the place, buy him out."

"How much does your place cost?"

"Well, it now stands us around ten thousand."

"Well, Jimmy, what would my end be?"

"Twenty-five per cent," Durante said, and then added, "But I don't want you to put up no cash, Lou. The rest of us will buy the fellow out and you can have twenty-five per cent of the place if you only just come in with us. You dance like nobody's business, and I know you'll do us nothin' but good."

Clayton thought this over. "Jim, I'd want to feel like as if I was coming in on an even footing. And I'm not coming in as a bully or a tough guy, and if I take twenty-five per cent, I'd just like to put up my end."

"That suits me."

"Further and more, if I do come in, I want you to know that I'm gonna be president, and I'm gonna be treasurer also, of the concern."

"That's good enough for me," Jim said. "You can handle the money. All I want to do is play piano."

Clayton decided to call upon Benevolent Charlie for some "scratch." Lou had several obligations to meet, mostly gambling debts. Gamblers do not wait complacently for money owed them. A loser is allowed but one failure to pay up, and sometimes not even that one lapse. Welshing is the deadliest of sins on Broadway.

Clayton also wished to buy some new suits, so that he would look presentable on the café floor. In those days the dapper dancer was not wearing sixty- or seventy-dollar suits. His suits cost him two to three hundred dollars each and were tailored in the Broadway fashion of wide shoulders and ample lapels.

"Jimmy," Clayton informed Durante, "I'm gonna give you

twenty-five hundred dollars, my end, and I'm stepping in and open-ing with you this coming Thursday night."

Durante has several superstitious fancies and has always regarded Thursday as his lucky day. "That's just great, Lou."

Clayton distributed cards among his friends along the Avenue. The Durant Club held only one hundred and ten patrons at a time, but after Clayton's first seven nights there he was able to give Jimmy eight hundred and ninety dollars as his share for the week, and similar dividends to Jackson and to their fourth partner, Frank Nolan.

Concerning these arrangements, Clayton said, "I also had eight hundred and ninety dollars for myself, after holding out five thou-sand dollars—which I call fall money. And I call it fall money in case anything happens. What I mean by anything happening is that I will have money to pay off the liquor that I order, or if the place happens to get knocked off by a revenue man, and in case we have any other trouble, so we can pay a lawyer or mouthpiece."

The Clayton influence almost at once affected the business. The strong-minded Lou could say "no" to a best friend. Some ob-servers thought him unduly aggressive and self-assured, but the fact was that you knew where Clayton stood at all times. He never lied. If he liked you, he let you know it by the many favors he did for you. If he didn't like you, he would tell you so at once, or else stay out of your path—and it was well that you stayed out of his. He never backed away from anything, and even the toughest of Broadway men could not intimidate him. You had to know him well before you saw him for what he was, and then you either loved and admired him, or feared and disliked him, with no in-between feelings about it. If he was your friend, you had a loyal tiger in your corner.

It so happened, then and on through the years, that Clayton's unyielding observance of his code of "don't push me around" made up for Durante's lack of purpose. Jim would shilly-shally, avoid decisions, try to please everyone, and get into all sorts of mixups. Clayton made decisions on the spot, for he was cool, sharp, and farseeing.

A great affection took root between these men. They have been called Damon and Pythias; but they were more than brotherly. As comedian Phil Silvers said of them, their loyalty and love, one for the other, seemed that of father and son.

Clayton, five or six years older than Jim, was much more mature and worldly wise. He sometimes became severely critical of Jimmy but permitted no one else to utter one word against the Schnozzola. And whenever Jimmy told Lou one of his white lies, Clayton would first scare the hell out of him and then give him paternal advice.

Not only did Clayton show executive ability as president and treasurer of the Durant Club, but he handled troublemakers with firm diplomacy. If diplomacy failed, this athletic gentleman could apply physical force. He weighed one hundred and sixty pounds but appeared much lighter; he was made of steel springs, it seemed, and had a lion-tamer's courage. When both diplomacy and physical strength could not offset the threats of a drunken customer, Clayton summoned the most persuasive of all defense weapons, the Mickey Finn.

Clayton always had in his pocket a dozen of Mr. Finn's pills. He called the sickening dose "little Michael." "Our customers were all kinds," he said, "from the elite down to the gutter bum. Because, when a person comes into your place, as long as he acts like a lady or a gentleman, that's all we required. Naturally I never would even think of going over and asking somebody, 'Would you mind telling what your vocation is?' If you wanted to come into our place to be entertained, that was good enough for us. And you could not come into our place unless we knew you, and if a person acted any other thing but a gentleman, I had little Michael ready for him.

"They called the Mickey a 'Shoo Fly.' It's not anything that puts you to sleep, like a narcotic or dope. It is known in the pharmacy world as a laxative for a horse. Being a laxative for a horse, you can imagine what it does to the anatomy of a human being if he gets boisterous or rough. And if somebody got out of line, and I didn't want a fight to start in our place and get us closed up by Uncle Sam or the local cops, I would ask the party to have a drink with me.

"In those days we served ice in a bowl, and when I spooned out a piece of ice for the rough party's drink, I'd spoon little Michael into the glass. And when that got into your glass—brother! You could be a lion singing bass, but a few minutes later I made a tenor singer out of you. You were a baby in my hands, because when Mickey worked you belonged to me. People mostly behaved themselves around me, because I got the reputation as the best Michael giver in New York City."

When Clayton joined the Durant Club he tried not to go against Jimmy's wishes. For example, a girl named Lily had the coatroom and the cigar and cigarette concession. Bighearted Jim had given Lily this privilege for nothing, instead of leasing it to some racketeer who hired girls for the purpose.

"I let Lily stay," said Clayton, "not only because Jimmy wanted it that way. I never changed many of Jim's policies. I did change one, however, right off the bat, and that was to have a drawing account of only two or three hundred dollars a week each. Whatever moneys we took in, we never would touch the pot until the first of the next month. And many a time came up, and many a spot came up, where I didn't have my rent at the hotel. But I never would touch that money in the box, because that was a rule made up amongst us, and I always was taught one thing in life, and that is, if your word is no good, you're no good, and I never wanted my partners to put the finger on me and say, 'Lou, you drew five hundred dollars. Why didn't you come and tell us, and let us draw five hundred? Because we could use five hundred the same as you can.' " Durante was quick to observe this trait of honesty in Clayton and was deeply impressed by it.

Until now Jim never had paid much attention to the cash register. Like all the other equipment at the club, it was an antique. Each evening when the club opened it contained what was called "the bank"—petty cash in the amount of five hundred dollars, to make change, because there was no tab-signing, no charge accounts, and no bookkeeping.

One morning, as president and treasurer, Clayton asked the cashier to stand aside while he checked up to see that the reading coincided with the amount of cash in the drawer. Durante was standing beside him. The ribbon showed that the club had taken in more than seven thousand dollars that night. The till, however, held seven hundred dollars less than the recorded amount. Lou asked the cashier, "Where's the rest of this money?"

The cashier consulted Frank Nolan, who offered the explanation, "This cash register is secondhand, and it jumps."

Clayton looked at Jimmy. "We're over seven hundred dollars short here, and the answer that I get from our partner Mr. Nolan is that the register jumps."

"Well," Jimmy said, "let's get somebody to fix it."

"Never mind that," said Clayton. "Let's see what happens to-morrow. Let's see if it will jump again."

The next morning the cash register once again was short of funds. Clayton asked the cashier about this discrepancy. Nolan interposed, "The register jumps. Like I told you last night."

Durante took the initiative. "Lou, go open the front windows."

There were two large windows overlooking Fifty-eighth Street, with panes painted green to hide the light from snoopers out in the street, and covered by black curtains.

Clayton went to the windows, parted the curtains, then opened one creaking window. Jimmy said, "Look out and see that nobody is passing."

"What are your intentions, Jimmy?" Clayton inquired.

"Just do what you're asked," Jimmy answered.

Clayton gazed out on the early morning street. Nobody was to be seen. Durante picked up the cash register and threw it out the window. "I'll tell you somethin', Lou," he said, "that damned register ain't never gonna jump no more!"

During the first week at the Durant Club, Clayton decided to take Jim away from the piano and put him on the floor as a comedian. As an employee at other clubs, whenever Jimmy had tried to say anything the bosses had stopped him. Now he was a boss himself. He could do what he wanted to do. President and Treasurer Clayton said so. Clayton hired a piano player called "Sticks" to play the Durante songs.

At the beginning of the floor show Eddie Jackson would be at one end of the room, or in the kitchen, and Jim would be at the other end. They used little megaphones, the kind that Rudy Vallee later on employed for his crooning. They would sing "echo songs." For example, when Jimmy sang, "I love . . . ," Jackson, from the other end of the room or the kitchen, would repeat after Jim the words, "I love . . ." And they went on with, "I love . . . I love . . . the birds . . . the birds . . . the bees . . . the bees . . . the trees . . . the trees . . ."

Then Clayton would slide onto the floor. He put Jim between himself and Jackson in the trio. They sang and improvised business and jokes, setting a pattern for night-club comedy that was imitated widely but never surpassed.

At about this time Durante wrote a song with Walter Winchell and Chick Endor, "She doesn't like a shady joke, she doesn't hike, she doesn't smoke," etc. These virtues were revealed in the punch line to belong to a cow.

And now Clayton coined the nickname for Durante of "Schnozzle," or "Schnozzola," or simply, "Schnozz." Durante says, "Clayton would run out to the kitchen, pretendin' to look for me, and when he found me he would grab me by the beak and yell that he has discovered oil. Then Jackson would ask where, and Clayton would say, 'In Jimmy's Schnozz.' Then Jackson would grab me by the nose, and then little by little we graduated, got bits here and there, and added to our routine. I wrote songs the first year like 'Jimmy, the Well-dressed Man,' and afterward, 'I Ups to Him and He Ups to Me,' and 'Who'll Be With You When I'm Far Away.' A man named Farrell wrote a tune like it, and I went and got the words a little closer to that melody, and then we got together and wrote the whole song over. Farrell was a colored fellow and a clever man."

Durante brought "jumping" music to the night clubs, tunes as distinctive as those of George M. Cohan, a Broadway saint who had two characteristics in common with Jim, lovability and vivacity.

Jeanne Durante had misgivings about Jim's taking in a new partner. In face of the huge returns coming in, she could not very well find fault with Clayton's efficiency or vision. She was polite to him, but did not feel close to him, ever. For his part, Lou liked Jeanne very much. He went out of his way to win her approval. But, as he himself put it, "No dice."

Notwithstanding his upbringing in poverty-ridden neighborhoods and his long association with gamblers and rough characters, Clayton had elegant manners, especially with women, most of whom admired him very much. He tried at all times to observe what he called the niceties of behavior when he was with women, and had style and class, as Broadway viewed it.

Jeanne was able to buy her first car, a runabout, and pay off the mortgage on the Flushing house. She had almost everything that a wife could want—except Jim. The success of the club kept her husband away from home more and more. He would not return to suburban Flushing until eight or eight-thirty of a morning. Then he would have breakfast and go to bed. Jeanne would have all day with Jim—but he would be asleep in a darkened bedroom. In the afternoons he would get up and go straight to the club.

Jeanne became extremely nervous and lonely. The Durante home stood in a wooded section of Flushing, the last house on the street. A fear of the darkness and the night caused Jeanne to lock her bedroom door while Jim was away. She would call the club when she wanted to go to the bathroom, and ask Jim to stay on the phone until she returned to bed, to tell him that she was all right. Sometimes these calls came in while Jim was out on the floor, singing or clowning.

The Durantes both tried to be patient, but Jeanne's growing nervousness, as well as her ill health, was not conducive to the happiness that she had sought in marriage.

"She also worried about whether I'd go out again," Durante says. "You know, on another flirtation. And I'd say, 'Toots, don't worry. There couldn't be.' And there was a lot of time on her hands. And she'd say, 'Jimmy, let's give this all up. Let's go to California.' "

Not only did Jim belong to the public, but Jeanne felt that she was being replaced, not by another woman to be sure, but by a man with great influence on Jim. The gentle Jeanne felt that gradually her man was drifting away from her. It was not that he had ceased to love her or she him, but she was being denied an active part in his life.

When Jimmy refused to permit Jeanne to continue her stage career, the disappointed young woman had aspired to become his business adviser. But Clayton usurped—to Jeanne's way of thinking—that place.

Jeanne still made an effort to become useful to her husband as a counselor. Among other things, she suggested that her old friend Sig Werner, the restaurant man, be permitted to run the kitchen at the club. "The people you've got," Jeanne told her husband, "are robbing you in the kitchen. You just go in early some night and see."

Jimmy did as Jeanne suggested. The waiters and busboys were sitting around eating steaks. The icebox door was open. He told Clayton of this, and Lou put a lock on the iceboxes. Lou refused, however, to give the restaurant management to Werner. Frank Nolan ran the kitchen.

This "veto" by Clayton hurt Jeanne's feelings, and it did not lessen her prejudice against him. Nor did Jimmy help matters by telling Jeanne little lies, saying that he was going to ask the Shuberts or the Albee theatrical managers to find work for her on the stage. He did not sense that Jeanne had a secret desire to work as a singer at his club. He also could not see that he was well on his own way to becoming a great entertainer. Even if he had, he would not have countenanced Jeanne's presence as a fellow performer.

"And that," he says, "was the biggest mistake I ever made."

Unknown to Jim, his wife became so unnerved and ill that she drank during her lonely nights. She had not, by nature or desire, been a drinking person; but in her extremity she sought release. In Clayton she obviously saw a rival, and she behaved as though she were caught in some strangely set trap, a triangle.

One June night the trio of Clayton, Jackson, and Durante went with their respective wives to Coney Island, to look for replacements in the Durant Club for the fall season. The Durantes had postponed their trip to California to allow Jimmy to play an early summer engagement booked by Clayton.

The wives of the three men were friendly but never became intimate. When the trio went on tour the wives seldom accompanied them. The cool-brained Clayton was aware that some of the most successful theatrical teams on Broadway had been disrupted by the petty jealousies and quarrels of wives. "We'll not risk that," he decreed. "This is a man's team, and a great team, and we'll not risk busting it wide open just because some dame, good or bad, don't like the color of somebody's eyes, or who sits where at dinner."

At Coney Island the Durante party heard a band doing a ballyhoo from a window of the Ritz, an upstairs joint on a Bowery corner. They went in and ordered soft drinks. A member of the band sneered, "Society people!" The leader, pianist Harry Donnelly, said, "No, fellows, that's Jimmy Durante. Let's fake one of his songs in the key of C."

They played "I Ain't Never Had Nobody Crazy over Me," and Jeanne Durante, her happiness revived for this little time, sang at the table. Jimmy, Lou, and Eddie got on the floor and did a turn.

After the impromptu act Durante asked Harry Donnelly if he would work that winter at the Durant Club. Jimmy had observed that Donnelly was an expert on cues and quick to follow a performer without rehearsal or discussion of "business." Donnelly also was a most amiable man, and in appearance resembled comedian W. C. Fields.

When Donnelly mentioned salary Clayton said, "The salary will be good, but when you work for us, never go home in the morning without first asking permission."

Donnelly took four members of his band with him to the Durant Club the next season. Jimmy already had a drummer, Jack Roth, a Long Island fellow of sound rhythm and an easy disposition. Roth, who had been with Jimmy since the Alamo, stayed with Durante, except for a few brief times, for all the years that followed. Donnelly remained with Jimmy until Durante went West to live.

The Durante band members looked like mugs and dressed that way. They played in a rowdy fashion, giving an impression of having an all-night jam session, with an every-man-for-himself mood. Clayton, Jackson, and Durante bounced many laughs off the bandsmen.

Donnelly remembers when Jack Roth left Durante's band temporarily to travel with Sophie Tucker's act. Jim hired another drummer. When Jack returned to New York, Durante tried to get up courage to fire the substitute drummer.

Donnelly was walking up the stairs to a rehearsal of the band when he heard Jimmy's voice and paused to eavesdrop.

"You see, Joe," Donnelly heard Durante say in a very loud tone, "I know you are a class-A drummer. But every onct in a while there has to be changes made, even in my business. Ross Gorman made a change, and now he's got his own band the way he wants. Henry Busse left Paul Whiteman—another change—so Busse can have his own band. And now it hurts me to tell you we've decided to make a change, and it has to be you. Sorry, partner, but get out!"

Donnelly was amazed to hear Durante speak so forthrightly, for everyone knew that Jimmy always tried to spare the feelings of colleagues. After a pause Durante began again, this time roaring even louder than before, "Don't gimme that, Joe! All right! All right! But my hands is tied. It's two weeks' notice, and that's final!"

Donnelly entered the room to find Durante alone. The softhearted fellow had been rehearsing to fire his drummer.

At the Durant Club the routines grew, the songs multiplied, and the madcap didos of the trio of Clayton, Jackson, and Durante became the talk of Broadway. Sime Silverman, founder and editor of the trade weekly *Variety*, played a major part in the "discovery" of these men, whom he called in his paper "The Three Sawdust Bums."

George M. Cohan, a man who seldom drank or went to night clubs, was induced by Arthur "Bugs" Baer, Bill Halligan, Damon Runyon, and two or three other cronies to visit the Durant Club. Cohan was so enchanted by the show that, on his way out, he put a hundred-dollar bill down and said, "Ring this up on the register."

The stars of Broadway productions would visit the club after their own performances, and of course the principal racketeers of the town made it their headquarters. Columnists Walter Winchell, Ed Sullivan, Jack Lait, Louis Sobol, Dan Parker, Bill Corum, and many others began to write about the "Three Musketeers of Broadway." Runyon was particularly fond of Clayton. Several of his race-track stories were based on incidents in Lou's life. And, indeed, Clayton's way of speaking cropped out in the dialogue of several Runyon characters.

As for Sime Silverman, that editor visited the club almost every night. He would buy all the cigars and cigarettes that Lily, the coatroom girl, had in stock, then distribute them to other patrons. Sime would spend as much as three or four hundred dollars a night.

Looking back on his long partnership and friendship with Durante, Clayton said, "I want to make it very plain and emphatic that during all those years of our association and partnership, there wasn't a piece of paper written between Durante and myself. There never has been a contract. We have cut up millions of dollars. Never at any time did Jimmy ever ask me for a contract, and at no time did I ever ask Jimmy for a scrap of paper to show our association together. He knew the ethics as I did, and that it was by the nod of our heads we did our business. And one time Jimmy gave me a picture of himself, and on that picture, which I treasure dearly, he inscribed on it ahead of his signature the only contract you might say that we ever had:

" 'To My Dear Pal and Partner, Lou, until Death Do We Part.' "

The Three Sawdust Bums

Durante's nose was on its way to becoming the most widely known promontory this side of Gibraltar. Eddie Jackson, Lou Clayton, and Jimmy Durante worked all night like jumping-jacks and prospered. They never quarreled about billing. Clayton's name stayed in the lead because he wanted it that way, and the others felt that the title Clayton, Jackson, and Durante looked well in print and sounded just fine in Broadway's big ears.

The trio had no paid publicity agent. Columnists gunned the woods for them. In each issue of *Variety*, Sime Silverman published a story telling of the capers of the "Three Sawdust Bums" in the smoke-fogged room over the garage on West Fifty-eighth Street.

The Durant Club paid not a penny for police protection, an amazing circumstance during Prohibition, when many law-enforcement officers, both national and local, had eczema of the palms. The "square" cops—and there were several—admired the partners for their refusal to put in the fix. Certain crooked officers, however, vowed they would get evidence against the Durant Club.

Before a speakeasy could be padlocked under the law, proof had to be established that liquor was served to, and paid for, by an investigator. Samples of seized liquor had to be brought to court and identified as such, and snoopers carried small flasks to collect the evidence.

Clayton kept a schoolmaster's eye on Durante, for the Schnozzola might let just anyone into the club. Jimmy promised to be careful and figuratively kissed the Book never, under any circumstance, to buy anyone a drink.

Whenever brawls started among the patrons Jimmy and Eddie would run downstairs and out of the building. Durante was peace-loving, and Eddie's nerves leaped when killers such as Mad Dog Coll and Legs Diamond patronized the club. The deserters would go to the all-night Child's Restaurant at Columbus Circle for coffee and cake and stay there until Clayton telephoned that the storm signals had been hauled down.

To prevent gunplay Clayton ruled that all marksmen turn in their sidearms upon entering. He reminded pistol-packers that if frisking police officers were to find guns on their persons, it might mean prison for violation of the Sullivan Act, which prohibited the carrying of firearms without permits. Detectives occasionally searched the Broadway shot-putters but discovered no iron evidence at the Durant Club.

The hiding place for pistols was a long box behind the bar in which the bartenders kept cracked ice. A gangster would surrender his pistol to Clayton in the washroom. He in turn would go behind the bar and bury the weapon in ice. He referred to these guns as "frappéd artillery."

Had it not been for this precaution, it is quite likely that shootings would have occurred at the Durant Club, as happened elsewhere on the Avenue, when mobsters chanced to run into enemies at play.

The club had two "plants," a plant being the hiding place where the owners stored illegal liquor. The big plant, with dozens of cases of bootleg liquor, was in Nolan's apartment, ten blocks uptown from the club. The little plant lay beneath a trapdoor of the cloakroom at the club. The checkroom girl stood innocently upon a rug covering the hatch. Five cases of Scotch and rye and bourbon, and three cases of assorted wines were kept on hand. When the supply ran low, Nolan would taxi to his apartment for replacements.

Traders in liquor bought and sold bootleg booze with few bookkeeping worries. A buyer would meet the seller in a hotel room or café to make a deal. If a man wanted five hundred cases of Scotch, the seller wrote the number twice on a dollar bill—the first entry on one side of the note's face and the duplicate numerals at the opposite side. The seller then tore the bill in halves. The buyer kept one part and the seller the other. The buyer paid cash in advance, and his half of the dollar bill was the receipt.

A truckman called at an appointed place, whether at a berthed boat just in from Rum Row off Sandy Hook, or a "drop" at a garage. His passport was his boss's part of the torn dollar bill. When this matched the other half of the bill, the liquor was surrendered without question. There were no records, receipts, or memoranda of any kind to incriminate buyers or sellers of bootleg booze.

It was a decade of loose money and blazing speculation on Wall Street. Along Broadway some of the newsboys had rolls of currency, and Avenue taxi drivers seldom carried less than a hundred dollars for change of "C" notes. There was much poverty and hardship elsewhere in the Great City, and beggars played fiddles or whined out above the laughter of Broadway, but in the main the Avenue seemed a midway of some huge and prospering carnival, where no one spoke of a tomorrow. The time was always a golden now.

Early in the mornings Wall Street brokers would stop in at the Durant Club to breakfast on ham and eggs and champagne before going downtown to count their paper profits. Racketeers, relaxing late at night, arrived with their Lollies dressed in mink coats and wearing diamonds. They drove to and from the night spots in expensive cars, with liveried bodyguards at the steering wheels.

Many of the easy-money boys took up golf. Lou Clayton learned the game. As in other matters that enlisted his attention, he studied it intensively. Whenever the weather permitted he would leave the club of an early morning and, instead of sleeping, go to a Westchester or Long Island golf course. He practiced until his game became that of a professional.

Clayton was left-handed. He began to play golf that way but soon decided to change to the right-hand clubs. When he felt ready, he began to bet on his golf rounds, or on separate holes, and some years won as much as fifty or sixty thousand dollars on the links.

Durante and Jackson became mildly enthused about golf, but neither excelled at this sport. Whenever Durante hit a ball into the rough he would refuse to play it. He would sneak back onto the fairway, surreptitiously drop another ball, and go on from there. His companions knew of course that he was cheating but let the happy trickster get away with it. Jimmy would carry but three clubs, all irons, and no golf bag at all.

Harry K. Thaw was an occasional customer at the Durant Club. Clayton felt apprehensive when this graduate of Matteawan Asylum arrived. He was not sure what might happen were Thaw to get out of line, as when he shot and killed architect Stanford White on the roof of the old Madison Square Garden back in 1906.

The Durant Club charged twenty-five dollars for a quart of

wine, and there was a four-dollar cover charge. The night of Thaw's first visit he ordered a quart of Mumm's. The waiter was about to open it when Thaw took the bottle from the server's hands, explaining that it was unlucky to have anyone open wine for him. Thaw put a hundred-dollar bill on the tray. The waiter gave him the seventy-one dollars change. Thaw said, "Keep it."

This may seem a sizable tip, but many customers strewed money at the Durant Club. Jack Kearns, manager of pugilists Jack Dempsey and Mickey Walker, frequently gave Clayton as much as five hundred dollars for singing a repertoire of ten torch songs.

Proprietors of other famous clubs visited the Durant Club in the early morning hours, among them Texas Guinan. She said she wanted to get a laugh before going to bed. Tex lived in Greenwich Village, and notwithstanding her wild manners in public, she was an abstemious lass. In her private life—what there was of it—she lived as quietly as a schoolmarm.

Patrons were greeted with informal, boisterous songs as they came into the room. Jimmy had written "Skeet, Skat," a song touched with the Durante lunacy. Sometimes, when a woman and man came in, the entertainers would interrupt a routine to sing, "Skeet, skat, skat, skoo. Skeet, skat, skat, skoo. Here comes a friend of mine. Sit him down at table nine. See that he don't buy no wine, Oh, skeet, skat, skat, skoo, skoot, skee, skat, ska . . ."

Jim would take the fellow's arm, and Clayton the girl's, and escort them to widely separated tables. Jimmy would sit down with the man, suddenly pretend surprise, and say, "What happened? I come in with a girl." And then they would seat the man and the girl together, while everyone laughed.

Off-color jokes never entered their routines. None of the partners had a "dirty mind," and Jimmy still deplores the actions of comedians who court applause by telling "blue" jokes.

"We made what to us was laughter all the time," Clayton said. "We wanted to keep you in the mood. When we got tired and felt we wanted to get off the floor, the orchestra, which we later enlarged to twelve pieces, would play. It was intimate fun. You were right up against one another. You'd come in at eleven o'clock and leave at seven o'clock the next morning. You wouldn't know where the night flew by, because at no time was there a lull in the place, and that's how we got sayings like 'There's a lull in the place.' 'What happened? The piano must be busted.' And those things were cues, and we'd start doing something. Eddie'd get out there and start singing a song. Or I'd get out there and fly across the floor. We never stole the play from one another while a partner was doing his turn. We knew how to build each other up."

Many persons now well known to the entertainment world visited the Durant. George Raft, at that time a Charleston dancer, was there almost every night. Durante once said to young Raft, "Georgie, you're welcome, and any time you're busted, kid, go right into the register and help yourself."

When George danced at the Durant the customers would throw perhaps seventy-five or a hundred dollars on the floor. Then he would go on to Texas Guinan's or some other club. But whenever he was short of money he would call at the Durant. The partners never counted him up, as the saying was, because they knew that he was a good boy and always would pay back what he had borrowed.

Members of the band, waiters, or busboys, were used to get laughs. A small Spanish fellow, Benny Rajos, had charge of the washroom. Jimmy, who could not pronounce his last name, called him Rajah. Sometimes Jimmy would say, "Ladies and gentlemen, I want to introduce Benny Rajah, and he's goin' places. He's in a place right now you all know. He's comin' out of his place."

Benny Rajah wore a tuxedo that looked more like an overcoat and an old silk hat. He wanted to be an actor. In his right hand he would carry a clarinet. Jimmy would ask him, "What are you goin' to do tonight? You going to impersonate somebody?" Benny would say he was going to give an imitation of Ted Lewis and play "When My Baby Smiles at Me." He would put his hand to his heart and try to imitate Lewis's way of singing, then drop the clarinet.

A frequent patron of the club was gambler George McManus (not the comic artist). McManus later was charged with the murder of the underworld financier and fixer Arnold Rothstein but was cleared in court of the crime.

McManus must have weighed two hundred and thirty pounds and stood six feet two inches. When drinking, he sometimes lowered the boom on persons who stirred his dislike. One night he got full of Scotch tonic at the club and chanced to see a former jockey, Tiny Cal. The ex-jock looked like a toy monkey alongside McManus. Clayton, hearing them exchange hot words, was afraid that the gambler would make a Salisbury steak out of Cal, who was backed against one of the black-draped brick walls. McManus let go a zooming right-hand punch. He had telegraphed his blow, as the boxing critics say, and Cal ducked. George's fist struck the drape-covered wall and folded up like a concertina. A bone of his forearm snapped.

It now occurred to Clayton that he had forgotten to put the McManus gun in cold storage earlier in the evening. He leaped between the men as the big fellow tried with his good left hand to get a pistol free of the shoulder holster.

Clayton recalled, "Seems I couldn't make headway with George, who kept yelling, 'Get out of the way, Lou! I'm going to bump off this rat!' But I said, 'Before you do it, George, would you please have a drink with me?' George decided to postpone the execution long enough to have a drink. And I slipped little Michael into his glass. In about five minutes little Michael took a-hold of George McManus. George wanted to go to sleep. He was tired and sick. He didn't want to fight nobody. So we carried him downstairs, hoisted him into a cab, and took the remains to the Astor Hotel; and, with the help of some pallbearers, got him up to a suite.

"George McManus was a money man and had pieces of floating crap games. I put my hand in his pocket, and I count down fifty-four thousand dollars. I take this fifty-four grand and I put it in an envelope. I close the door from the outside after I have first lowered the transom; and outside I throw the key with a note through the transom, and I say in the note: 'I got your money. When you awaken, call me at my hotel, and I will go down to the box and get your money and give it to you.' "

The next afternoon Clayton received a telephone call from a weak-voiced McManus. Lou went over to the Astor to give him his money. The still-muddled gambler asked, "What happened, Lou?"

"All I can tell you, George, is I saved you from the electric chair. You wanted to kill Tiny Cal, and I stepped in between you, and you got little Michael. Here's your money."

"I'm going to tell you something, Lou," said McManus. "I'm going over to the priest to take a pledge never to touch another drop."

Of McManus and Prohibition drinking, Clayton said, "McManus was one of the most lovable men God ever gave breath to, but

when liquor got into him, I don't imagine he could handle it any
better than anybody else, because John Barleycorn fears nobody.
No matter how big you are, how tall you are, or how much you
weigh, it seems to give people who get full of that stuff a different
complex. I know myself sometimes I like a drink or two, and sometimes three or four. I happen to be a different type. I like to get on
your shoulder and cry. I like to tell you the sad stories, or I want to
be put to bed. Many a time I fall asleep on the settee in the Durant
Club, and they'd look for me. 'Where'd Clayton go?' And here
I'd be, in the beautiful three-hundred-dollar dinner suit, lying under
a settee, and all I say is, 'Leave me alone, will you please?' And I
was no good if I drank too much, and neither is anybody else, ever.
And we wanted nobody to get drunk in our club. We wanted them
to have a good time. And if they got too drunk we wanted them
to go on home."

Although both Durante and Jackson now lived in houses of their
own, Clayton never owned a home. He had become used to living
in hotels and out of wardrobe trunks.

Eddie Jackson bought a house in Brooklyn for sixty thousand
dollars. A prize-fight trainer, Pete the Goat, told him he should
have a gymnasium, so he purchased a wrestling mat, bar bells,
pulley weights, a medicine ball, and other equipment. After one
hour at his machines Jackson gave up, and thereafter used the room
for house guests. A one-legged man named Charlie Cooper went to
spend the night at Jackson's house and stayed on in the gym for
several years, emerging from it nightly to act as Eddie's chauffeur.

When Jackson gave his sister a thousand dollars as a present, his
worried mother said, "My boy, I hope you are getting this money
honestly. Please never do anything to bring disgrace on us."

The trio worked very hard, not only at the club but at numerous
benefits or at special performances at the homes of wealthy patrons.
Their band, all but drummer Jack Roth, stayed at the club to play
for the dancers between shows while the trio fulfilled outside
engagements.

Jeanne's antipathy to Clayton became more marked than ever.
"Theirs was a beautiful love, and a sincere love," Clayton said of
the Durantes. "But wives are very peculiar, and women are very,
very peculiar. When Jeanne was in a furnished room with Jimmy
up on Fifty-second Street, she was very happy. Now, when they

had this beautiful little home in Flushing, it seemed like something was lost. She didn't care anything about money; all she wanted was the companionship of Jimmy. And I don't blame her or any other woman, because that companionship from a man of that kind is beautiful. And I know that this woman at first tried to like me; but I lost what I wouldn't call affection, but her friendship. There were times when Jimmy wouldn't come home until late in the morning, because he was working; and Jeanne would call me and ask me would I come out to the house; but I also was working."

Once Jeanne called Clayton and asked him to come to the house, it was important. He went. "Lou, how much money are you fellows making?" Jeanne asked.

Clayton was the kind of man who believed that when anyone questioned him there always was a very particular reason behind the query. "How much did Jimmy tell you he was making, Jeanne?"

She named a figure somewhat less than the two thousand dollars a week that Jimmy was averaging.

"Well, Jeanne, if that's what Jimmy is telling you he's making, then that's what he's making."

Clayton always believed that his refusal to discuss Jim's business with Jeanne cost him any friendship she may have had left for him. "What I mean by friendship was she would never abuse me, and never do anything to hurt me; but when I would see her, I would love to walk over to her, and exchange salutations, and say, 'Hello there, Jeanne, how are you? How do you feel?' But she'd always ignore me. Well, I'm the type of man if you ignore me once, sometimes I think that you didn't hear what I said, and I try to repeat what I said. But if you ignore me again, why, I will just take it for granted that you do not want me to talk to you, and I will not talk to you any more. And that woman never spoke to me but one time again. I don't think Jeanne spoke to me but once in fifteen years. If she did, it wasn't anything that I would sit down and say was complimentary.

"I finally asked her, 'Jeanne, why don't you be friends with me? Did I do something?' And she looked at me, hurt and bitter, and said, 'You took my love away from me.'"

Clayton knew exactly what she meant by this: he had taken Jimmy in hand and made him successful. He did not think that she should dislike him for this but would not say so to her. Nor did he point out that he had made it possible for Jimmy to give her what

Clayton called the niceties of life, the luxuries a woman usually desired.

"But no," Clayton said, "that wasn't what she was after. She'd have been tickled to death if Jimmy was making fifty dollars a week, just so he'd stay home with her. She really adored her man. She didn't want money, or sables, or any big cars. She was not a greedy woman. But she blamed me for his success. When I tell you that I lost her respect and friendship, it hurt me. And good women always get plenty hurt when they marry men who belong to the whole world.

"When Jeanne started to drink, it was because it was the only way she could give vent to her feelings. She was so alone, and you know what this show business is. When you become a success in it, you become a servant of the public. No time is your own. When Jeanne did go out in public with Jimmy, when they went to a restaurant or to the theater, someone would walk over to Jimmy Durante, compliment him, slap him on the back, touch his nose, or shake hands with him, or ask for an autograph. And Jeanne always felt that that was time taken away from her. That was her time, and she wanted it. There comes an hour in every person's life when he or she wants to be alone with some loved person, and if anyone steps in on that hour, he or she is an intruder. And that's the way it seemed to Jeanne Durante with her Jimmy. She resented it very very much."

During the years of silence between Clayton and Jeanne, and even after she died, he never said a word against her to Jimmy or to anyone else. He just went ahead with his plans for his idol, and never wavered in his belief that Durante would become a star, a great comedian. "God gave Jimmy Durante his great talent," Clayton said. "A thousand Lou Claytons never could have put that talent into this man. But I loved him, and I knew then, as I know now, that he was a true genius in his own way. And he was so sweet and fine that I never could get enough of this man."

Jeanne made a few good friends, neighbors in Flushing. At first she tried to plan little daytime get-togethers, with Jimmy present, but he was so tired from his violent exertions each night—and he never had time off from the seven nights a week—that he became an unhappy host in his home. Jeanne soon learned the futility of this course and planned no more social hours at home. She was a gallant woman, but ill health and defeat plagued her.

Of the quarrels that Jimmy and Jeanne sometimes had, Clayton explained, "Naturally a little squabble would start, but they would be patched up just as soon as Jimmy and Jeanne had left wherever they were. Jimmy's naturally loud voice made it seem that he was angrier than was the case. They never were thinking of a divorce, or of court, or of separation. There wasn't anything like that."

When Jimmy and Jeanne went to Clear Lake in the summer of 1925 their little differences seemed to vanish. They fished together and were happy. They visited the home in Pasadena which Jeanne and her stepfather had bought, and all seemed to be well with them. Jeanne again urged her husband to stay on permanently in California and forget Broadway and the night clubs. But Jimmy said no, he couldn't do it. They returned to New York, and Jimmy and his partners resumed business in September at the Durant Club. Jeanne's melancholy cloud of frustration again descended.

Prohibition enforcement agents frequently searched the Durant Club for liquor but never found the plant. When some clever officer got by the door, Clayton would recognize him for what he was, make clucking sounds, and the partners would retire to the kitchen for a conference. The waiters were instructed not to serve liquor to the intruder or to anyone else near his table.

The friendly Jimmy Durante had a habit of giving everyone a big hello, whether he knew that person or not. One evening two gentlemen appeared downstairs. The doorman did not know these men and said so. One of them replied, "Well, go get Durante. His brother and me went to school together."

When Jim came down one of the fellows shouted, "Hello, Jim, old pal!" And the other chap called out warmly, "Jimmy!"

Durante responded in kind. "Well, well, hello, and how are yah? So glad to see yah!" Durante turned to the doorman. "What do yah mean, not lettin' these men in?"

When the doorman said he did not know the gentlemen, Jimmy bawled him out. "You *should* know them! They're friends of my brother's. I've known 'em since I was a kid."

So up the stairs they went. A worried Clayton whispered, "Say, Jimmy, just who are these guys?"

"Aw, Lou," Jim said, "they're friends of Al's. He went to school with them."

"Are you sure, Jim?"

Durante seemed annoyed. "Lou, am I sure?"

"Well," Lou agreed reluctantly, "if you say so, Jim, I guess it's okay."

Jimmy went out on the floor to do his number, then joined his brother's "friends." They bought Durante a drink. He sipped it out of politeness and bought another round. One of the fellows took a small bottle from his pocket and poured his drink into it.

"Gee," Jim said, "what's that? You are maybe chemists?"

The man nodded. "Yeah. We're chemists—for the Prohibition Department!"

The next day, while padlock proceedings were under way, the partners met in the deserted club to divide their assets, including thirty-two thousand dollars in cash earned that month. They kept the club bankroll in a safe instead of depositing money at the bank. Large deposits or withdrawals would have been a tip off to government agents that somebody was dealing in bootleg booze.

While Clayton was casting up the figures and preparing to share the money, Nolan put in a claim for an "extra piece" to cover the rental of his apartment.

This show of greed astonished Clayton. "Frank, I don't think you're justified in nicking us for your apartment. You were living there."

"I know that," replied Nolan. "But I was making a storehouse out of it, wasn't I? I was keeping your liquor up there, wasn't I?"

"You wasn't keeping *my* liquor," Clayton observed. "It was your liquor as much as mine, or Jimmy's, or Eddie's. We didn't take a hundred per cent of the tips we got from the people who wanted us to sing special songs. When we'd walk over to a table and sing a request song, we always rang the tip up on the register, and you took down twenty-five per cent of that. So why charge us for your apartment?"

When Nolan insisted upon the "rental," Clayton said, "Frank, I'm going to cut this pot up just the way you want it, but as far as I'm concerned, I'm backing out of the combination."

Durante interposed, "Not without me, you're not, Lou, because if you go, I go." And Eddie Jackson said, "I'm going too."

"Well then," said Clayton, "I'll tell you right now. This combination stays as Clayton, Jackson, and Durante, because from here on we're going to move, and move big."

VIII

Just Rolling Along

SOON AFTER the padlocking of the Durant Club, Lou Clayton left a floating dice game and walked up the Avenue for a breath of air. He had taken down ten one-thousand-dollar banknotes that morning when a Broadway bone specialist, Nick the Greek, crapped out after eight successive passes. Clayton carried his winnings in secret pockets built into his clothes at such strategic places as the trouser cuffs and inside the fly.

Somewhere near the Astor, Clayton chanced to hear a greeting thrown his way by "the Quaker," a man so called because he shook like a bowl of gelatin whenever rough lads threatened to muss up his person. The Quaker owned a controlling interest in the Dover Club at Fifty-first Street and Sixth Avenue.

The Quaker asked if Clayton would like to saddle up his trio at the Dover. Lou replied, "Let me take a gander at your room."

They traveled in a taxicab to the club, which was above a garage. Lou appraised the room. "It looks very massive to me. I'd say you seat two hundred and fifty or sixty people in here."

Clayton observed that the interior had brick walls with drapes hung over them; not black drapes as at the Durant Club, but dusty rose. He made a note of the big bar, the comparatively large kitchen, and a small office, situated between the kitchen and the two dressing rooms for the "talent."

"We'll sign your trio up for two weeks as a tryout," the Quaker offered.

Clayton wanted three thousand dollars, but received the reply, "Oh, don't make me laugh! We only do three thousand business here, tops." Then he countered, "I'm gonna give you seventeen hundred and fifty a week."

"That's the only proposition?"

"No. I'll give you the one thousand seven hundred and fifty clams, and fifty per cent of all over ten thousand."

"That's a pretty good spread you're taking for yourself," Clayton said, "but I like the combination, and I think I'll take a draw here."

When a Broadway gentleman said he would "take a draw," it meant he would commit either his bankroll or his personal safety, or both, to a hazardous undertaking.

A landing halfway up the stairs interrupted the climb from a double-door foyer at street level to the Dover Club room. To the left of the landing, a stout door shielded a small private room, which had in it makeshift toilet facilities—a wash basin, a cold-water faucet. A low cot lay near the plumbing. Expertly grooved floor-boards beneath the cot concealed the club's big plant.

Unknown to Clayton at the time, a mustard-complexioned chap known to the Avenue as Mr. Bamboo had a key to this sideroom. Mr. Bamboo slept here during the hours when the club was closed. He not only slept above the plant, but also enjoyed himself as a Campfire Boy, a smoker of opium. The room insured his privacy as he cooked "Chinese dumplings."

Clayton said of the Dover Club venture, "The first week we did seventeen thousand five hundred dollars. That meant seventeen hundred and fifty salary for the trio, and also a bonus of thirty-seven hundred and fifty of the business over the ten-grand guarantee—in all, over five thousand for the week."

The Quaker called the trio to his office. "You ast for three thousand a week. So I'm giving you the three."

"Oh, no!" Clayton replied. "Now that I see the traffic we are doing, I'd like a different proposition."

"Well," said the Quaker, "how would you like it if I give you fifty per cent of the place?"

"There's three of us," Clayton said. "There's only one of your-self. Instead of taking fifty per cent, we'll take sixty per cent of the place, with a drawing account of two hundred dollars apiece, no-body ever to touch the big pot till the first of each month; and I'm to be president and treasurer. I'll take the receipts out of that cash box every morning. And I'm going to hold out five thousand in case we take a fall. You can go wherever you want to around the premises, but at no time take charge of us. All we want you to do is see that the room is conducted like ladies and gentlemen should be conducted, and we'll do the entertaining. The only thing to be charged against us is that which we derive a profit out of: that is, the liquors, the waters, and we will pay for the linen used while we are in the club, and the electric lights and the dining-room help. All other obligations, the kitchen and upkeep, we assume none of that."

The Quaker surrendered. "You got a deal."

Clayton, Jackson, and Durante stayed at the Dover Club for a season and a half. To use Clayton's phrase, the four partners cut up a total of two hundred and fifty-eight thousand dollars the first year.

The Quaker had as his bodyguard and bouncer a squinty little sound-big named Zimp who was paid ten per cent of the Quaker's forty per cent take. Zimp pretended to be a very bad package. He carried a huge Western-type pistol thrust in a shoulder holster, and saw to it that the butt of this weapon showed beneath his bulging lapel. At first he did not attempt to bother the trio, because, as Clayton said, "We didn't come under his jurisdiction." But he tried persistently to impress Clayton with gabble about his supposed adventures in the underworld.

In the early mornings, after almost everyone had gone home, Zimp would bring out his pistol and flourish it in imitation of William S. Hart. As Clayton counted up receipts at a table near the bar, Zimp would spiel about safaris in Hell's Kitchen.

"Why don't you clam up?" Clayton would say. "Someday you'll collapse from a solid lead backside."

Zimp would shoot at an incandescent light bulb above one of the tables against a wall opposite the bar. Although he emptied his pistol in target practice on various mornings, he never hit the bulb— just drilled holes in the rose hangings.

From time to time Clayton hired an old seamstress, Mama Rosenburg, to repair the drapes. The dear old lady was mystified by the holes and once asked what might be causing them. "Moths, Mama!" was Clayton's reply.

Of that first season at the Dover Club, Clayton said, "That's the time Durante started coming out with songs like 'I Can Do without Broadway, but Can Broadway Do without Me?' 'Everybody Wants to Get into the Act,' 'Again You Turna,' and 'Broadway's a Phony.'"

This last song was inspired by a Sidney Skolsky newspaper column about Broadway's fickle heart. It seemed that the very persons who enjoyed most the pleasures of the white-light district liked to hear songs condemning the street which comedian Joe Laurie, Jr., has called "Headache Avenue." Durante adapted the Skolsky motif to his own hoarse indictments of the Big Artery, Coffee Pot Canyon, Orange Juice Gulch, and the Double Crossroads of the World, where people sought you out to pat you on the back but were only looking for a spot to knife you. But it was his street, Durante sang, "the heart of the world."

Whenever Jimmy got up to do "I Can Do without Broadway," Clayton interrupted, "Jim, have you ever been off this Avenue?" And Durante answered, "This is a great street when you're going up, but when you're going down, take Sixth Avenue."

"That's an awful nice street you picked out. Why don't you go a little bit to one side?"

"Well, I'll tell you something, Lou. They've had me over to First already, and a little bit more and they'd had me in the East River."

Not only did the trio appear for long hours at the Dover Club seven nights a week, but their outside engagements were heavy. "It wasn't all easy sailing," Clayton recalled. "It was a tough life, a rough life. But we liked every minute of it. I was good and strong then. And Jimmy was strong. And we had our youth, and we could stand it. But now that we've learned what life is, I don't think you could print enough money for us to go through it again."

Jimmy had a touch of illness at about this time, a bilious attack. Perhaps his gall bladder revolted at the pie crust he nibbled between meals. He always carried these tidbits in his coat pocket, and his partners saved their leftover crusts for him. Durante never was a glutton at table, but he certainly liked pie crust. "When we were up at the Alamo gettin' our forty or fifty, plus tips," Durante told Jackson, "I could have ate cast-iron sausage, and nothin' happen. Now we're drawing down two thousand apiece or over, and it looks like healthy people shouldn't ever get in the big money."

The management of the Palace Theatre, foremost of the vaudeville houses, wanted to bill the trio for a week but turned down Clayton's demand of three thousand for the act. Sime Silverman, the wise little gamecock of *Variety*, advised them always to ask for big money. He foresaw a day, not far off, when Clayton, Jackson, and Durante would become box-office champions.

"Of course," Clayton said of the entertainment at the Dover Club, "we now were using talent outside of ourselves. We had a line of pretty girls singing and dancing. We had a clever girl by the name of Julia Garrity; we had the Smith sisters, and we kept changing talent all the time. From ten o'clock at night that room was kept jumping until seven, eight, nine o'clock the next morning, or as long as there was somebody in there. Because at that time Jimmy made up the slogan, 'Anything for a laugh!'

"I well remember a little secretary came up there one afternoon, and I'm sitting there, and I don't know what happens when Jimmy Durante says, 'I'm goin' to engage this girl.'"

"What does she do?" asked Clayton.

"She's a singer."

When the young woman exercised her pipes Clayton moved away with the announced intention of bouncing down the stairs ten steps at a time.

"Oh, Lou!" Jimmy called out. "Come back here, will you?"

Clayton turned to ask, "Just *what* are you going to do with this doll?"

"What am I gonna do? We'll make the room crazy with this girl."

"Jimmy—" Clayton began, but Durante broke in solemnly, "We'll call her Mademoiselle Fifi."

"So what?"

"Watch!" Jimmy exclaimed. "That's all I'm askin' yah to do is watch. Just sit down and watch what goes on." Durante went on, "Lou, let me tell yah somethin' for your information: this gal speaks five or six different languages. I'm gonna have her sing a song in French, and while she's singin' this song in French, that's where Eddie and yourself—yah can do whatever yah want out there, but just jungle us up. I'll have the trumpets blare, and we'll holler, and from then on it's every man for hisself, and we'll have lots of fun."

"I hope you know what you're doing."

The first night Mademoiselle Fifi sang the patrons did not want her to leave the floor. Sime Silverman grew hysterical at his table. Eddie and Lou hissed, and Mademoiselle Fifi turned around to say, "Mr. Durante, if you don't shut the steam off, I will queet!"

Jimmy replied, "That's not the steam, Mademoiselle Fifi, that's the bartender putting some siphon water in the highballs."

Then, as Mademoiselle Fifi resumed her warbling, Jackson strutted across the floor. As he made his exit, Clayton, from the opposite side, came on and danced wildly out of view.

Mademoiselle Fifi asked Durante, "Who is dees?"

"Don't pay no attention to him," Jimmy replied. "That's a crazy man, going from one war to another."

"Concerning Mademoiselle Fifi," Clayton said reminiscently, "she couldn't sing a lick, but what we would do when this girl was singing was bounce laughs off her. We would spray seltzer bottles and throw other things, but never touching her, but just to break her up."

Mademoiselle Fifi was about five feet seven inches tall, had the figure of a Nell Brinkley girl, and was a brunette. She had an enormous appetite but never seemed to gain weight. Customers used to buy wine and dinners for her as often as three times a night.

"Where this girl could pack this food," Clayton recalled, "was beyond my sense of recognition. One night she happened to be sitting with Sime Silverman and ordered all three of her favorite dishes: chicken à la king, chicken à la Mexico, and chicken sandwiches on toast. I don't know what possessed me when she ordered another chicken sandwich on top of everything else. I run into the kitchen, and I pull out my dinner shirt, and I say to the chef, 'Cut off enough of this tail, and put this between two slices of toast, and then put a piece of lettuce on it.' The chef does like I say, and then cuts the sandwich quarterly. When the waiter comes in to get the wine and sandwich I go back to the table where sits Sime and Mademoiselle Fifi. And she takes a bite into a quarter of this sandwich. Naturally she is chewing on the end of my shirt. She keeps on chewing and chewing and masticating it, but cannot swallow down this cloth."

"Pardon, Monsieur Clayton," said the lady, "this here chicken is like rubbair!"

"Mademoiselle Fifi!" Clayton exclaimed, "I don't think you are justified when you say what you say in front of Sime Silverman, one of the greatest newspapermen in the country, and also insult Jimmy and Eddie and I with your saying that the chicken is tough."

"Pardon," said Mademoiselle Fifi, "I say nossing about Durante! I say nossing about Monsieur Jackson, or you, Monsieur Clayton. All I say is, the chicken is tough!"

Clayton got to his feet. "Well, that's enough! We run this place, Mademoiselle Fifi. And when you talk around so the customers can hear about our chicken, well—"

"Look," Mademoiselle Fifi tearfully interrupted him, "I can no swallow zee chicken. It is like rubbair!"

"Mademoiselle Fifi," said Clayton, "you better take a rest. You are fired!"

The Mademoiselle was retired for two nights and then rehired at an increase in salary.

Many of Jimmy's jokes lose flavor in print. He has told many of them for years, but they always stay fresh as he repeats them. Everything he says or does on stage springs from a personality as warm and as broad as the Gulf Stream.

Durante will not tell a joke unless he can understand it himself, and he likes jests that portray in clown's colors the raw, banging violence of mankind's daily struggles with the world. Notwithstanding his "dese" and "dose" manner of speech, Durante has creative gifts, crudely packaged perhaps, and the faculty, sharpened by the rough-and-tumble grind of show business, of knowing where laughter may be found.

It seems an odd circumstance that other comedians do not envy Durante or become jealous of his success. Red Skelton, regarded by many as heir apparent to the title of that old master of comedy, the late W. C. Fields, has said of this, "It's because none of us can steal from him. Imitations of Durante fall flat, for he is in a class by himself."

The comedy at the Dover Club might be described as catch-as-catch-can. There was hat-throwing, piano breaking, and the mad little clown with the prowling walk defying the world and its injustices—and yet not really hating the world despite the rages he simulated as he beat the air with his arms and cried out like a hoarse Ajax.

Clayton and Jackson ably abetted the zany fellow during these shenanigans. Clayton, who looked like an Indian, would affix feathers to a hatband, and together with Jackson, also costumed as a redskin, would scream, "The Americans are coming!" The velvet portieres would part at the entrance to the club, to reveal these "Indians" in a ludicrous pose. Sometimes Paul Whiteman, Ted Lewis, Eddie Cantor, George Jessel or other celebrities took part in these tableaux, and Jimmy would cry out, "*Every*body's tryin' to get into the act!"

Headwaiter Leon Emken (later a partner at Leon & Eddie's) made sure each night that warring racketeers were seated safely apart. He created barriers by assigning socialites to tables in the midst of the Rover Boys and among the lady furtrappers of the underworld. The presence of smart-set patrons put a damper on gangland tempers.

Remembering that early morning when Lou Clayton first entered the Durant Club, Jimmy decided to revive "Willie the Weeper," with the trio acting it out. He called this turn "The Hop Fiend's Easter," and changed the name of the principal character to "Jimmy the Weep."

For this routine the waiters would line up two rows of chairs in the center of the small dance floor, five chairs on either side. Clayton would lie down on one rank of chairs. Jackson would give him a sawed-off broom handle with a tin cup nailed to one end of it, a simulated "hop pipe." Then Eddie would make "toys" of candle wax, little balls, and pretend to cook opium pills over the flame of a candle set in the neck of a soda-water bottle. Eddie borrowed a hairpin, straightened it, and used it as a "yen-hock," the needle upon which the supposed dream beads were toasted.

As Clayton lay upon his side he sang that he owned "a silver mine, a diamond vine, a sapphire bush, and a railroad fine." At a knock at the door leading from the kitchen Clayton would leave off singing to ask, "Who is it?"

"It must be one of our customers," was Eddie's reply.

Enter Jimmy, in a big raccoon coat and a slouch hat pulled down to the bridge of his great nose. A green spotlight played upon this scene. Clayton would say, "Take your hat off, Jimmy, and your coat. And make yourself at home."

Jimmy removed the raccoon coat. Under this he had on another fur coat with a fur collar, and under it still another overcoat, and under it yet another, a Prince Albert. Beneath the Prince Albert he wore a swallow tail coat, and under it a dinner coat.

"Brother, you sure did expect a storm!"

"I didn't expect it, I brung it with me."

Then Jimmy'd take his hat off, and Clayton would ask, "Why don't you lay the straw and make yourself at home?"

Jimmy the Weep would reply, "I think I will. All I want to do is smoke four or five pills. I just want to get feeling good."

Jimmy would lie down on one bank of chairs and Clayton on the opposite row. At the head of the aisle Eddie would hum happily over the candle, and Jimmy would look at Jackson and shout, "I don't like the look of that chef!"

"Oh, Jimmy, the chef's all right," Clayton would reassure him.

"I just don't like his face!"

Eddie would put on a hurt expression. "I think he's talking about me, Lou. I'll dip a couple in oil on him"—meaning he was going to make the customer ill.

Sometimes Eddie would poke the broomstick pipe in Durante's mouth, but more often in his eye, or hit him on the nose with it. These mishaps sent Jimmy into yowling rages.

Clayton would quiet the Weep, then ask about his travels.

Jim would start out, "Well, I'll tell you. I was three days on the road and four days from home—"

"Just a minute!" Lou would interrupt. "You're three days on the road and four days from home? Why, you lost a day someplace."

And Eddie would cut in, "No, Lou, he never lost a day. He filled it in with a Sunday concert."

At this Jimmy would bounce up, and Clayton would fall to the floor and tackle Durante's legs, and Jimmy would scream, "Look out, Lou! Let me at him!"

Lou would drag Durante to the floor and wrestle violently, pull Durante's nose, and Jimmy would say, "Lou, Lou, this is your partner! This is Jimmy! This is Jimmy, Lou! Stop it!"

Then Clayton would say, "For a second I didn't recognize you."

"Put the bum out!" the orchestra members would chorus.

Jimmy would stagger about, shouting, "Somebody called me a bum! Me, the Great Durante! Me, Jimmy the Weep—they're calling me a bum!"

"Jim," Clayton would call out, "you just don't know what you're saying! Nobody called you a bum. We got a few songwriters back there in the bunk. They're feeling kind of high. And they just wrote a new song: 'Bum, bum, bum-bum, bum de bum-bum, bum de bum-bum.' "

"Oh," Durante would say, "that's different, Lou. Because I let nobody call me a bum. How much do I owe you?"

"Oh," Clayton would say, "forget about it, Jim. You had six toys at five dollars a toy. You owe me ninety dollars."

"Let me take ten dollars cash, will you, Lou, for sure?"

Clayton would start to put Jimmy's clothes on him, but Durante would seize them, bundle them up, and announce, "I'm going home to take a sleep." As he made his exit the orchestra played and Eddie and Lou sang, "He's sitting on top of the world, rolling along, just rolling along."

At about this time in the mid-twenties a new racket was intro-

duced to Broadway. Known as "the Snatch," this form of kidnaping was perfected by two extremely tough brothers. The procedure
was to capture moneyed gamblers, club owners, or bootleggers and
hold them for ransom under threats of torture or death.

The Snatch appealed to the easy-money greed of underworld
copyists of the kidnap pattern. The victims ordinarily knew the
names of their captors but very seldom reported the facts to the
police. Their friends paid off and then waited until matters could
be rectified in consonance with their own code of a set of teeth for
a tooth.

One evening as Clayton went halfway downstairs to tap the big
plant he heard the sound of running water inside the secret room.
He snapped on the light. The Quaker was standing at the wash
basin, much perturbed and disheveled, his trousers and his drawers
off.

"What are you doing?" asked Lou.

"I'm washing my drawers."

"You're washing your drawers?"

"Yes."

"I don't understand that."

"Well then," the Quaker gasped, "to be plain with you, they just
snatched me on the Avenue."

"Go on!" Clayton said. "Know who it was?"

The Quaker thought a while. "I imagine I know who it was all
right, but I don't want to take nobody into my confidence."

"All right then," Lou said. "But what are you washing your
drawers for?"

"Well," the Quaker said, "to be truthful, Lou, you can picture me
gagged and lying up there on the bed in a certain hotel with my
hands tied and waiting for these two gorillas to give me a hot cigar,
where it'll do the most good, if I don't call up somebody to bring
thirty grand down to them. While one of the guys is lighting up
his cigar and the other is called to the phone to talk to some broad,
I works my hands loose, suddenly jumps off the bed, and dives
right out of the second-story window. Almost bust my guts. And
now you ask me *why* I am washing my drawers!"

Not long after this episode Durante received a threatening letter.
He was threatened with kidnaping if he failed to pay twenty-five
thousand dollars to "someone who will get in touch."

"There was only one way you could kidnap Jimmy Durante,"

Clayton said, "and that was I'd have to die first. So when Jimmy Durante would drive home from the Dover Club I would tail him in my own car. And I said, 'Don't worry, Jim. I'll be behind you right up to your door in Flushing.'"

Clayton stayed home one night with a severe cold. Early next morning Jimmy drove his car into the Flushing street on which he lived. A sedan went past him and then stopped on the road, broadside.

Durante, an excellent driver, put on his brakes, quickly shifted the gears into reverse, backed away, then turned and raced off, his horn going full blast. He had glimpsed three men in the sedan. They did not follow him, perhaps because it was broad daylight and traffic was growing thick. After half an hour of cruising Jimmy went home.

Lou, after making inquiries along the Avenue, became convinced that Vincent Coll, a member of the Dutch Schultz bootlegger "mob," had been in the car. Broadway knew Mad Dog Coll as the most irresponsible and desperate outlaw of all the bullet boys on the gangster scene. Although he had "the frozen stare" he was on the whole a good-looking fellow, barely twenty years old. Persons out of the know would not have believed that this werewolf lad with the pompadour hair and the even white teeth could in an instant become a savage mankiller. He, more than anyone else on the Avenue, caused members of rivals mobs to wear bullet-proof vests. No one knew just what the unpredictable young man might decide to do at any moment.

Clayton's first intention was to kill Coll. Jimmy made him promise not to try this and advised him to stay away from the gangster. Clayton, however, unarmed except for a spring-blade pocketknife, set forth one afternoon for Coll's hangout in the Bronx. Clayton brushed past the doorman.

Mad Dog was playing pinochle in a back room. Clayton ignored the other players and looked Coll in the eye. He asked with quiet emphasis, "Do you know anything about that sour bid to snatch Jimmy Durante?" Perhaps ten seconds went by as the men stared at each other, then Clayton said, "Maybe you're hard of hearing?"

Coll affected a smile. "I got no way of knowing what's on your mind, Lou."

"Here's what's on my mind," Clayton said. "Anybody that touches Jimmy Durante will be beaten to death by these." He held out his strong hands. "And if that certain party has got good white teeth, that person won't ever eat again with their own teeth. For Clayton will nail him or them by appointment or otherwise." He turned and left the cardroom, his back to the Mad Dog and his gorillas.

Broadway bubbled over with the news that Lou Clayton had faced down Mad Dog Coll. "Don't ever go up against Clayton," was the advice given wide and far on the Avenue. "He'd take a draw with the devil."

A few days later Coll spotted Clayton in front of Lindy's and approached him with a mortician's smile. "Lou, you got me all wrong."

"Maybe I have, and maybe I haven't," Lou replied. "But I want to predict something for you: a person that lives by the gun will die by the gun."

Coll put on his most charming manner. "Lou, I just happened to see Benevolent Charlie, and he told me to tell you he wants to see you right off about something."

"Did he give you a note to hand me?"

"No, just said to tell you. And I got my car right acrost the street."

"Benevolent Charlie always knows where to find me," Lou replied, "and if he wants me, the telephone has been invented a long while ago."

Clayton turned away contemptuously and hailed a passing taxi-cab. He never got into a cab waiting at the curb unless he was well acquainted with the driver. At the Dover Club he telephoned Benevolent Charlie, who informed him, "Why, no, Lou, I never saw the Mad Dog today whatsoever; and I didn't say I wanted to see you, which of course I'm always glad to. What he wanted was to take you for a ride, or snatch you to save his pride from the other day. Watch your step."

When time came to close the Dover Club in May of 1926, everyone concerned was glad to take a rest. One wearied of the constant trouble that lay beneath the veneer of gaiety, for the rackets were rolling high and wide.

As for Jeanne Durante, news of the threat to kidnap her Jimmy had reached her somehow, and her state of mind did not improve with this fresh problem. Durante took Jeanne to consult their family doctor, Dr. Shirley Wynne, afterward Health Commissioner under Mayor James J. Walker. Dr. Wynne recommended that Jeanne go as soon as possible to California to recuperate.

Just before the club closed its doors that May, Clayton ran into another bit of trouble. Two regular customers, good spenders known as Charlie and Cap, frequently had brought their sweethearts, twin sisters, to the Dover. Headwaiter Leon had warned Clayton that these sisters were "bad babies."

Unescorted women were not permitted inside the club. One evening, however, Clayton received a buzz from the outside doorman, Sam Thorpe. The two sisters had arrived. There were two separate doors at the bottom of the stairs, an outside one and, four or five feet inside of that, another door with a peephole in it, guarded by a husky fellow, Red Cohn.

Sentries Thorpe and Cohn knew how to protect themselves, as the saying was. They were diplomatic but rugged whenever someone came down the stairs after taking on too much Prohibition juice. Roisterers sometimes did not want to get into a cab and would cause a loud disturbance at the door, a very fast way of having the club closed by the law.

Clayton went downstairs to ask the sisters what they wanted. It seemed their gentlemen had stopped in somewhere along the Avenue to see about business but were to join them at the Dover.

"Come on up, girls," Clayton said, against his better judgment.

The room was packed, so Leon assigned the unescorted pair to a place on a settee near the bar. Clayton then went onto the floor to dance to "When My Sugar Walks down the Street." Of a sudden he heard a commotion.

Whenever trouble started as the trio was performing, they signaled the orchestra to play noisily. The cue was the upturn of hands behind the back of a performer. Lowered hands meant to play softly. There were many other signals, of course, such as the flicking of "dust" from one's coat lapel. An upward flick meant that a party was all right. A downward flick meant "get rid of him, but fast."

Clayton raised his hands behind him as he went into his dance. The orchestra hit it hard. Lou danced over to the settee. The sisters were quarreling. He put his fingers to his lips, and one of them called him a vile name.

Eddie and Jimmy took over the entertainment, and Clayton sat down to pacify the girls. "Waiter," he called out, "bring these nice ladies a drink." Then he asked, "What seems to be the trouble?"

Ignoring Clayton for the moment, one sister called the other "a two-dollar prostitute." The reply was, "Yeah? That goes double, and I never see you send Mama a few dollars."

At Clayton's suggestion that the girls moderate their language, one sister picked up a petit-point pocketbook and struck her twin in the eye, which soon resembled a Blue Point oyster peeping out of its shell.

Clayton calmed the girls eventually. Soon afterward he was called to the kitchen, and the tipsy girl who had wielded the pocketbook followed him.

Clayton turned to ask, "Just what is it you want?"

"I want a kiss."

"You want a kiss? Why, you ought to be ashamed of yourself! You're Charlie's girl."

She called Lou another name. He walked into the office and slammed the door shut behind him.

The girls stayed at the club until seven o'clock closing time next morning. Bodyguard Zimp had gone home without shooting at the lights, and the only person left downstairs was Red, the inside doorman.

"Girls," Clayton said, "come on. Let's go downstairs."

They refused, so Clayton took them by the arms and called out to Red, "Open the door down there!"

Clayton and Red put the screaming girls into a cab and gave the driver a ten-spot. Clayton returned upstairs, and then the buzzer began to sound.

Lou called down, "Look through the chute, Red. Don't open that door for nobody."

Red peered out to see a policeman, who said, "Open the door before I break it down!"

Clayton came on down. The policeman was standing outside with the twins. There also was an audience of some eighty or ninety persons who had been on their way to work.

As Clayton opened the door the policeman said, "You better get your hat and coat. I have to take you down."

"For what?" Lou asked. "I haven't done anything."

"That's the man, officer!" yelled the girls. "Arrest him!"

At the station house the sisters charged Clayton with assault and battery. The one with the swollen eye said that Clayton had hit her and caused the "mouse." Lou was released on five-hundred-dollars' bail.

Next day a lawyer for the sisters informed Clayton that he could fix the case for twenty-five hundred.

"Twenty-five hundred dollars! I wouldn't give you twenty-five cents. I didn't do anything. I'd give twenty-five thousand dollars rather than have this happen, but all I ever did was steer these two tramps to the street."

The case was transferred from Police Court to Special Sessions, with three judges sitting on the bench. Lou refused to retain a lawyer, although William J. Fallon, "the Great Mouthpiece," offered to represent him free of charge. Lou cross-examined the girls, and they contradicted themselves. The judges threw the case out of court.

Years after this Clayton met these "ladies" when the trio was working in a Saratoga gambling casino. As pretty as you please, they "exchanged salutations" with him in the dining room, and, without being invited to do so, sat down and asked if Clayton would buy wine.

He would be delighted to do so. When the wine arrived he slipped little Michael into each sister's glass. After a few minutes the girls ran a dead heat to the Ladies' Room. That was the last Clayton ever saw of them.

The Great Pete

SEVERAL MONTHS before the Durantes left New York for their California holiday in 1926 Jeanne put ten thousand dollars in a safe-deposit box. For reasons of her own she rented the box in the name of Mrs. Mary Peel, her maternal grandmother.

That summer Jeanne wrote from California to her young friend Jenice Werner: "I put away some money in a bank vault in Seventh Avenue, and I can't remember for the life of me which bank it was. Will you please find out so that I can send the bank people a check for the rental?"

Miss Werner undertook a two-day quest among Seventh Avenue banks until she found the right one. "She did not tell Jimmy about this deposit," Miss Werner recalls, "until they went to live in California in 1931. He couldn't believe she had kept the ten thousand dollars intact. To prove that she had, she drove with him to the Pasadena bank, where the money was now deposited, parked their car, went in and got the ten thousand, and then came out to show it to him. He nodded happily, and Jeanne went back to redeposit the money. Half an hour later there was a holdup at the bank. Jeanne had been displaying the money at a time when the robbers probably were arriving on the scene."

The Schnozz and his wife entrained for the East in September of 1926. The holiday had refreshed Jeanne's spirits as well as her body. As the train approached San Bernardino the Durantes were in the club car. Jimmy likes to look out of windows, whether in a hotel or on a train, and now was admiring the orange trees against the background of mountains.

As most western travelers know, firebreaks rise along the sides and cross the ridges of California mountains. These pathlike clearings minimize the hazard of forest fires.

When Jimmy saw the firebreaks he called out, "Can you imagine anybody drivin' a car up them steep roads?"

Fellow passengers stared in amazement at Durante. Jeanne got up from her chair and left it to the Schnozz to explain his ignorance. He could see by the expressions of his companions in the car that he had made some big blunder.

"You see," said the only man in the world who could not pronounce "cat," "us perfessors don't get out of the chemical lavatory too often."

Just before Thanksgiving the Quaker told Clayton that he wanted two hundred dollars for turkeys as a present for two detectives on the Avenue. Clayton pointed out that a hundred dollars per turkey seemed expensive and sarcastically suggested that the Quaker buy birds of paradise.

The Quaker had intended the Thanksgiving remembrances for a Lieutenant W. and his partner, a sleuth known as Camera Eye. Lieutenant W. had gone to grade school with Durante, liked Jimmy but not Clayton, because Lou played dumb whenever the lieutenant sought information about Broadway's boys and girls.

The detectives were sitting in the club one night as a waiter passed by with perhaps a dozen beakers of something for the customers.

Lieutenant W. called to Clayton, "I want to buy a drink."

"What will it be?" Clayton inquired. "Ginger ale?"

"Damn you!" The officer rose from his chair. "You know I want whisky!"

"You must know we don't serve whisky," replied Clayton. "It's against the law."

The lieutenant pointed to a waiter. "What's that he's serving?"

"Oh," replied Clayton, "that's ginger ale."

"I'm going to get you, Clayton! And when I do, it'll be for keeps! And I think I'll punch you in the nose right now."

"If you ever get the idea of punching me," said Clayton, "just put your gun and blackjack down, and no matter how big you are, I'll punch back."

"I want to see Durante," said the detective.

Clayton gave a birdlike signal for everyone to be on the alert, that trouble was brewing, and for the partners to go to the kitchen for a conference. Clayton went off ostensibly to find Durante.

In the kitchen he said to his partners, "Look, that copper is going to cause trouble; and don't let anyone, under any conditions, serve him a drink."

Durante objected. "Now look, I went to school with the guy. Why don't you be nice to him?"

"Because," Clayton said, "he doesn't like me, and he's out to get us."

"Aw, Lou," said Durante, "we was pals when we was kids. He couldn't!"

"He couldn't, eh?" said Clayton. "Well, he's the type that would send us all to the electric chair."

"Lou," Durante said, "I always try to go by your advice, but this time you're dead wrong."

Durante went out to placate his old schoolmate. The lieutenant complained bitterly about Clayton's rudeness. He said all he had wanted was a bracer. Schnozzola personally got two drinks and served them. Whereupon his former schoolmate brought a bottle from his pocket and into it he poured the drinks. "All right, Jim, get your hat and coat. We're going to headquarters!"

Durante almost fainted at this show of disloyalty.

Armed with evidence, Lieutenant W. said that he was entitled to search the premises. He found several bottles of liquor beneath the floorboards of the cloakroom, as at the Durant Club. He selected a bottle of gin, a bottle of whisky, and some wine. Looking around for a container in which to put the evidence, he spotted a black valise with the initials "L.C." He put the bottles into this bag.

Lou appealed to Camera Eye not to pinch Jim. That officer replied that he was helpless, that he loved Jim, "But what can I do, Lou? Jim served the drinks."

The Schnozz was booked at police headquarters. Clayton begged the sergeant not to lock up Jimmy, and the sergeant fixed bail at two thousand dollars. Clayton then picked up his grip with the booze in it and sauntered toward the door. Lieutenant W. set up a furor, and the sergeant asked what was going on.

"This is my property," Clayton said. "See my initials on it?" But he was compelled to leave his grip at the station house.

Next day Jim was tried in Special Sessions Court. Sentence was suspended, but the bench ruled that if the Schnozzola ever served another drink, he would go to jail.

"I'm brandied as a criminal!" moaned Durante.

Durante never poured another drink except in his own home until the repeal of Prohibition. "That's twice, Lou, I've been a sap," he said. "I'll never go against your judgment again."

One of the patrons at the Dover Club was a towering fellow known along Broadway as the Great Pete. In the early twenties he had been a doorman or "lookout" at floating crap games, and sometimes stood in as a stick man, or supervisor of the rolling dice, when such referees as Fast Mike or Smiley Lippman failed to show up at the tables.

One evening Clayton won several thousand dollars at craps and gave the Great Pete a gratuity of two hundred and fifty dollars. The Great Pete invested this at another game up the Avenue and ran his stake into sixty thousand dollars.

This burst of luck convinced the Great Pete that he no longer should serve either as a lookout or a substitute stick man. During the next two years he had considerable luck with the freckled cubes and was supposed to be holding as much as two hundred thousand dollars in his kick. He patronized the best cafés, became a liberal spender, and was well liked.

The Great Pete could crush your hand while "exchanging salutations" with you and thought it a grand joke when you said, "Ouch!" Long ago he had become friendly with a Mrs. Schiffer, the widowed mother of a temperamental miss named Alice, who one day would marry Legs Diamond, gangster, hijacker of fur and liquor trucks, and notorious hoodlum. Alice did not like the Great Pete because of what she considered his ill-advised fondness for her dear mother.

Upon her marriage to Legs Diamond, Alice neglected to confide in him that she knew the Great Pete. Mrs. Diamond was a peculiar lass: a practical joker on the one hand and very hot-tempered on the other. It was said that she rigged up an electrified chair at her house in New Jersey, and whenever one of Mr. Diamond's callers sat in it, she would turn on the juice. She did this, said she, to rehearse Mr. Diamond's cronies for the electric chair at Sing Sing.

These references to the hot seat up the River did not alleviate Legs Diamond's ulcers of the stomach, an ailment second in severity only to his occupational disease of leaditis. Before he was done forever with the cares of business, this gangland metallurgist had collected some thirty-two bullets in his otherwise worthless body. He had as much lead in him as the east window of Westminster Abbey. Mr. Diamond liked to swim but never dared try it, of course, and whenever he stepped upon a scale the indicator would pop up as if to ask, "What happened?"

Legs received his nickname when, as a sneak-thief boy, he over-turned and robbed pushcarts and then dodged off faster than a varsity halfback.

At the Dover Club the Great Pete always deported himself quietly, and no one cared to pick a quarrel with him. It was well remembered how he had seized two husky rousters one night on the Avenue and cracked their heads together. When they came out of Bellevue Hospital they mumbled constantly in what seemed to be the tribal idiom of the Hottentots.

The Christmas season of 1926 brought to a close one of the most colorful and active years that Broadway and the Big Town ever had known. It had been a Coolidge year of Wall Street bonanzas and a busy mint. Al Smith was Governor of New York State, and the high-stepping Jimmy Walker Mayor of the Big Town. Down the bay and at City Hall, the Honorable Grover A. Whalen had greeted a succession of celebrities, from hero Captain George Fried of the S.S. *President Roosevelt* and his crew to Queen Marie of Rumania.

So many reservations were made for New Year's Eve at the Dover Club that the seating list was closed three days ahead of time. More than a thousand Broadway and Park Row personalities wished to spend that evening in the gay, mad atmosphere of the club that Clayton, Jackson, and Durante had made famous.

On the Eve the Dover Club was jammed. Social unequals, the Piping Rock boys and the White Rock boys, got up to participate in the entertainment, and the ladies and the flossies became sisters under the gin.

Between shows there was dancing on the small floor. The grape flowed, and tobacco smoke gave the room a Vesuvian aspect. Paper hats, balloons, and noise-making instruments had been distributed among the guests, and the band played on.

Among the tables of socialites were the ones pre-empted by gangsters and racketeers. Upon entering the club, the gangsters had held on to their folded topcoats long enough to conceal the transfer of pistols to Clayton. One after another, he placed these weapons on ice. He even persuaded several friendly detectives to let him keep their guns "in escrow" until the night was done.

Pasty-faced Arnold Rothstein, gambler and fixer, known as Broadway's pawnbroker, had the place of honor at one of the two tables reserved by Mr. and Mrs. Diamond. Legs' lieutenants and their molls were celebrating at the expense of their ulcer- and bullet-ridden chief.

Zimp swaggered about the room, the butt of his Western pistol showing. Clayton wondered just how this fellow would act if real trouble were to arise. He felt that Zimp would dog it if anyone gave it to him in spades.

At ten o'clock the Great Pete, accompanied by a dapper fellow known as Jocky Fall Off, entered the room. Pete and his guest were assigned by Leon to a small table near the bar. They ordered wine, and were chatting amiably until Alice Diamond danced past their table in the arms of Arnold Rothstein. The spirit of the season overcame the Great Pete. He rose and smiled at her. Alice turned her head away, then danced inside the squirming throng on the floor.

Jockey Fall Off asked, "What's the matter, pal?"

The Great Pete shook his head. "She won't let bygones be bygones concerning her mother. Well, drink up."

The Great Pete reminisced with Jockey Fall Off about this and that and sent wine to friends at nearby tables.

Shortly before midnight the bandsmen prepared to play "Auld Lang Syne." The Great Pete decided that it would be a nice gesture to go over to the Diamond table with the season's greetings.

The first blare of the trumpets set off a tempest of singing and shouting. The men stood up or leaned over to kiss the women or to shake hands with other men. The Great Pete's opening words at Diamond's table were, "Hello, Alice. A happy New Year to you!"

Alice did not answer him; that is, until he added, "And how is your Mama?" an inquiry that seemed to trip a trigger in her head. She called the Great Pete a name. Diamond, full of wine, mistook the intentions of the big fellow for those of a masher. He got up, lead and all, to face Pete.

Arnold Rothstein was well aware of the situation and might have served as a peacemaker. But Rothstein never "put himself in the middle"; instead of saying "the word," he got up, moved away, and was last seen at the cloakroom, putting on his topcoat.

Clayton did not observe the beginnings of trouble in the vicinity of the Diamond party. He was bouncing from table to table, and so were Jimmy and Eddie, exchanging greetings with everyone in general. The women were kissing and hugging the entertainers.

Amid the hullabaloo of horns, rattles, laughter, and songs the hot words that fell upon the Great Pete were lost. The room was a ball of fire, and the band was playing.

Legs Diamond finally shouted, "You're making yourself too promiscuous!"

The Great Pete was astounded. He turned to Diamond as though to explain something. Alice picked up a wine bottle from an ice-bucket and hit the Great Pete on the top of the head. He went down. Blood flowed from a wound in his scalp. He got up to put bear hugs on his foes.

From several quarters of the room Diamond's friends closed in. When the Great Pete hugged Diamond, one of Legs' henchmen slugged him till he let go and fell. Other gangster factions entered the free-for-all. A rose wall-hanging came loose and for a few moments covered several combatants.

Women screamed. There was a stampede for the cloakroom and the street. The detectives called for their guns, but Clayton refused to restore their weapons to them. Besides, he was very busy with his hands. Plates were thrown and tables overturned. The cash register toppled with a clang.

Jackson and Durante, according to their custom, fled the premises. It was said that Eddie did not stop this side of the Williamsburg Bridge.

The fight lasted for an incredible hour. At its close not a plate or glass was left intact. Jockey Fall Off wound a napkin about the bleeding head of the Great Pete and took him to the Polyclinic Hospital. Other casualties were given first aid, then sent on in cabs to their homes or to the doctor's.

The guests had gone out without paying their checks. It was Clayton's opinion that the club lost twenty thousand dollars in unpaid bills. No one was arrested, because the attending detectives were friendly patrons, and Clayton advised them to let the boys settle matters in their own way at another time and at another place.

In the early morning hours Clayton lifted the cash register from the floor of the wrecked club. He smiled mirthlessly as he thought of Zimp. That braggart had deserted the room during the first few minutes of the fight.

Clayton then thought of Rothstein and said to himself, "Rothstein could have saved us all this trouble if he'd just said to Legs

Diamond, 'I know the Great Pete, and he's all right.' But no! And now we lose a small fortune."

. Someone had made away with Clayton's topcoat. In the checkroom he found a wide choice of overcoats, left by fugitives from the fracas.

In the cold early hours of New Year's Day the city resembled a ghost town, with only a few cabbies and an occasional drunk to be seen. Clayton felt quite alone in the world as he rode uptown in a taxicab. Then he thought about Jimmy, and that made him "feel warm again."

At the hotel Ida had hot coffee and oatmeal prepared for her husband, and then put him to bed.

According to Clayton, he lay awake, "worrying about what could have happened. Somebody could have gotten killed in that free-for-all. I knew that the Great Pete wouldn't bring any charges against anybody, because that was his slogan and the ethics of his life, which was to say nothing. The next day the Great Pete showed on Broadway with enough bandages on his head to make him look like one of them Indian rajahs. Nobody bothered him when he went around, and he didn't bother anybody else. Naturally his friends wanted to intercede for him, and Jack Diamond's friends wanted to intercede for Legs, and they held a conference and decided to forget the whole thing. And that saved a lot of killings all the way around."

The trio decided not to open the club the next night, because they had nothing in which to serve drinks or food. Clayton visited the club at about ten o'clock on the evening of New Year's Day, and there was the Quaker, sitting with Jimmy Durante and Eddie Jackson on a surviving settee at the back of the wrecked room.

Durante pointed. "There's Lou now."

Lou took off his hat and overcoat and handed these and his walking stick to Leon. "Good evening, gentlemen," he said ironically. "And happy New Year."

Jimmy looked grave. "Lou, the Quaker here tells me that you used a lot of language last night not befitting a gentleman to girls, to our entertainers."

When the Quaker said that Zimp had made this charge, Clayton observed, "I knew all along he was a yellow-bellied fox, because he had a pistol on him, but he ran out of the room last night." He sneered at the Quaker. "And you ran out of the room! I was tickled to death that Jimmy got out, and Eddie got out, and if I'd have had any brains I'd have got out. But no! I stay and try to pacify these people in this Hey Rube, and I only got the arms and legs God give me to protect myself. And now you say I used bad language!"

Zimp left the room, muttering to himself.

Under Clayton's questioning the girls of the chorus said he merely had asked them to stay out of their dressing room as much as they could. There was a coin-box telephone in the dressing room, and Clayton didn't want the girls to overhear the bootlegger's number, were he to call up for liquor during the evening. He merely had said, "Will you girls please stay the hell out of this room to-night? And thank you very much."

Clayton informed the Quaker, "You better go and get three new whores, because I'm quitting. And when I quit, my partners quit."

"Lou," Jimmy Durante objected, "I think you're losing your head. I don't think that's the right thing to do, just walk out on him. Let's do things like gentlemen."

"What do you call that, Jim? What do you want me to do?"

"Let's give these people a two-weeks' notice," Jim said.

"If that's the way you want it, Jim, that's the way it's gonna be."

The next evening Zimp said, "Lou, I understand you're going to quit in two weeks?"

"That's right, brave boy!"

"Well, what's going to happen to me?"

Clayton looked him in the eye. "What do I care what happens to you? Since when am I your guardian?"

"Well," Zimp said, "you know I got ten per cent of the Quaker, ain't I?"

"You haven't got ten per cent of us," said Clayton. "What are you trying to bring out?"

"Well," said Zimp, "don't you think I ought to go along with you three fellows and get ten per cent?"

"For what? Muscle? I don't stand for muscle. Nobody muscles me. I don't stand for it."

Zimp got angry. "Well, I'll tell you something! If I don't get ten per cent after I quit the joint, I'm going to shoot you in the leg, and you'll never dance no more."

Remembering the recent shambles, Clayton held his temper. "Zimp, you better not shoot me in the legs. You better hit me between my two eyes. Because if you shoot me in the leg, and I can't dance any more, I'll shoot you right between your two eyes! Now get outta my way!"

During the next weeks the trio did not work too well. They endeavored not to shirk, but the atmosphere somehow had changed. There was a lack of good fellowship. The punch laughs did not go over, and everything they did seemed forced. Their friends asked, "What's the matter with you three fellows? What's happened?"

When Jimmy and his partners left the Dover Club, Jeanne Durante made Jimmy promise never to buy into another place of that kind. She recalled her prediction that he would have trouble with the government, or in other ways, then added, "Tootis, why should you have the big headaches over selling liquor illegally? Don't you realize what it is to do that?"

"You're right, Toots," Jimmy replied. "I don't want ever to have a piece of a night club again as long as I live."

X

X

The Hollow Leg

HUMORIST Arthur "Bugs" Baer once remarked that Durante and Jackson were "scared to death of Lou Clayton." Of this Durante says, "Yeah, that's right, but— There's a but there. I'd argue with him, and he'd fight, even when I was right. But then I'd say, 'Lou, take this deal, will yah please?' And he'd say, after he'd looked at me for a while, 'Well, Jimmy, if that's the way you want it, that's the way it's gonna be.' Even if we stood to lose fifty thousand on the deal, he'd want me to be happy. That was the main thing with Lou."

The Schnozzola says that Clayton knew him better than Jimmy knew himself. "I know every move he makes too, just like he knows every move I make. He knows when I lie to him, when I don't look him in the face. When I'd want to get outta somethin', he'd say, 'Wait a minute!' Aw gee, there were so many fine qualities in that man. A lot of people thought him aggressive because he fought for his rights. He was very, very sensitive. He wasn't like me. All three of us had different dispositions. And he was honest to the core. He had terrific principles, and he wanted the other fellow to have 'em too. If he had ten thousand in his pocket, and you wanted ninety-nine hundred of it, there it was. But he made one point, which was, 'Give it back. Give it back, for you took it. If you're gonna put your hands in my pocket, then you gotta respect me and pay it back.'"

As an illustration of Clayton's belief that a borrower should pay back a debt—and he would let a man set the date himself for restitution—one remembers a time when Tony the Rock borrowed five thousand dollars from him. Tony's nickname was given him because he was one of the last of the Broadway boys to wear a diamond stickpin in his necktie. He had obtained this large stone from one of the rich widows upon whom he specialized for his upkeep at the gaming tables.

Ten years after Tony neglected to pay back the Clayton loan, he was dancing one night in a Hollywood café. Clayton chanced to be dining there, saw the Rock, and sent a note to his table, suggesting a meeting in the gentlemen's washroom. As the Rock entered that place with a big hello, Clayton whipped out his springblade pocketknife. He seized Tony's necktie and lopped it off above the place where the diamond glowed like a headlight.

Clayton pocketed the trophy. "Want a receipt?"

The Rock gasped, "No! No! It's all yours, Lou!"

By 1927 the Durantes had been married for almost six years. They were deeply in love, but Jeanne's continuing ill health and loneliness and her resentment of Lou Clayton marred their complete happiness.

Jeanne could not become reconciled to the fact that she had little influence in respect to the larger decisions governing the Schnozzola's activities. Whenever Durante asked what she thought of a business deal, Jeanne would reply, "Well, go ahead, Tootis, Clayton has made up your mind to do it anyway."

Concerning their situation during these years, Jim says, "Lou never said a wrong word about my missus. Here was a woman who used to have something to say about my career, and along comes a guy who does it so big. I know women are that way. It's nothing against anybody. And a man don't know. As I sit down and I think back, a man really don't know a woman. They don't know even one. We think sometimes by bringing home the envelope, by giving them the money, that's enough, but it really don't mean a thing. There's a picture on my dresser which was me the first time I started to play piano. And every time I look at that picture it takes me back. How little I knew. She had put on that picture a subscription, 'In the days when.' And I never miss thinking those were the happiest years of our life when she said, 'I wish you was a piano player.' And I think back that she wanted to work with me, and I didn't know; and I'm not saying this because she was my wife, she was a great entertainer, with a beautiful voice. And what a mistake! I keep on repeating to myself that taking her out of the business was such a mistake; and if I'd let her stay in it, she would have become a star in her own rights. And the big success I got with Clayton, Jackson, and Durante kept dragging me away from her."

Durante did, however, belatedly pay attention to Jeanne when

she asked him never again to own part of a night club. Clayton
said that he would go along with this decision. Lou told his partners
that he was going to "book a place" and get three thousand dollars
a week net, a thousand dollars each, and added, "It will only be
a matter of time till I jack up that salary."

Johnny Hodge, principal owner of the Parody Club on East
Forty-eighth Street, offered the trio a job in January of 1927. They
opened the Thursday after they had closed at the Dover. Leon the
headwaiter, Jack Roth the drummer, and Harry Donnelly the piano
player went along with Clayton, Jackson, and Durante.

The room, accommodating about four hundred persons, was in
the windowless basement of the building. An electric-fan ventilator
was supposed to bring fresh air into the place. It was more luxuri-
ously furnished than the Durant Club or the Dover, and Jimmy
called it his upholstered cellar.

The staunch discoverer and friend of the trio, Sime Silverman,
could be seen at the Parody four nights out of seven. Sime was not
much of a drinker and would feel good on two glasses of wine. He
had an expensive stop-watch, and it pleased him to flip it across
the floor when Durante began his act. The watch would strike
against the bandstand. Durante would pick it up and send it to
Tiffany's next day for repairs. It cost eighty or eighty-five dollars
and took about two weeks' time to mend Sime's watch. Then, the
very next night after the watch was returned, Sime would fling it
against the bandstand. Clayton finally kept the watch to cut down
on expenses.

On opening night at the Parody Club the Quaker, Mr. Bamboo,
and Zimp had a table. The Quaker nodded to Lou, but Clayton
refused to greet him or his companions. Jimmy, of course, was his
usual friendly self. Zimp told the Schnozz that Clayton had
snubbed him.

A few nights later Zimp came in again, to try to touch Durante
for a thousand dollars. Clayton threatened never to speak to Jimmy
if he gave the cheekster one white dime and escorted the angry
Zimp to the stairs.

At about this time three gun boys were on the prowl for the
Quaker. The "enforcers" chanced to be sitting in the club one evening when Zimp again applied for admittance. On being refused,

he sent in a demand that Durante give him five hundred dollars. The Quaker's enemies overheard this and went outdoors to take care of Zimp. He had gone.

That night Zimp had a few whiffs of the pipe, then went uptown to Lenox Avenue to play pinochle. It so happened that Mad Dog Coll dropped in at the rear of the cigar store where Zimp was playing cards and kibitzed over his shoulder. When Zimp played the ten of clubs to knock out the ace, instead of playing the king of clubs for that purpose, the Mad Dog said it was a very silly thing to do.

Zimp glanced up and sneered, "Why don't you mind your own business?"

There were more words, and the hop-happy Zimp slapped Coll's face. The Mad Dog inquired, "Would you please wait here for a few minutes?"

"I don't know whether I'll wait or not," said Zimp, "but don't hand out no more of your advice."

Coll said over his shoulder, "I won't bother you with advice."

"That's better." Zimp resumed his study of the cards.

In about five minutes Coll reappeared and shot Zimp in the head. The body was found by the police some days later in the Harlem River.

As for the Quaker and Mr. Bamboo, they eventually fell upon evil times. A fire at the refurnished Dover Club gutted the room and the garage under it. The Quaker carried no insurance, and had gone for his roll to recondition the club.

Early in 1930 a foreign agent of Mr. Bamboo and his associates purchased in Europe enough narcotics to fill two trunks. The agent shipped the trunks from Le Havre in the hold of the French Line luxury ship *Ile de France*. An English gentleman, known as a Joe Blow, was commissioned to accompany the trunks to New York as their dummy owner. A Joe Blow is an intermediary who undertakes the delivery of something without having had actual contact with goods consigned to interested parties.

Mr. Blow, who came aboard ship from a tender off Plymouth, England, had never seen the trunks. His own two pieces of hand baggage were placed in his cabin. The purser gave him the two claim checks for the precious trunks in the hold.

When one went through the United States Customs, a government inspector pasted a stamp on each piece of luggage that passed examination. The stamps were uniformly of one color, an off-white. After the stamps were affixed, porters would wheel trunks or other luggage to the gate of the pier shed, where a second Customs man canceled the paper stamps with an inked rubber stamp. The baggage was then clear, except for one formality: a passenger had to surrender claim checks, if any, to an employee of the steamship company.

Joe Blow got off the ship and went to the letter "B" at the pier. His two bags were inspected and stamped. He did not ask the inspector to examine the trunks, of course, so they remained locked and standing among many other pieces of baggage that awaited examination on the busy scene.

At the outer gate Mr. Bamboo greeted Joe, received from him the claim checks for the bonded trunks, and went inside to claim them. Leaning against one trunk was a Customs agent, resting from the effects of a late night out. For perhaps twenty minutes, Mr. Bamboo sweated it out. Finally, after the crowd had begun to thin out, the Customs man moved groggily off.

Mr. Bamboo sidled up to the trunks, backed against each one in turn, and, as he did so, pasted bogus white stamps on them. Having done this, he called porters to wheel the trunks out to the pier gate. An unsuspecting Customs man canceled the stamps, and Mr. Bamboo was entirely in the clear, except . . .

In his excitement he neglected to give the French Line employee the claim checks. He was walking along happily, although somewhat damp with perspiration, and his porters were trundling the trunks behind him, when a French Line employee called out, "Monsieur! You!" Mr. Bamboo did not stop to think about surrendering the claim checks. He took to his heels. Bystanders merely glanced at the fleeing man, then, like true New Yorkers, went about their own business.

Mr. Bamboo leaped into a taxicab, pulled his hatbrim down over his eyes, and crouched low in the seat. After meandering about town in various cabs and subways to shake off his fancied pursuers, he rejoined his confederates at a hotel rendezvous. He reported that he miraculously had escaped the law.

The syndicate members expressed alarm—also disappointment. The trunks contained three hundred thousand dollars' worth of goods bought on the European market, and were worth who knows how much in America.

For days the unhappy merchants lay low. Joe Blow had planned to return home in style, but he too hid out. When no squawks were heard and two weeks had gone by, they became convinced that Mr. Bamboo had fled the pier gate without good reason. They decided to get the trunks. Hadn't they been duly stamped and cleared?

A member of the syndicate contacted a government employee. He told this man that the trunks contained two hundred dollars' worth of liquor in all and asked if he would see to it that the pieces were surrendered legally but quietly. They already had been double-stamped, he reminded the employee, who was offered a gratuity of one hundred dollars.

This employee had but two more years to serve as a government worker before' he was eligible for a pension. It appears from what afterward occurred that the man worried about the proposition and decided to open the trunks. To his dismay he saw that they contained narcotics. Rather than be a party to the delivery of these drugs, the agent confessed. Although promptly sacked, and his pension rights revoked, he escaped prosecution because he belatedly had done a courageous thing.

Investigators traced the trunk's means of entry to the *Ile de France* and determined which cabin Joe Blow had occupied under an alias.

The next time the liner arrived in port, officials learned that Joe Blow was a short, blond fellow with thick-lensed spectacles. The agents questioned the ship's photographer and looked through every negative pertaining to the voyage in question. Finally they settled upon the picture of a boxing bout. There, among the photographed audience, and in the front row, and very happy indeed, sat Joe Blow the sportsman.

The pictorial evidence was uncovered the day after Joe Blow sailed to England aboard the *Berengaria*. Government agents wired his description to all European-bound ships. Scotland Yard returned Joe Blow to New York to stand trial on a narcotics charge.

When he was arraigned before Federal Judge Henry Goddard, Joe set up a big to-do that, as an English citizen, he should have an English lawyer to defend him. Judge Goddard, however, assigned a rising young New York attorney, Charles L. Sylvester, to represent Mr. Blow.

The defendant would not talk to his attorney at all, thinking him a government agent. Mr. Bamboo got in touch with Sylvester and said, "We'll do anything for this boy as long as he don't mention us." He also revealed that, during a recent trip to Paris, he and Joe Blow had purchased two unusual amber necklaces for their respective lady friends. Mr. Bamboo gave Sylvester one of these necklaces as a token, to convince Joe Blow that his attorney was the real McCoy. But still Joe Blow would not talk. He was convicted after a trial before Judge Frank Cooper in United States District Court on April 18, 1930.

From that time on Customs provided stamps of several shades, instead of merely one, and used them without previous announcement of color on various days of the week, to prevent a recurrence of Mr. Bamboo's smuggling conspiracy.

Lou Clayton frequently lectured his partners on the hazards of gambling. He permitted them to risk a few dollars now and again on the ponies, on dice games, or at cards, but he made them promise never to go up against professionals.

Durante and Jackson would have liked to have been successful gamblers, but they had easy-mark dispositions. They went to much trouble to hide from Clayton their occasional betting sprees. Neither Jimmy nor Eddie had personal bank accounts at this time; they allowed their wives to keep their growing wealth in their own names.

Jimmy thought over the problem of where to keep the money he "pinched out" of sums acquired beyond his weekly salary. He eventually confided in Jackson that he had hit upon a hiding place as safe as Arlington Cemetery.

"I just read about an employee with a wooden leg out in the Denver mint," Durante said, "and he abscondled with thousands in gold in his leg."

"How's that affect us?" asked Eddie.

Durante made sure that Clayton was not listening in. "Charlie Cooper has a wooden leg!"

Cooper, the doorman at the Parody, was the man who worked after hours as Jackson's chauffeur and slept in his gymnasium. He agreed, after no little persuasion, to cache the money inside his artificial limb. "It's got to be folding money though," Cooper stipulated. "I don't want to sound like jingle bells. Besides, my leg is heavy enough without loading it down with coins."

Sometimes Banker Cooper had on deposit as much as three thousand dollars. It required ten minutes or more for him to undo the leg from its moorings, so he requested the capitalists to give ample notice whenever they proposed to withdraw their money.

Before the trio separated for their summer holiday, Clayton agreed to do his friend Benevolent Charlie a favor. The benevolent one had a luxurious gambling casino and restaurant at Saratoga and asked that the Parody Club stars play at his establishment for two weeks at five thousand dollars a week.

"Gladly, Charlie," Clayton said, "but I want one thing clear: never under any circumstance are you to let Jimmy or Eddie play the wheel or shoot craps in your room. I'll do all the gambling that's necessary."

"They'll be as safe as in a church," said Benevolent Charlie.

The Durante troupe had been at the Saratoga spa for two or three nights when Jackson met an old Brooklyn friend, an ex-streetcar conductor known to gambling circles as Carbarn Frank. As this gentleman emerged from the gambling room Eddie said, "How did you make out, Frank?"

"Oh, I rung up a few fares tonight, Eddie," said Carbarn Frank.

"Shooting craps?"

"No, sir. Roulette. I got a system."

"Well," Jackson said, "you and me know one another for years. How about giving me that system?"

"If you won't tell a soul."

"Not even my rabbi."

"All right. It's only five numbers you play: seven, eleven, thirteen, nineteen, and twenty-nine. Play them numbers, Eddie, and stick to 'em for about an hour only, and you can't miss."

Jackson informed Durante of this unbeatable system. The Schnozzola became excited. "After the first show, Eddie, we'll slip away from Lou and put twenty dollars apiece on the wheel."

While Clayton was having a bath and rubdown between shows the system players all but ran to the gambling room. The doorkeeper halted them with, "You can't come in here."

"Why not?" asked Jimmy.

"We don't allow the entertainers to gamble here."

"But," protested the Schnozz, "Lou comes in here! Clayton comes in here!"

"That's all right, but *you* can't come in."

Durante gave the doorman ten dollars. "You didn't see us."

The doorman turned his back. The confident Jimmy said, "Eddie, go over to the first table and buy a stack of yellow chips." But the banker was just out of yellow chips. "Well," said Durante, "Go to the next table and buy a stack of green chips."

The second banker said there were no green ones to be had. At the third table, where white chips were dispensed, Jackson received the same answer. Durante said, "Something smells bad here. Let's go see the boss."

Benevolent Charlie greeted Jimmy with a big hello, complimented him on his performance that evening, and asked how he was feeling.

"It's not how we feel. But we'd like to know one thing."

"What's that, Jimmy?"

"Eddie and me want to play a little roulette. We want only to try our skill, and, well, they don't want to sell us any chips." Durante turned to Jackson. "Eddie, show him that forty dollars." Then he asked Charlie, "What's wrong with our money? Ain't it no good?"

"I'll tell you the truth, boys. Lou Clayton don't want you to play. And I told all the dealers and the manager not to let you lose your money here. Just keep on entertaining."

"Aw gee, Charlie!" Durante cried out, "just let's lose this forty. Jackson's got a system."

Benevolent Charlie laughed. "System! What's your system?"

"Oh," said Jackson, "I tell nobody."

"Well," said Benevolent Charlie, "go ahead."

The boss went over to the floor manager and okayed the two gentlemen. Within the hour they had won four hundred dollars. The next night they took down another three or four hundred. Their luck continued for a third time. "Eddie," said Durante, "Now I'd like to try my own system just once."

"Play it yourself, Jimmy. I'm sticking to a sure thing."

Each man played his own system, and both plans went sour. They lost what money they had not deposited in Cooper's leg and, besides that, signed an IOU for fifteen hundred dollars.

"I only hope Clayton don't find out," said Durante. "Let's be awful careful."

About three o'clock in the morning Jackson and Durante went outside. They ran into Eddie's banker-chauffeur.

"What's wrong with you birds?" Cooper said. "You look a little pale."

"We're not feeling too hot," Durante said, then brightened. "Charlie, come into the washroom with us a minute."

"What for? I don't need to."

"Oh, yes you do," said Eddie.

In the washroom Durante said, "Now take your leg off."

"What for? You nuts?"

"Never mind," Jackson said. "Unscrew the leg."

"But my God! Not in here?"

"Right here," the Schnozz commanded. "We want to make good on an IOU before Clayton gets wise."

"Now off with the leg!" Eddie said. "We was saving it in case of a tie, and now we got tied."

"But suppose somebody comes in when I'm doing it and—"

"Nix," said Jackson. "Do you want to keep your job or don't you?"

The losers withdrew enough money to pay up at the casino, and Durante decided to take out an extra five hundred.

Later that morning Durante knocked at Eddie's door. "Where's Charlie Cooper stayin'?"

"Near a garage." Eddie gave the address. "Why?"

"I dropped seven hundred more," the Schnozz confessed, "and I got to pay for an IOU for two Cs."

Next day Clayton said, "Smart guys, eh? Well, I knew all about it, and I let you get roughed around on purpose. Had enough?"

"Yeah," said Durante and went on to inquire, "Is there anything to a system, Lou?"

"There sure is," Clayton said. "And it's this: no matter who you are, if you play long enough against the percentage the house takes on each spin of the wheel or each roll of the dice, you are bound to get knocked out."

That summer Clayton and his wife went to Lake Placid, where he played golf. Jackson, his wife, and their baby daughter went to the Catskills for their holiday. And the Durantes set out for Clear Lake.

The Durantes returned to New York in September of 1927. The Schnozzola told Jeanne that he would like to handle his own money, because he wanted to keep a bankroll in his pocket. Aside from the cash in Charlie Cooper's leg, Durante didn't have access to much spending money at any one time. He told Jeanne that he felt left out of things as he watched other Broadway gentlemen peel off banknotes in public places.

On October 15 of 1927 Jimmy took Jeanne to the office of Dr. Wynne on East Fifty-third Street for a physical checkup. Jimmy that day had two banknotes in his pocket, a thousand-dollar bill and a dollar bill. Jeanne was carrying a velvet handbag with but forty dollars in it. She was wearing her diamond engagement ring, the small stone that Jimmy's mother had given him some years ago, and her wedding ring.

The receptionist at the office was informing the Durantes that the doctor was busy in the next room when four armed bandits walked in. "Stand up against the wall!"

One holdup man stayed behind in the reception room while the others went into the examination room, where a male patient was lying face down on the table, nude except for his undershirt. The doctor was ordered to stand against the wall, the patient warned not to move even a muscle. The Durantes and the receptionist were herded into the examination rom.

Jimmy addressed the terrified man on the table. "There's ladies present! Can't you put your pants on?"

The gang leader advanced on Jim as though to shoot him. "Shut up! And stand back!"

Mrs. Durante fell to the floor as if in a faint. Jimmy moved to help his stricken wife but was hurled against the wall. "Another move out of you, and I'll shoot that big nose right off your face!"

"But my wife, she could be dead!" Durante protested. Then, as a magnificent non sequitur, he blurted out, "And besides, this is awful unmodest as a situation."

The robbers took Dr. Wynne's valuables, then found the patient's wallet in his pants, lying on a chair beside the table. One of the men shook Mrs. Durante but decided to let her stay as she was on the floor. Jimmy's two bills were taken, and the gangsters left the premises.

The patient draped himself in a sheet, and Dr. Wynne prepared to minister to Mrs. Durante. She amazed everyone by springing to her feet, giggled, then triumphantly exhibited her velvet bag. She had thrown it beneath the examination table while pretending to faint and had hidden her rings in her mouth.

While the doctor was notifying the police the Schnozz looked at his wife and said, "Toots, I guess I shouldn't handle our money after all. This proves you know how to take care of it."

Some weeks after the holdup the bandits were arrested. Durante and Clayton were asked by a fellow known as the Chinaman, an active operator in bootleg circles, to decline to identify the robbers, as a personal favor.

Durante obliged, but only after his money had been returned. Dr. Wynne, however, identified the bandits. They served time in Sing Sing. Years afterward they went on a rampage out West, were convicted, and perished in a prison fire.

It seems a curious circumstance that Jeanne Durante behaved so bravely, when we remember how frightened she was to be left alone. In the face of actual danger she always became very courageous. On several occasions when she came home to find robbers on the premises, she behaved coolly and outwitted them. Once, when the Durantes were living on Olympic Boulevard in Los Angeles, she returned alone from Palm Springs. Jimmy was in San Francisco, playing a benefit. As she entered her bedroom she heard footsteps. Then the alarm clock sounded in the kitchen. This puzzled her, for it was an old alarm which she never wound and which she kept as a kitchen convenience. She waited a while, and the alarm went off again. She was smart enough to know that someone in the house had set it off in the hope that she might come to the kitchen to be robbed and probably tied up or assaulted.

It was Durante's ambition to play the Palace Theatre. But whenever Clayton had asked for three thousand dollars, the manager had said, "Who knows you?" Now, when the management again offered to book the trio, Clayton upped the price to thirty-five hundred dollars.

"Knock it off at their price," Durante urged.

"No," replied Clayton, "and the next time they ask, the salary will be five grand."

"That's ridiculous!" exclaimed Schnozzola.

"You 'tend to the joke department," said Lou, "and Eddie to his singing. I'll look after the business end."

Loew's State Theatre, three blocks north of the Parody Club, met Clayton's demands for thirty-five hundred dollars a week for two weeks, the trio to play four shows a day.

Clayton called up Mr. C. B. Dillingham at the Globe Theatre. The previous spring the celebrated impresario had commissioned playwright William Anthony Maguire to write a book for a musical production to be called *Ripples* and had contracted for the services of Clayton, Jackson, and Durante. Clayton now wanted to know where they stood in respect to the contract. "Suppose I give you ten thousand dollars," Dillingham said, "and tear up the contract? I don't know when Maguire's going to give me the book, if ever."

Durante never had been on the stage, other than to perform at a night club. Clayton, of course, had appeared at the Winter Garden, at the Palace, and with the Georgia minstrels, McIntyre and Heath, in *The Ham Tree*. Comedian Joe Laurie, Jr., an authority on vaudeville, remembers that McIntyre and Heath, one of the oldest partnerships in show business, never spoke to one another offstage and died within a few months of each other.

Eddie Jackson too had been in vaudeville and traveled as far West as Kansas City, Missouri, where he had been stranded with Dot Taylor and her young son. They had to eat popcorn for three days.

At about four o'clock one morning the trio called at Silverman's apartment on West Forty-sixth Street. The six-story *Variety* building originally had housed the dressmaking firm of Madame Frances (a gentleman named Nate Spingold). An inner circle of perhaps a dozen friends, among them Mayor James J. Walker, had gold keys to the Silverman top-floor apartment.

"As you know, boys," Sime told them, "this act is to be in a theater, not a night club. You have to rehearse each number and get the act timed exactly right."

The next day they rehearsed at the club, and that night did the show as they would do it at Loew's State. They stayed two weeks at Loew's and broke all records.

Many producers now wanted to hire the trio. The Shuberts made offers, and Florenz Ziegfeld. The Palace booking agent informed Clayton that the thirty-five hundred salary would be his for the asking.

Clayton said, "The price is five grand now."

"Please, Lou!" Jimmy almost screamed. "Take it! Knock it off!"

"No," said Clayton. "Be a good boy and shut up!"

The vitality of the three men was amazing. They did as many as twelve turns a night at the Parody Club and also appeared in four shows afternoons and nights at Loew's State.

Durante advised Lou to give up dice playing, not only because sleep was precious but the financial hazards were great. But Lou said he could not quit, that gambling was his curse, and that he would have to live with it.

One night Clayton shot dice in a Park Avenue game of which Arnold Rothstein had fifty per cent, as the silent partner of a man known as "the Herring." Clayton had a lucky two hours and won ten thousand nine hundred and fifty dollars. Chips had been used instead of cash in this game, and the Herring gave Clayton a check to cover his winnings. When Clayton presented the paper at the bank he learned that the Herring had but a thousand dollars on deposit.

That night at the Parody Club, Rothstein said to Clayton, "Understand you won some money last night?"

"That's right, A. R., and I got a no good map for my winnings."

"I'll cash that check for you," offered Rothstein, "if you take a twenty-five per cent discount."

Clayton snorted. "I book a winner, and you say you'll cash the check if I give you a discount. No. I understand you got fifty per cent of that place, A. R., and I'd better get my money, because if I don't I'll guarantee you I'll disgrace you all over this Avenue."

Several times that week Clayton made it his business to denounce Rothstein in person. This effrontery annoyed the man against whom most citizens of the Avenue were afraid to speak openly. A. R. telephoned one night. "Come over to my office tomorrow, Clayton."

The Rothstein offices were more or less soundproof, except for a papier-mâché wall that separated the Brain's private quarters from a room occupied by his chief hatchetman, Fats Walsh.

No sooner had Clayton arrived than Rothstein began to call him names. Clayton replied coolly, "A. R., you're supposed to be a big shot on this Avenue, but to me you got the heart of a gutter bum."

Bodyguard Walsh entered Rothstein's office, his right hand in his coat pocket. Clayton knew that Walsh was not caressing a bean-shooter.

"Did you want to see me, Mr. A. R.?" asked Fats.

"No, I'll send for you when I need you." Rothstein turned to

Lou. "Well, I suppose you'll be going down to the D. A.'s office?"

"All I came here for was to get my money, A. R. I want ten thousand nine hundred and fifty, and I'm gonna get it, because if I don't, A. R., I'm not going to any D. A., but I'm gonna disgrace you. Everybody on this Avenue will know you're a welsher."

"You think you'll get away with these tactics?"

"A. R.," said Clayton, "you squealed on Whitey after he stuck you up at the Somerset Hotel at a private crap game. You went to the D. A. and turned him in, but I don't squeal on nobody. I'll just disgrace you in front of your face."

The reference to Whitey seemed to move Rothstein to conciliatory action. He cashed the check, and never again spoke to Clayton, nor Clayton to him.

At this time Miss Fanny Brice, New York's foremost comedienne, was a headliner at the Palace Theatre. She fell ill, and the management hurriedly sought a replacement on the bill. When Clayton was approached he said that the price for the trio would be five thousand five hundred dollars.

"I'll tell you what," he said. "We'll take a draw with you. If we go in there and do business, you give us the fifty-five hundred. If we don't break your house record, then you don't owe us a quarter."

The agent nodded. "You've got a deal, except we'll pay five thousand; but if you break the record held by Beatrice Lillie, we'll give you a bonus of five hundred."

The trio was billed in the spot next to closing. They were supposed to do forty minutes, but the audiences would not let them offstage for an hour and a half. The Palace decided to cancel the last act, for no one could successfully follow the Schnozzola and his partners. The first week they broke all records, received their bonus, and were held over for three successive weeks.

From then until 1930 they were frequently booked at the Palace. They always clicked there, and did so, let it be remembered, when sound came to motion pictures and hastened the death of vaudeville.

Sime Silverman, of course, was delighted at the success of his protégés. He had a waggish disposition and sometimes wrote disparagingly of the Sawdust Bums, expressing wonderment that they had been hired at the Palace. Durante turned the joke on Sime, served defamation of character papers on him, and, with Lou and Eddie, picketed the *Variety* offices. Silverman threw a picket line in front of the Palace. The management begged both parties to call off their joke, because many patrons took it seriously and refused to cross the picket line at the box office.

During one of their subsequent appearances at the Palace the trio introduced their greatest act, the Wood Number. Durante had created this after reading a trade-magazine advertisement picked up by Jeanne in the club car while en route from California to Chicago. The lumber company advertisement said that wood had played a mighty part in civilization, that without wood life on earth would be unthinkable.

Jimmy composed the number to the tempo of Kipling's poem "Boots." The cue for it was Clayton's remark that the Schnozzola's head was made of wood. Jimmy would reply that he was delighted to know this, since wood was the most valuable thing known to civilization. In the course of the act all kinds of wood products were brought on stage: furniture, boards, curtain poles, pencils, violins from the pit, a tree stump, a ricksha, and even an outhouse. During the violent collection of these objects Jimmy and his partners sang, "Wood . . . wood . . . wood . . ."

When offers for engagements came in, including a bid from Paramount Pictures, Clayton said to Durante, "We shouldn't try to eat all the pieces of pie at one time. Sit back for the best piece, and it will come."

At Christmas time. Jimmy said, "Lou, you know that ten thousand we got from Mr. Dillingham? Well, he's such a swell guy, and we've done nothing for that ten thousand. I like to be a giver, not a taker. Suppose we send him back that check?"

Clayton sent the check, along with a note: "Please accept this as a Christmas present from the Three Sawdust Bums of Broadway." Mr. Dillingham, himself a true gentleman, saw to it that everyone on Broadway heard about the Christmas present the trio had given him.

XI

It Was Chilly in Minneapolis

IN THE spring of 1928 Durante became dissatisfied with the Parody Club management. One March afternoon Jimmy and Lou found Eddie Jackson almost in tears, and Johnny Hodge, proprietor of the Parody, glowering at him.

"What seems to be the trouble, Eddie?" inquired Durante.

Jackson indicated Hodge with his thumb. "Let him tell you."

Hodge objected to Jackson's song "There'll Be Some Changes Made."

"Eddie has a couple of hundred songs," Clayton cut in. "Why pick on that one?"

"Because," said Hodge, "I'm tired of it."

"Well, let me tell yah somethin', Mr. Hodge," replied Durante, "when yah pick on Eddie, you're picking on me and Lou."

Clayton notified Hodge, "We're gonna pull out of here this May."

During the remainder of the season Mr. Hodge, although sulky, relied upon Clayton to quell disorders in the rathskeller.

It seems remarkable that—except for the brawl that had wrecked the Dover Club—violence spared the places where the Schnozzola performed. Before this age of reckless living reached its close, there were murders at the Club Abbey, the Hotsy Totsy Club, and several places elsewhere on the Avenue, but not in cafés where Jimmy's warm personality and Clayton's firm ways kept troublemakers in hand.

One evening Big Link, a former Hudson Duster, arrived at the outer door of the club. Two weeks before this the Link had shot a gentleman, one Johnny Blue Eyes, in the leg, and Johnny was at the moment sitting at a table at the Parody with another gentleman, the Silver Fox.

Johnny Blue Eyes was an exceptionally handsome, well-built young man. The Link also was large and collegiate in appearance. Unlike most gangsters, the Link had come of a well-to-do family.

Some quirk had turned his mind to crime. He drank heavily and used drugs. Charged with Peruvian snow, he became a wildie.

Johnny Blue Eyes and the Silver Fox were having caviar and chopped onions when Proprietor Hodge whispered to Clayton, "The Link is on the upstairs sidewalk with his forty-five."

Clayton signaled to the band to play loudly, then went up to the street. The Link was arguing with doorkeeper Charlie Cooper. "Link," said Clayton, "why don't you go home like a good boy?"

The Link waved his shooting-iron. "Not till I see two certain parties you got downstairs."

"You're putting gray hairs in my head, Link," Clayton said, "and you're a link I wish I could take right outta the chain of my years. Please give me your gun."

"All right, I'll give you the gun!" snarled the Link, pressing the muzzle against Clayton's stomach.

Lou decided to talk. "Think what you are doing. All I'm trying to do is save you. Link, somebody is going to get cooked, and you'll wind up on the front burner."

The Link relented. "All right. Loan me twenty-five dollars."

Clayton ran downstairs, got twenty-five dollars from the cash register, came up again, gave the money to the Link, and put him into a taxicab.

Lou returned to the cellar room to find Johnny Blue Eyes and the Silver Fox waiting for him. They demanded their sidearms, which he had persuaded them to leave in cold storage.

Clayton returned their weapons. "Now, please blow."

"That is our intention." Johnny Blue Eyes winked.

The Link, full of liquor and well frosted with cocaine, meantime had gone downtown to Greenwich Village. He decided to visit an upstairs cabaret on West Eighth Street. On the stairs he met an undersized fellow, known as Philly the Fly, coming down with a very tall girl on his arm.

The Link sneered, "Why don't you get this broad a job as first baseman for the Yankees?"

The Fly talked back, and the Link slapped his face. Philly's girl steadied her little escort, called the Link a no good son of something, and at the curb outside the café got into a taxicab with Philly.

Half an hour later the Fly returned alone to the café. He stayed inside the downstairs vestibule, exchanging prize-fight gossip with the doorman, until the Link, now very drunk, appeared on the stairs. He never walked the whole way down. The Fly fired but one shot, and the Link's body did what the boys called going over Niagara in a barrel. Someone interested in protecting the café's good name managed to get the body into a cab and away from the neighborhood.

Now Johnny Blue Eyes and the Silver Fox appeared on the scene. "Did you see the Link tonight?" Johnny asked the doorman.

"He just left here."

"Oh. Know where we can get in touch with him?"

"I'd say yes to that."

"Well then, where?"

"A hundred to one," said the doorman, "you will find the Link on a marble couch at Bellevue Morgue."

"Oh," said the Silver Fox. "I knew he'd get tired out sooner or later."

A police siren sounded from somewhere on Sixth Avenue.

"Let's get out of here," said Johnny Blue Eyes.

"It would be the reasonable thing to do," the Silver Fox agreed.

Among the musicians at the Parody Club was a young man named Benjamin A. Gilbert, a student at the New York Medical College attached to Flower Hospital. He had been working his way through school by playing the trumpet for dances at the Knickerbocker Hotel when Harry Donnelly, Durante's piano player, asked Benny to try out at the Parody.

Jimmy gave him the job. "If ever you need money for your intuition, just let me know, because you'll stay with our combination till you finish medical school, and you'll be my boy."

Gilbert was at school from nine in the morning until five in the afternoon. At seven-thirty he played the supper show. It got so that he couldn't concentrate on his studies unless there was noise. He would bring his lecture notes and his anatomy charts and clinical pictures to the club and place them between sheets of music so that he could study during the orchestra's rests. He finished work so late that he had to attend classes dressed in his tuxedo. The dean of the medical school wondered about this.

One night the dean saw the student tootling in Durante's band at the Palace. Next day he gave Benny the option of leaving medical school or resigning from Durante's orchestra.

Durante called upon the dean and pleaded with him to let young Gilbert continue his studies as well as his musical duties. The Schnozzola promised to do anything at all for the hospital, sing, play, or appear at benefits. Durante said nothing to Benny of this visit.

The trio said farewell to the Parody Club on Memorial Day, played vaudeville engagements at the Palace, then at Newark, and in Keith-Albee theatres uptown. The booking agent for the circuit's Midwestern theaters signed the three to play Cincinnati, Chicago, and Milwaukee. The wives were to stay home until their husbands returned from the road tour, their first out-of-town appearance.

At Cincinnati a racing-wire operator, Gambling Boy, met them at the railroad station. He told his friend Clayton, "You're not going to make a move without me. I'm going to be with you every time you leave the hotel, and take you wherever you want to go in my own car."

"Well," Clayton asked, "what's your reason for that?"

"You'll learn the reason when you get back to Broadway."

Whenever the trio got into Gambling Boy's five-passenger car, their guardian would put all three of them in the back seat. Durante always liked to ride in the front seat, but Gambling Boy would say, "Get in the back, Jimmy."

Another fellow, a strangely silent character, rode in the front seat with Gambling Boy during these trips. Clayton did not ask any questions concerning this man, nor did Gambling Boy volunteer an explanation. The trio left for Chicago still in the dark.

The Chicago engagement went very well, professionally and socially. Jackson's old friend of the bookbindery days, Al Capone, was maharajah of gangland. Durante and Clayton hitherto had not known that Eddie—who quailed whenever a gunman came into a club where he was coonshouting—was a great favorite of Scarface. The Chicago overlord insisted upon lending the trio a beautiful automobile—armor-plated—a chauffeur, and an armed guard.

When Eddie admired Capone's battleship on wheels, the flattered gangster offered him a present of one just like it. Jackson declined, and Scarface grew angry. Durante smoothed his feelings by saying that Eddie couldn't drive a car, especially such a heavy one.

Jackson roomed with Durante on this tour. Clayton liked to sleep by himself and engaged a room on the other side of the sitting room of the Durante suite at the Bismarck Hotel in Chicago.

One night Durante, ordinarily a good sleeper, called out, "Eddie!" Eddie turned on the lights. Jim was sitting up in bed. "Yes, Jim, what is it?"

"Eddie, you know somethin'? We're gettin' fifty-five hundred a week here. A king's transom. Do you think we're worth that kind of money?"

"I guess we are or they wouldn't pay it, Jimmy."

"That's a lotta money, Eddie. Where do we come off gettin' it? I just don't think nobody's really worth that kinda dough."

"Well, Jim," said Eddie, "we pack the theaters."

"I still can't believe it, Eddie. Me and you, workin' back in the old days, were just makin' a living. And now look. Headlinin' theaters! New York and Chicago talkin' about us! I don't understand that much money."

If Jimmy wondered if the act was worthy fifty-five hundred dollars a week, he would soon find out. At the end of their successful Milwaukee engagement the trio received a telegram from an old friend, Ben Piazza, then a vaudeville booking agent and later a casting director in Hollywood. He asked them to do him a great favor and play a week in Minneapolis.

Jim asked his partners what kind of show town "Minneanapolis" was. "Have you ever played it, Eddie?"

"Sure, I played it years ago with Jackson and Taylor."

"What kinda audience they got out there?"

"A little tough, but so far we been lucky on the road, and I don't see why we should miss there."

"Oh, great!" said Jimmy. Then he asked Lou of his experiences.

"It's a great town," said Clayton. "I played it three times. Georgie Burns and Gracie Allen are there, and might stay over a day or two to catch our act."

"All right then," said Durante, "let's knock off the week at Minneanapolis."

Concerning a time that still stands out as a sore memory, Jimmy says, "Our routine consisted of such numbers as 'I Can Do without Broadway, but Can Broadway Do without Me?' 'Jimmy, the Well-dressed Man,' and Eddie doin' his strut, and numbers like 'I Ups to Him,' and I don't remember what we finished with. And I liked that town very much. We had with us a kid workin' as a kinda secretary, Jack Harvey. He's one of our writers now.

"There was an act on ahead of us called 'The Cowboy and the Girl.' Now I'm standin' in the wings, and they got lines like 'Roses are red, violets blue, horses neck, do you?' And this act was gettin' dynamite laughs.

"And so we are in high spirits, and I go out there. I look down at Georgie Burns and Gracie Allen in the audience, and they applaud like mad, but we get little applause from anybody else. And then I open with 'Jimmy, the Well-dressed Man.' Believe me, in all the years I been in the business—nothin', just nothin' happened. I got on a raccoon coat, and I remember hearin' someone in the audience sayin' out loud, 'He's not well dressed.'

"And then we do 'I Know Darn Well I Can Do without Broadway,' and I come to a line where Shubert is supposed to be standin' in the wings, and he comes out and says, 'Jimmy, put in both knees, and Jolson goes.' Nothin'! Nothin' at all! And that was our biggest laugh in New York.

"Now we're discouraged. Discouraged. Jackson didn't go so good with his number either. Lou got some applause for his dancin', but everythin' was kind of sour and we go off. To make things tougher, this kid Harvey is out on the street one day, and he walks against the lights, and a cop gives him a ticket, and he calls the cop a hick. And then headlines come out that one of the boys in the band called a cop a hick and we think this is a hick town. Well, I coulda died.

"Harvey was locked up. He needed ten dollars' bail or somethin'. I didn't let him have it. I says, 'Let him rot there!' None of us went down to the jail. We let him get out the best he could. And the act went very bad, and on top of this the guy callin' a cop a hick, which was out of line. I said to Lou, 'Aw, please, let's drop the whole business and go home!'

"Well, Burns and Allen are awful good people but they come to our dressin' room and they simply got to laugh about this. They had done well, and they always did do well. And around the bookin' offices in New York, every time Lou would show up, the booker would say, 'Do you want us to book you in Minneanapolis?' "

The Minneapolis fizzle awakened the Schnozzola to the realities of American taste for comedy beyond the small area of Times

Square. "We hadn't given them what they wanted," he says. "It was before the big broadcastin' days, and sound was just comin' inta the movies, and I found out that Broadway and New York ain't the whole world. There's a great big country outside of it, and each place has a solid humor of its own, and you got to have an act that is right down to earth.

"It wasn't the fault of Minneapolis. It was our fault. And I was very happy a long time afterward in 1934 when Minneapolis voted me the best comedian in pictures. I loved 'em for this. I loved 'em for teachin' me a valuable lesson."

When the trio returned to New York after the Minneapolis episode they were met at the train by two high rollers, the Chinaman and a chap known as Long-shot Abraham. They borrowed twenty-five hundred dollars from Clayton at the train gate at Grand Central Station.

A few days later Clayton met these men on Broadway, and Long-shot Abraham brought out twenty-five hundred dollars and counted it down, to repay his debt. "We only wanted to know how we stood with you," he explained. "To see if you would risk your dough on us."

Clayton was offended by this test of his friendship. The Chinaman placated him. "We knew we had your confidence, or you would not of gone for the bite."

An idea now occurred to Clayton. "How come you boys knew the exact hour and the train Durante and me and Eddie Jackson was going to come in on?"

The Chinaman explained. The silent man who had ridden in Gambling Boy's car in Cincinnati was a fugitive gangster from Detroit, called the Dimmy because of his thick wits. In Detroit he had hit Long-shot Abraham's brother under the heart with a bullet, but the victim had survived. The Dimmy fled to Cincinnati. He was unaware that Gambling Boy was a good friend of Long-shot Abraham. Also, he revealed to his host that he planned to snatch Durante or one of his partners at the earliest opportunity—which was why Gambling Boy had put the three men in the back seat, so that the Dimmy could not split them out, as the saying was. Someone eventually caught up with the Dimmy and made blue portholes in him.

The Clear Lake interludes were becoming shorter and fewer for

Jimmy and his Jeanne. They had barely arrived there in the late summer of 1928 when a telegram arrived from Clayton. He had booked the trio for three days at a Red Bank casino operated by a bootlegger known to the rum empire as Lonesome Tom.

"Three days!" Jeanne exclaimed. "Why leave here for only three days?"

"Lou wouldn't call me in unless it was important."

So back they went to New York, arriving home just before Labor Day. Lonesome Tom told Clayton he could not guarantee the trio three thousand dollars for a split week but offered to turn over to the comedians the "plates," or cover charge, for a room that seated four hundred. Clayton accepted this proposition upon ascertaining that the cover charge was four dollars a person. The trio made almost five thousand dollars on the covers that holiday week end.

Lonesome Tom asked Clayton if he would care to entertain him at cards between shows. Lou consented to play a series of Klaberyash, a Hungarian card game, and relieved Tom's loneliness to the extent of twenty-five thousand dollars.

Each morning before going to bed the trio played a round of golf on the nearby Shrewsbury course. One morning Clayton, Jackson, Durante, and Lonesome Tom made up a foursome. Tom was a fine golfer, as was Clayton, so the two made side bets. These wagers did not apply to Durante or Jackson, duffers.

A railroad station stood near the fourth tee of the course. As the foursome prepared to tee off there, a train crowded with passengers pulled in at the station. Clayton drove a long one down the middle. Jackson teed off next and did fairly well. Lonesome Tom whacked a dandy. The Schnozzola took a stance, swung like Casey at the Bat —but came up empty. He solemnly went through with the false shot, pivoted, then posed with the club at his neck, looking into the distance where the ball should be.

Clayton gazed in wonderment at Jimmy. "Hey, what are you looking at?"

"Yeah," said Jackson, "the ball is still on the tee!"

The Schnozz shouted angrily, "Pernt out there the same as I'm doin', will yah please? Don't let me stand this embarrassment. Everybody on that train is lookin'!"

The others looked, "pernted," and then all four sportsmen walked off, leaving Jim's ball on the tee.

"Gee!" said Jimmy. "I never felt so good about anythin' as get-tin' away from that there train."

Durante and Jackson resigned at the fifth hole. Clayton and Lonesome Tom continued on with the round, during which the casino owner dropped about sixteen hundred dollars. Lou promised Tom revenge on the morrow.

Next morning, as Clayton was approaching the first tee, he observed the caddies standing about at the caddy house. None of them came over to take Clayton's bag. Lonesome Tom was in the building talking to the golf pro.

"Say," Clayton called out, "when are a couple of you boys going to get on our bags?"

No one moved. Clayton went over to consult the fellow who had caddied for Durante the day before, "Get on my bag, son."

"Not me, Mr. Clayton."

"Why not?"

"I'm waitin' for the big-nosed fellow."

"Why wait for *him?* He can't even hit his head with a hammer."

The caddy nodded. "That's it. He plays five holes and gives me twenty-five dollars. That's the kind of a guy I want. For you I'd walk eighteen holes and only make five. I'm no dummy."

Clayton promised the boy a ten. After a twelve-hundred-dollar day, he sought out the Schnozzola. "You've ruined all the caddies here. And you ruin everybody you touch. You'll never go to heaven because you spoil everybody. And if I get to heaven first, I'll tell St. Peter not to let you in, because I'll say that's Jimmy Durante's unforgivable sin, ruining people everywhere just like he did the caddy at Shrewsbury Golf Course."

XII

Sued but Glorified

THE TRIO began the autumn season of 1928 at the Silver Slipper on West Forty-eighth Street. Big Bill Duffy was front man at the Silver Slipper. Together with his friend Owney Madden, known among liquor lads as the Duke, Big Bill controlled several cafés, including the Cotton Club.

The Duke was an undersized fellow but had a world of "moxie," a term denoting physical courage. In 1923 he came out of Sing Sing Prison with a grudge. He maintained that he had been sent up the river on a bum rap, as an accomplice in the killing of Little Patsy Doyle, and that he had had no part in the murder. Certain newspapermen of good repute felt that Madden, whatever his other sins against society, had been made a scapegoat for Little Patsy's fadeout.

Alfred E. Smith, who ran for the governor's office the first time in 1921, heard the stories that Madden had been poked away on prejudicial say-so. He promised Big Bill Duffy to look into the matter. Soon after his election Smith had the Duke transferred from Sing Sing to the Tombs, there to await possible executive clemency.

On his way to the Tombs at Christmas time, the Duke asked permission of his guard to visit his invalid mother. The guard agreed to this filial excursion, put the prisoner on his honor, and fixed a place and time for them to meet late that night.

At the appointed hour the Duke could not find his guard, an alarming circumstance, since failure to appear at the Tombs before midnight might well be construed as an escape. At ten minutes of twelve the Duke and Big Bill came upon the blotto guard in a Bowery barrel house and all but carried him to the Tombs. The man on duty at the outer door refused to admit Owney. After some parley and a telephone call to Sing Sing, identifications were established.

A month or so later Governor Smith advised Big Bill that he could not parole the Duke because of opposition by the press. Madden returned to Sing Sing, served out his time as a model prisoner, and eventually came forth "looking for evens" with society. Bootlegging on a vast scale became his revenge. The Duke had a flair for executive work and for inspiring loyalty among his followers.

Unfortunately for Clayton, Jackson, and Durante, someone at the Silver Slipper had sold a drink to a Prohibition enforcement officer a few days before they reported for work. Ten days after opening night the law sealed up the Silver Slipper. The three performers sought a new job.

Clayton was walking along Broadway one day when he happened to run into the Chinaman. "Lou," the Chinaman said, "I have a chance to go into the café business; but I wouldn't think of going into it unless I had Clayton, Jackson, and Durante,"

"What café are you thinking of going into?"

"I'd like to take over the room above the Winter Garden."

That café, formerly the Folics Bergère, now was called the Plantation. The Chinaman explained that he needed partners to bankroll the venture. His principal scratch man, he said, was Frankie Marlow, prize-fight manager, gambler, horse owner, and partner in the Silver Slipper with the Duke and Big Bill Duffy.

"Well," said Clayton, "if we go to work there, we're going to work for you only. And if ever you have any words in that place with your partners, and you leave, we leave. I hope that's understood, because we are not the personal property of anybody."

The Chinaman asked if Lou would like a piece of the café. Clayton replied, "I don't want to, and my partners don't want to. We want to work under the same conditions as though we was partners amongst ourselves, but not of you people. Don't tell us when to come, when to go, but we'll keep the room good and hot."

The trio opened to good business at the newly renamed Les Ambassadeurs. A week or two later they learned that the proprietors had not put up any actual money for the venture, banking on the popularity of the trio to keep the club afloat.

The Chinaman owned fifty per cent of the place. It was thought that Frankie Marlow owned the other half, but Marlow had disposed of twenty-five per cent of his share to Larry Fay, a gentleman who specialized in many things, including a fleet of rum trucks that ran the Canadian border blockade. Fay also operated a racket by means of which he collected a percentage on raw milk delivered to dealers in Manhattan. Just recently he had disposed of a taxicab syndicate, with scores of ornate vehicles and strong-arm drivers who monopolized choice locations such as Grand Central and Pennsylvania Stations. Fay assigned "pieces" of his quarter-share of Les Ambassadeurs to Johnny Blue Eyes and the Silver Fox.

The trio's first knowledge that Larry Fay or his henchmen had anything to do with Les Ambassadeurs came one early morning when the Silver Fox went behind the counter to play piano on the cash register. The Fox's preoccupation with the no-sale key enraged Marlow, who ordered him away from the money till. The Fox explained that he was only taking care of the interests of his boss, who was in Florida at the moment, making some Cuban connections for the furtive importation of rum.

One word led to another, and finally Marlow said he wanted to bow out of the picture. He recited several complaints, among them the fact that he could not spell Les Ambassadeurs correctly when he made out the paychecks.

Fay returned from Florida that week. He listened gravely to Marlow's beef that the Silver Fox played chopsticks on the cash register, then offered to put up seventy-five hundred dollars to buy out Marlow.

Marlow's career from that time on was a rugged one. In June of the next year he was slain by killers imported from Chicago at a fee said to have been thirty thousand dollars. This contractual price included the assassination of another gentleman of the rackets, Frankie Yale. Marlow's well-ventilated body was found among some barberry bushes near Flushing Cemetery in Queens.

That fall, as Clayton remembered the incident, a handsome young fellow at Les Ambassadeurs received a check for twenty-eight dollars. Clayton overheard the husky customer say to Leon the headwaiter, "I won this afternoon, and I'm going to win tonight." The young man was a Columbia football star and had played that day at Baker Field. At the next table sat Johnny Blue Eyes, wearing a fine coat of Florida tan, with two muscular cronies in attendance.

Clayton went over to the football player's table. "How are you, partner? What's your trouble?"

"Well," said the football player, "I sat down here and had only ginger ale, and I got a check for twenty-eight dollars."

"Well, they wouldn't present the check to you if it wasn't right."

"I'm not going to pay it!"

"Okay," said Clayton. "Sign the check if you don't want to pay it, and I'll pay it for you."

"I won this afternoon, and I'll win tonight," the young man said. "I want to see somebody make me pay it!"

Johnny Blue Eyes walked over, although no one had sent for him. "What do you mean, you won't pay your check?"

The young fellow looked at him. "Why, you fairy-looking bum! What do *you* want?"

Johnny Blue Eyes swung and missed.

Clayton afterwards said that until this incident he had never seen a tiger on the loose. "But I saw one that night. This fellow bounces out of that seat like he is in the electric chair. He flies at this Blue Eyes. He hits him. He must have thought he is a football. He knocks him back on his heels, and Johnny never stops falling until he hits the wall. That's where Leon is standing. I lock the fellow's arms up, and he says, 'Clayton, get out of the way! Because I'll throw you right over the roof.'"

Clayton let go of the young bull and watched him leave the room under his own power.

Ten minutes later Clayton was called outside. The young man was stretched out on the sidewalk, almost dead from wounds made with a tire-iron. Johnny Blue Eyes' hoods had revenged the flattening of their pal.

Clayton lifted the young man, put him in a taxicab, and gave the driver a ten-dollar bill. "Take this poor kid wherever he wants to go."

Business was so good at Les Ambassadeurs that Fay decided to open the Gaslight Café on the Bowery, with singing waiters and busboys in imitation of the Gay Nineties. The trio had no active part in either business, but it disturbed them to see Fay taking cash out of the till to put into his Bowery venture, which was consistently losing money.

"He's using one hand to wash the other," said Clayton. "And it harms our morale."

At this time Jimmy Durante went to Midtown Hospital for a minor operation. Clayton suggested that the trio lay off for a while. Fay refused to consider this and proposed that Jimmy be brought in an ambulance to perform at the club each evening.

An angry Clayton said, "Jimmy don't move out of that hospital till he's good and well."

The bosses engaged actor Jim Barton to substitute for Durante and changed the name of the club to the Rendezvous. It was the same café, the same room, and the same cobwebs. The change in name came about after the son of a state official had been beaten up outside the club.

Clayton had warned Fay and his partners time and again against rough tactics inside the club. He now promised that they would walk out immediately if sluggers continued to waylay customers who happened to have spoken out of turn.

When Jimmy left Midtown Hospital he decided to do the Wood Number for the first time in a café. The act was a riot, but the management did not appreciate it. During the wild collection of wood Clayton chanced to get his fingers underneath the molding of a mirror and added the wooden part to the pile. The shouting Durante brought in wooden salad bowls and a meat block from the kitchen. When the Silver Fox stepped in to prevent further damage the audience though his didos a part of the act and applauded. The Fox tried to punch Clayton, but Lou, an excellent boxer, ducked and then clinched with him.

"What's the matter with you?" asked Clayton. "You going crazy?"

"Going crazy? You're breaking up the jernt, ain't you? I'm going to kill youse guys!"

"Get the hell out of here, will you please!" said Clayton. "This is a number we're doing. What's the matter with you? Sit down there and get a thrill out of it. We're going to give you a touch of high life."

With that, Clayton went into the gentlemen's washroom, tore the seat off of one of the stools, and brought it out to give to Jimmy to throw onto the woodpile. After fifteen boisterous minutes the busboys and waiters began to clear the floor of wood.

Fay asked Durante, "Listen, how often is this going on?"

"Just once a night," said Durante.

"Just once a night! You're expecting to do this number again tomorrow night?"

"Why not? Maybe we'll do it tomorrow night. Don't you like it?"

"You going to tear that molding off every night?"

"If there's any molding there to tear off, I am going to tear it off," said Clayton. "What you going to do about it? You're lucky we didn't tear everything apart and throw the tables and chairs out there."

"You threw everything but the customers out there," said Fay.

"Maybe tomorrow night we'll throw them in too," said Durante.

"Do we have to build you a new room every night?" inquired Fay. "That's what we're trying to find out."

"Just leave us alone, will yah please?" said Durante. "By the way, Mr. Fay, you have changed the name of Les Ambassadeurs just after we have memorized it, and now we got to turn around and find out how to spell Rendezvous."

An old friend of Clayton's and Durante's, Lou Irwin, later a successful Hollywood agent, brought a young lady to the Rendezvous to try out as a singer. Her name was Ethel Zimmerman, and she had been trying to get into show business for quite a while. During the day she worked as secretary for Caleb Bragg, Wall Street broker and sportsman. At night she sang at an obscure café called Little Russia, where Irwin had heard her and decided that she would go far.

"It seems that all these singers are secretaries or stenographers or something," said Clayton, thinking back to Mademoiselle Fifi.

"Aw," said the Schnozz, "let's hear her anyway."

Miss Zimmerman gave her sheets of music to Harry Donnelly, and the three partners sat back to listen.

"We picked up our ears like donkeys," says Durante. "This girl was dynamite!"

Clayton changed the young woman's name to Merman and hired her at a salary of eighty-five dollars a week. She stayed with the trio for several months and then went on to bigger and better things. Later on, George White, who once had rejected the little lady when she auditioned for his *Scandals*, gave Ethel Merman a contract for twenty-five hundred dollars a week and a percentage of the gross on business done over thirty thousand dollars.

"Miss Merman," said Durante, "is the world's greatest salesman of lyrics. That's for sure."

In the spring of 1929 the trio was engaged for Florenz Ziegfeld's production *Show Girl*. They canceled their plans for the usual summer holiday. Durante told his wife, "Toots, Mr. Ziegfeld is going to glorify my nose."

William Anthony McGuire adapted this musical comedy from a novel of the same name by J. P. McEvoy. George Gershwin composed the score and his brother Ira and Gus Kahn wrote the lyrics. During rehearsals Ziegfeld suggested that Durante supply a song of his own.

Jimmy was at the club one night when a friend of his, a police captain, came in and sat down in a corner. The officer was a stern and self-sustained fellow until a quart of wine replaced the blood in his heart. Then he would suddenly remember that his wife had grown cold toward him, despite the fine house he had bought for her in Westchester. With tears flowing out as the wine flowed in, the captain would confide to his pal Jimmy Durante that he had been so very happy in the old days when, as a patrolman first class, he and his colleen had resided in a furnished room in Greenpoint.

Tonight the captain was babbling, "You can have your six-room, seven-room, eight-room, twelve-room home. Let me be happy in my little one-room home. You can have your fourteen-room, sixteen-room, twenty-room home. Just let me alone in my one-room flat."

"Say," Jimmy consoled him, "don't let anybody knock your house."

The captain sobbed on, "You can keep your thirty-room, thirty-six-room, forty-room home. So I tell you, I gotta one-room home, and my wife she likes to make pretty pillows for the settee. You can go on being proud while you have a one-room, two-room, six-room, ten-room—"

"Captain," Jimmy interrupted, "is there a lawn in front of your one-room, two-room home?"

The captain collapsed on the table, and Jimmy and two busboys took him to his car.

The next day Jimmy appeared at rehearsal with a new song, "My one-room, two-room, three-room house." When *Show Girl* had its out-of-town opening in Boston that June, the Schnozzola sang the number successfully.

Some years afterward Jimmy once again presented this song, but this time on the radio. Poet Alfred Kreymborg brought action against the Schnozz for plagiarism and copyright infringement. He asked for one hundred thousand dollars in damages, alleging that the material for Durante's one-room epic had appeared originally in 1916 in the poet's volume of verses called *Others*.

The complainant's attorney, Harry Weinberger, who some years before had successfully defended playwright Eugene O'Neill in a plagiarism action, said in United States District Court that Durante had taken a fine poem and ruined it by means of comical recitation. He charged that if Walt Whitman were alive, he too would be exposed to Durante's ruinous whims.

"Whitman?" asked the Schnozzola in a loud whisper to Clayton. "Wasn't he District Attorney in the Gyp the Blood case?"

Weinberger recited from Whitman's "Salut au Monde," and Durante urged his counsel to object. "It don't make no sense!" said Jimmy.

Judge Patterson ruled in Durante's favor, holding there had been no infringement of copyright. The next day Clayton found the Schnozzola in his room at the Astor with several sheets of paper before him on the writing desk, scribbling busily.

"What you doing, Jimmy?"

"Shh!" Durante looked up at the ceiling. "I'm ruinin' that poet Whiteman."

Clayton picked up a sheet of paper and read: "I sing of America, of the United States, of the Stars and Stripes, and of Canarsie. I sing of railroad cars, of hotels, the breakfasts, the lunches, the dinners, the suppers, the soup, the fish, the entries, the game, the puddin', the ice cream, I sing all. I eat all. I sing in time of Carter's Little Liver Pills. No subject is too small for Nature's poet. I want to go back. I want to go back. Where? I don't know where. I don't know when, I don't know how. But I want to go back. You've heard. I want to go back to that tumble-down shack. I want to go back to Caroline. I want to go back to Mammy. I want to go back to Miami, Maine. In fact, I want to go back. No one is sendin' me back. No one is pushin' me back. No one knows where is this back. But if I find the back, my idea will be complete . . ."

Clayton seized Durante by the nose and lifted him from the chair. "Cut out this literary work, will you?"

Before the *Show Girl* players left for a Boston workout, Fay asked Clayton to defer the trio's wages for two weeks. The partners had been getting three thousand dollars a week, and now two paydays had gone by with no money from Fay.

Clayton came upon Jimmy outside of Lindy's one afternoon. "I just left the Chinaman," said Durante.

"What about it?"

"He wanted to give me the six thousand they owe us, but I never took it."

"Why didn't you? That six thousand rightfully belongs to us."

"Well, Lou, you know I was stuck up once when I had a thousand-dollar bill. I ain't carried no money like that since. And if I walk up and down this Avenue with six grand in my person, they're apt to kick my brains out."

"I wish you'd taken it," said Lou, "because you know how I'm situated. I've been knocked out plenty by the dice."

"And you know how I'm situated, Lou. You can always have my money."

"I don't want your money. I want *our* money."

Lou sought out the Chinaman and had him deposit the six thousand dollars in a joint account for the trio.

The night Ziegfeld's *Show Girl* opened in Boston, and Ruby Keeler, the feminine lead, entered her dance to "Liza," played by Duke Ellington and his band, a great commotion arose among the audience. Al Jolson, Ruby's new husband, came running down the aisle, singing the chorus. This unexpected event pleased the first-nighters and flattered Miss Keeler.

In the wings Durante asked Clayton, "What's going to happen when Jolie ain't here to sing this song? It's marvelous when he sings it, but the nights he's not here there'll be a big difference."

Show Girl moved into New York in July. Most of the drama critics commended the team of Clayton, Jackson, and Durante for their first musical stage performance. Louis Sobol, drama critic of Bernarr MacFadden's *Graphic*, and Walter Winchell, then reviewing shows for Hearst's *New York Daily Mirror*, gave cheers. Burns Mantle, critic for the *Daily News*, however, could not understand Durante's humor or his popularity. He called the Schnozzola a lesser Leon Errol and described him as "foggy-voiced and crudely clownish."

Mantle never did yield to the Durante fun. Such outstanding reviewers as Percy Hammond of the *New York Herald Tribune*, and Ashton Stevens of the *Chicago American* liked Durante. Stevens at first was slow to appreciate his genius, but then beat the drum for the Schnozz, as he has continued to do ever since. "He would be a great comic," Ashton Stevens said as late as 1942, "even with a snub nose."

The wider theatrical public delighted in Jim's mispronunciation of big words. There was another picturesque element to his way of speech, his misplacement of emphasis. He put importance upon lesser words in a sentence, and the effect was astoundingly comical.

Ruby Keeler withdrew from the cast because of ill health toward the latter part of July and was replaced by Fred Stone's gifted daughter Dorothy. The show closed in October during a general diminution of theatrical business. Night-club attendance also declined that October, when Clayton, Jackson, and Durante resumed work at the Rendezvous. The authorities were enforcing the three o'clock closing law, which may have had something to do with the public's desertion of the night spots.

The Rendezvous receipts held up comparatively well. Still the trio felt unhappy over Larry Fay's frequent interferences with their act. He also became embroiled in legal and financial jams, and these confusions were reflected in his management of the Rendezvous.

Clayton informed the Chinaman that the Three Musketeers planned to leave. The Chinaman himself had many troubles, and besides had to work hard as a lieutenant in Waxey Gordon's beer business, an affiliation that led to his quarrel with Gordon's rival, beer baron Dutch Schultz, in the Club Abbey in 1931. During that melee someone stabbed the Chinaman with a broken peanut bowl and sent him to the hospital. In 1933 he was found dead in the street of an upstate town. He was found *in* the street in the truest sense of the preposition. His body had been placed in a new roadbed and concrete poured over it and leveled off.

While Clayton was shopping for a new café job a motion-picture offer came from Paramount Pictures. Paramount had brought a scenario from playwrights Ben Hecht and Charles MacArthur, to be produced by Walter Wanger at its Astoria Studios. Hecht and MacArthur were good friends of the Three Musketeers.

One cold October day Clayton, Jackson, and Durante set out in Lou's sixteen-cylinder Cadillac to talk contract with the Paramount people.

On the way across the Queensboro Bridge, Clayton said, "I'm going to hit them for a real bundle."

"Oh," advised Jimmy, "just take a good salary and knock off the job, Lou. Don't go so far up into the sky for your figures."

"Just leave it to me," said Clayton. "We're not going to work for peanuts in the movies."

XIII

Money to Burn

O N THEIR arrival at the Paramount Studios in Astoria, Long Island, Clayton told his partners that he would show them how to make a business deal. They entered a conference chamber worthy of the late Rameses II, a room designed originally as a private office for Adolph Zukor, pioneer motion-picture potentate.

The spendid decor almost frightened the Schnozzola out of his wits. Jackson began to perspire from nervousness. Clayton seemed as cool as an Eskimo—and, indeed, he resembled a thin one—and pushed his pals into the presence of three regents of the Paramount Picture empire: Walter Wanger, Jesse Lasky, and Monte Bell.

The gentlemen of the cinema rose from beside an Empire period table to greet their visitors. Wanger, long a night-club devotee, had been responsible for the meeting. He had insisted, against some opposition, that Durante's looks on the screen would not scare patrons away from the picture theaters.

Mr. Wanger outlined the plot, if any, of *Roadhouse Nights*. He explained that a mighty cast had been recruited for the venture, including Charlie Ruggles and the sultry café nightingale, Helen Morgan, who sat upon pianos and sang about a heartless, wandering lover, a cad known as her Bill.

Miss Morgan was a client of agent Lou Irwin. In fact, she had been responsible for his career as a talent merchandiser. Irwin had come from New Orleans to New York in 1923 as a jeweler. One of his customers was Helen's mother, who urged Lou to procure for her little girl a job in show business.

Irwin obtained an audition for Helen Morgan at the Playground on West Fifty-second Street off Broadway. The timid girl drank a glass or two of champagne to bolster her courage. When time came for the tryout her legs gave way. Waiters lifted her up on the piano, and she sat there to sing. And that is how Helen Morgan happened to sit on pianos forever after.

As soon as Wanger had outlined the Hecht-MacArthur story and eulogized the cast, Clayton asked, "What is your business proposition, gentlemen?"

"Well," Lasky replied, "the picture will take about four or five weeks to shoot, so we'll give you seventy-five hundred dollars a week for four weeks—thirty thousand dollars in all."

Bell placed a contract and four carbon copies of it on the table. Durante looked at Clayton. Clayton looked at him and then at Eddie. Underneath the table the Schnozz nudged Clayton with his knee, a signal for Lou to accept the proposition, to knock it off.

"Gentlemen," Clayton demurred, "you are offering us seventy-five hundred dollars a week. Right? We get fifty-five hundred or six thousand dollars doing personal appearances at the Palace Theatre, where we entertain only around two thousand to four thousand people a day. In a café we get three thousand dollars a week, and we entertain around four hundred people a night there. Now you offer us seventy-five hundred dollars a week to entertain millions of people."

Durante kept kneeing Lou, who paid no attention. "I don't think the figure is right," Clayton concluded.

"Well, then," Wanger inquired, "for what figure would you want to make the picture, Mr. Clayton?"

"We'll take fifty thousand dollars for the four weeks," Lou replied, "or twelve thousand five hundred dollars a week."

Durante bounced out of his chair and looked at his wrist as if to see what time it was. Clayton knew that Jimmy had no wristwatch. In fact Jimmy had but a very cheap pocket watch, the one which, at the night club, he sometimes placed upon the floor so that Clayton could drive a box of matches off its face with a golf club.

"Did you cut yourself or something?" Clayton asked with simulated concern.

The Schnozzola blushed. "Pardon me, gentlemen, I have an apperntment to phone somebody special."

"Jimmy," said Lasky, "why don't you use one of these phones on the table?"

Still looking at his bare wrist, Durante said, "No, this is too private. I don't want you gents to hear the number I am goin' to call."

Picture magnates were quick, on or off the screen, to manage that boy got girl, so no one blinked as the Schnozzola almost ran from the room. Jackson, muttering something or other, followed after him.

Lasky addressed Clayton. "Well, that's all right. It's fifty thousand you ask, and fifty thousand you'll get."

With a signed copy of the contract in his breast pocket, Lou said good-by to his benefactors and walked out, expecting that Durante and Jackson had taken a cab and gone about their own business. But Jimmy was leaning over the desk of the receptionist to let her feel for herself that his nose was a real one. Clayton nudged him as he went by; Jimmy looked around to see who it was, then followed Lou to the car. Jackson followed him. Clayton drove several blocks before anyone said a word. Then Jimmy blurted out, "I can't understand your attitude, Lou!"

"Attitude? What's my attitude?"

"You should have knocked it off, Lou. And I don't like your refusin' seventy-five hundred dollars a week. What was your reason?"

"Because," said Clayton, "I didn't think it was enough money. Does it have to be a bigger reason than that?"

Durante grunted. "It's a big enough reason."

"I can't understand you," said Clayton. "I take you into a swell office among gentlemen of class, and all of a sudden, as soon as they mention a figure, you look at your wrist and run out like you was shot."

Clayton turned his head and stared a challenge at Jackson, who shrugged. "I'm not saying a word!"

"Well, Lou," Durante griped, "if you can't use seventy-five hundred dollars, I can. And Eddie can too. That's a difference of ten thousand dollars to each of us. Thirty thousand in all. I got big medical bills for Jeanne. And the way I hear it, picture work ain't so hard."

"Well," replied Clayton, "the way you hear, and when you go to do it, is a different thing. It don't just come down to the heading of hard work with me. It comes down to trying to get the best bargain I can. And for your information, when you're entertaining a million people in pictures, and you're only entertaining four thousand people in night clubs and vaudeville, well, it's two different things. Don't go hungry so fast, will you please?"

Meanwhile Clayton kept right on driving. "Just listen to that motor! Pure class!"

Near the Queensboro Bridge Durante said, "Do me a favor, will yah? Drive us up against the curb."

Clayton put on the brakes. The Schnozzola got out of the car on the right side. Lou got out on the left. Then Eddie, who had been sitting in the back, got out, and the three men gathered on the sidewalk.

"What's on your mind?" Lou asked calmly.

"I just want to tell yah," said Jimmy with great indignation, "I don't feel like ridin' any farther with yah. I'm gonna get a cab. You shoulda signed that contract."

"Who said I didn't?"

"Yeah?" said Jimmy skeptically. "Well, got it with yah?"

"I didn't take that contract at seventy-five hundred dollars a week. And besides I'm freezing. So go on and get your cab."

"You don't have to yell so loud, Lou," said Durante. "It's so cold out here I can't hear what you're sayin', but your breath will freeze right in the air, and I'll be able to read it."

"You will, eh?" Clayton brought the contract from his pocket. "Well, read this!"

The terms left Durante speechless. He passed the contract to Jackson, and, forcing Clayton against a building, began to search his pockets.

"What you putting your hands all through me for?" asked Clayton.

The almost hysterical Durante yelled, "I want to see if yah got a gun, because, brother, the way yah ask for twelve thousand five hundred a week, yah must have a gun! Yah ask them for it without even smilin'. Don't yah *ever*, as long as we're together, invite me into an office again. D'yah hear? Anytime yah go to talk business, I don't wanna be there. I just can't stand it!"

The trio returned to the Silver Slipper for a second and much longer season with Big Bill Duffy.

Patricia Grudier was in the chorus line at the Silver Slipper. She afterward became the second wife of Damon Runyon. Runyon was at the Silver Slipper almost every night. He would sit with Clayton and then go with him to various gambling games, where Damon liked to kibitz. Clayton and Runyon frequently attended the Madison Square Garden fights, which the great storyteller reported for the *New York American*.

The trio also accepted an engagement at the Palace that late autumn. This meant round-the-clock activity for the tireless men. They would be done at the curfew hour of three o'clock at the

Silver Slipper, then appear on the Astoria set by nine. At four o'clock they would be back in Manhattan for a matinee performance at the Palace. From there they would go to the club. After the first show at the Silver Slipper they would play the Palace once again at ten o'clock in the evening, then return to the club to work until three in the morning.

At the Palace, Clayton did a soft-shoe dance set to the muted background music of a trumpet played by Benny Gilbert. Gilbert, with graduation approaching, was getting less sleep than almost anyone else in the combination. True, he was not in the Paramount picture, but he had to be at the hospital or attend classes all day.

One night the medical student became so sleepy that he let the mute fall out of his trumpet while Clayton was doing his number, so Lou danced louder. When Lou danced louder Benny thought that he wasn't playing loud enough. Lou held his temper because the young man soon would graduate and leave the band.

Benny had married his childhood sweetheart, Ann, and when the time came for his graduation, he and his wife asked Durante what they could do to show their gratitude.

The Schnozzola replied, "There's only one thing you can do for me. When any patients in distress come to you, don't let 'em go to any charity places, but you treat 'em free."

Perhaps Flower Hospital should rear a monument to Benny, for it was through him and another young intern that the wealthy Wendell sisters became fond of the institution. These elderly spinsters lived in a brownstone mansion on Fifth Avenue. At one side of the old house, hidden behind a high wooden fence, was a yard used by their pets as a romping ground.

One day a Wendell cat fell ill. The sisters, who seldom left their mansion, took the cat to the old Flower Hospital. Benny Gilbert and his friend had a way with animals. They treated the cat, and it recovered. When the Wendell sisters died years later, they left a fortune to Flower Hospital, and a new hospital was built uptown.

When Gilbert received his degree Jimmy spoke to Dr. Shirley Wynne, the Health Commissioner, and obtained a job for Benny in that municipal department. It was at about this time that Jeanne Durante again became quite ill. Dr. Wynne decided that surgery was imperative. A Dr. Draper performed the operation at Flower Hospital. Dr. Wynne assisted, and the newly graduated Dr. Gilbert looked on. Dr. Wynne thought it best for the time being not to tell Jimmy Durante how dangerously ill Jeanne was.

"If I remember correctly," Dr. Gilbert says, "there was a growth on Mrs. Durante's intestines, and there also was a liver condition, and in addition to that an ulcer of the stomach. I remember the doctors saying that it would be a miracle if she lived for a long time."

Durante was very attentive to his wife during her hospitalization, or as much so as the demands of his work would allow. After the operation Jeanne began to gain weight and continued to do so until about 1940, when her weight suddenly began to decline.

"Jeanne Durante's trouble was largely intestinal," says Dr. Gilbert, "and she also had low resistance. No one knew the exact cause of that. There could be so many causes. She was ill most of her married life and frequently complained of various symptoms. I think it was more of a neurosis that started everything. Of course her illness worried Jimmy a great deal, but you would never have thought that he had a care in the world when he was working. His mind was so full of worries over Jeanne that it was most amazing for those of us who knew his great troubles to see him give his spirited shows."

Work on *Roadhouse Nights* began several weeks after the October crash on Wall Street. Just how much money each of the trio lost in the market is not now easily determined. According to Clayton, he himself had a marginal interest in many stocks. He often had advised both Durante and Jackson not to wade too deeply in speculation, but they had champed at the bit and wanted to be part of the bullish throng.

Jeanne Durante owned real estate: the house in Flushing, the little house she had bought in partnership with her stepfather in Pasadena, and the small place she had built on the Clear Lake property owned by her stepfather and mother. She also had kept intact the ten thousand dollars in the safe-deposit box and had perhaps forty thousand dollars in cash and securities in her own name. None of these assets was lost in the crash.

As for Jackson, his wife had most of his money in her own name but had consented to his putting some thirty thousand dollars into the stock market.

Clayton was hurt most of all the partners. He said of this time,

"All I kept on doing was sending my broker margin. I put my hands on money I never knew existed. I got under the rocks. I got into shoe boxes. I had money all over the hotel. But one day I went out of the hotel without a quarter in my pocket. I got knocked out."

During this time of financial doom and breadlines, and just before the trio opened at the Palace for a return engagement that winter, Durante said to Clayton, "I want yah to do me a favor. Go down to the printer and have some money printed."

Clayton didn't know what Jim was talking about. "What are you going to do? Going to get yourself arrested for passing out counterfeit money? Will you make yourself a little more explicit?"

The dictionary's foremost antagonist shouted, "Who are you hangin' out with? What are yah discoverin', a new language? What is that 'explicit'? Make yourself a little more plainer."

"Well," said Clayton, "what do you want me to go to the printer for?"

"I want yah to get some money printed up. Get a hundred thousand dollars printed up. I just wrote a new song."

"What's the song?"

"A money song."

"How's it go?"

The Schnozzola hummed a bit, then sang the lyrics, "Money to burn, money to earn, money to throw away, money for you, and money for her, and money for him. Hurray!"

Lou peered at his friend. "Are you nuts?"

"Everybody's busted," said Jimmy. "What the hell! Let's cheer 'em up! Get all this stage-money printed, and we'll put bills in every pocket, and we'll have this money stickin' out of every pocket, our inside pockets, our little lapel on top, in our pants pocket, in our back pocket, and we'll have a great big canvas bag in the middle of the theater over the dome in the orchestra. And at a certain cue, when we holler, when we come to the lyrics that we've got money to burn, money to throw away, one of the prop men will pull a string which they have gutted all the way out to this here bag in the dome in the center of the theater, and this bag will open up and all this money will fly down and around."

The act caused a great commotion. The audiences at the Palace were still large, and, though most of the people sitting there were downhearted, they felt cheered when the Three Broadway Musketeers came in singing, "We got money to burn, money to earn, money to throw away!"

The trio kept on earning big money, what with their Silver Slipper engagement, the Palace shows, and their salary as motion-picture actors. The month they worked at Paramount their income from all sources was more than twenty thousand dollars a week. However, Jimmy's generosity with comrades who were down and out kept him strapped, and Lou simply had to keep his hand in at dice. Jackson took his money home to his wife.

Durante also was supporting his father, his sister, and her family. Bartolomeo had made but one appearance as a guest at a night club, the Dover. The late hours were too much for him. When someone asked if he had thought his son was funny, Bartolomeo replied in Italian, "Let's not get into an argument."

After *Roadhouse Nights* was released early in 1930 the old man attended the picture show and sat through it three times. He did not understand the medium but kept looking at Jimmy with great interest. When asked for his opinion of the picture, Bartolomeo uttered what might well have been the most profound criticism ever offered of the cinema—or of modern civilization for that matter.

He said simply, "Talk! Talk! Talk!"

XIV

Gone Are the Days

WHATEVER THE demerits of the 1920s, the storytellers find in that decade the most nostalgic memories of the half-century. The era tripped along like a Merry Widow until October of 1929— and then tripped.

And the year 1930 became a great wake. Business in the theaters collapsed, except for the motion-picture showhouses, where many of the eighty-six thousand unemployed heads of families in Manhattan sought diversion from their woes that warm spring. The Broadway night clubs, of course, were hard hit, although Clayton, Jackson, and Durante continued to do comparatively well at the Silver Slipper.

One night a man in a high hat, white tie, and tails entered the club, to brace Eddie Jackson.

"I'm a juggler," he told Eddie. "The best in the world."

With a wink Eddie introduced Jimmy to the world's best juggler, and the Schnozz decided to play a joke on this Silk Hat Harry. "How much money do you want?"

"Well, I'll take five hundred a week."

"Five hundred?" said Jimmy. "You must be good!" It now was about ten-thirty o'clock. "When do you want to go on?"

"Oh, right away."

"I'll tell you what," Jimmy said. "We'll put you on about half-past eleven. That's the time we try out new entertainers."

At a quarter of twelve the neglected gentleman said to Durante, "I'm ready to go on now, and I'll take four hundred instead of five."

"We'll put you on at a quarter to one," the Schnozz replied. "That's an hour around, but you can see we're all jungled up here."

"Oh, my act won't take long, and I've decided to charge only three hundred. I'll just go out there and kill the people and then come off."

"Kill the people, eh?" said Eddie.

148

"We'll let you go on at a quarter to one," Jimmy ruled.

Clayton, Jackson, and Durante put their heads together. "This fellow is crazy or something."

At a quarter to one the man insisted that he go on and announced that he had reduced his fee to two hundred dollars.

"Well," Jim said, "we can't put you on till a quarter of two."

To this the fellow replied, "Maybe I'm asking too much money. What if I take one hundred dollars?"

"Wait until a quarter of two," said the Schnozzola.

At half-past two the man said desperately, "May I have a sandwich? I'll not charge you a cent, because I haven't eaten in two days."

Jimmy was ashamed. He ordered a big meal, wine and cigars, then gave the fellow a hundred as an "option" on his services.

Theatrical managers tried to shore up their business during the year that followed the Wall Street debacle. But many Broadway houses became dustbins when the Avenue's financial angels lost their golden harps. Instead of going out at night, New Yorkers were listening free of charge to Amos and Andy on the radio or making home brew or bathtub gin.

Clayton, Jackson, and Durante played many charity benefits that year, and in the early autumn went into rehearsal for *The New Yorkers*, a Cole Porter musical produced by E. Ray Goetz. The cast included Hope Williams, Ann Pennington, Marie Cahill, Richard Carle, and Frances Williams. The Schnozzola and his accomplices did the Wood Number as a finale to the first act, and also used the Money to Burn creation. When the show opened in New York on December eighth it was well reviewed. But two weeks after the opening Goetz's backers demanded that he ask his performers to agree to a reduction in pay. He was not the only manager touched by a desire to reef his sails. The year was ending on a note of great apprehension for almost everyone in the Big Town.

The iron-minded investigator Judge Samuel Seabury had begun his long inquiry into political corruption, a quest that eventually would unseat the gay and dapper Mayor Jimmy Walker, the beloved though misguided pixy who had been master of the revels since 1926. Appropriately enough, or so it seemed, this year marked the two hundredth anniversary of the cuckoo clock.

Many strange circumstances had made newspaper headlines that year. The disappearance in August of Judge J. F. Crater, a mystery never solved, seemed a symbol of dark days and dark deeds. When the Bank of the United States failed on December 11, 1930, Broadway managers, among others, began to comprehend that the panic, alias the depression, had come to stay for some time.

Goetz informed Clayton, Jackson, and Durante that the show was incurring an overhead expense of forty-odd thousand dollars a week and asked that the trio accept a salary reduction of twenty-five per cent.

"We are not partners in this show," replied Clayton. "We are working as Clayton, Jackson, and Durante. We have an Actors Equity contract. I signed the contract in good faith, and there are no loopholes with me, because I don't throw any curves. If you so much as take out a twenty-five cent piece, let alone twenty-five per cent of our money, we won't be here for the next show."

The trio received full compensation during the twenty-three weeks the musical play remained on Broadway.

Durante and his stage partners continued on at the Silver Slipper and in the cast of *The New Yorkers* until May of 1931. The Schnozzola gave freely of his time and his money, as always, to help fellow actors who were among the unemployed, but he had his own personal woes. Two unnerving events occurred on successive days.

At six o'clock one morning early in February, as Jimmy was driving home, a black sedan with four men in it tried to force Durante to the curb. He managed to shoot past the car and at the same time honked his horn and called to a neighbor who had come out to get the morning milk. The black car sped away from the scene.

This kidnaping scare weighed heavily upon Jeanne, who urged Jimmy once again to leave New York for California. She pointed out that a thousand gangsters had been slain in New York since Prohibition began. Jeanne feared that Durante one day might fall an innocent victim of gangland's ceaseless wars. "Why ask for unhappiness?" she said.

Jimmy suggested that his wife bring her father and her Uncle Bill from Toledo to New York, to make her feel less lonely. He then went to sleep. That afternoon he returned to the club. Early next morning Durante drove home—with Clayton following him in his own car. He waved good-by to Lou at the gate and went inside.

Jeanne was waiting up to tell him that his sister Lily had telephoned that one of her three sons, nineteen-year-old Michael, was desperately ill.

Durante called up Dr. Wynne, then drove with Jeanne to Brooklyn. They stayed at the Romano home until the boy died of spinal meningitis late that afternoon. A very sad Durante, tired and sleepless, made the funeral arrangements before reporting to the theater.

The doorman gave Jimmy an unsigned letter which read: "You were very lucky night before last, but it won't be that way next time. In the second act tonight wear a red carnation, which will mean you want to get in touch with us."

"Wear the carnation," Clayton advised Durante. "Then we'll get in touch all right, and I'll kill anyone that makes a move."

After the show Clayton stayed inside the theater for a few minutes to confer with Goetz. Durante went outside, where a gentleman of the Avenue known as "Lumps the Grabber" gave the Schnozzola a big hello.

"Jeez, Jimmy!" said Lumps. "Please accept the apology of everybody concerned."

"Everybody who?" asked Durante.

"Just forgive 'em, Jimmy. They're awful sorry this letter happened, because they all love you, and merely wanted five grand, and got hopped up and impulsive. And now they want you to know they're awful sorry, and will you forget and forgive?"

"I'll forget and forgive," said Jim. "But you better keep outta Clayton's way. He never forgets, even if he sometimes forgives."

"Thanks," said Lumps the Grabber. "You don't happen to have a C note on you at the moment?"

"It so happens I got four C notes," said Jimmy. "And I'll split 'em with you." With that, Durante gave Lumps two hundred dollars. "Go buy some carnations with it."

This experience made Eddie Jackson more nervous than ever. He was afraid to go anywhere alone. "Eddie really had nothing to worry about," Durante says. "The mugs loved him as much as they did me. But he wouldn't believe it. One time he said, 'Jimmy, I'd like to get out of this whole business. I'd like to break away and go into some little business, even if it's only a tailor shop. Even if I get only fifty a week, and I'd be contented."

One of the regulars at the Silver Slipper had a sweetheart who frequently visited backstage at the theater where *The New Yorkers* played. This beautiful girl was known as the Princess. Her sweetie, although fiercely jealous, gave her furs, a motorcar, and, according to Lou Clayton, enough diamonds to light up the business district of a city as large as, say, Troy, New York.

Sometimes the Princess would lend her diamonds to Frances Williams to wear on stage as she warbled the lyrics, "I'm taking no chances sitting on my Frances in the Great Indoors."

One night Clayton returned from the theater to the Silver Slipper to find the Princess's lover sitting with several of his rugged constituents in a corner at the left side of the bandstand.

"Did you see my girl tonight?"

"No, I didn't see her," Lou replied.

The jealous man called Clayton some nasty names. Lou waited until the man cooled off a bit, then said, "You will never have an opportunity to call me any names again, because from now on I will never talk to you."

Clayton walked to a table behind the bandstand where he usually sat with Eddie and Jimmy. Durante now came into the room, and the Princess's sweetheart asked the Schnozzola to sit down. "That partner of yours is a rat!"

The Schnozzola was amazed. "Wait a minute! What happened?"

The Princess's lover said he had asked Clayton a question and that Lou had lied when he said he had not seen the lady.

"Well," said Jimmy, "it's possible she was there, and he still didn't see her. You know we're pretty busy out there on the stage."

"He must of saw her there. She was with somebody else."

Durante became annoyed. "Well, if Clayton said he didn't see her, he didn't. And I don't think he's interested in whether he would see her or not. And I think you're wrong in accusin' Lou of anythin' like that, because that ain't in his make-up. If he'd seen her, he wouldn't have said nothin'. But if he didn't see her, he would say so; and that's what he told you."

Durante left the group. Two of the Broadway Othello's supers followed him to the trio's table with the message that their chieftain wished to see Clayton.

"You tell him for me," Lou replied, "that I wouldn't walk over to his table if I knew this was the last breath I was sending a message with."

When *The New Yorkers* closed in the early summer of 1931

Metro-Goldwyn-Mayer Studios offered James Durante a five-year contract. Irving Thalberg, a pleasant young man of extraordinary talents as a motion-picture producer, explained that his studio was prepared to hire Durante but not the other members of the trio. The proposed pictures were to be made in California.

Jeanne Durante was jubilant, for at last she and Jimmy could find a permanent home in California, away from the hurly-burly of Broadway, the all-night separations, and the worries of gangland threats.

The prospect of breaking up the closely bound triumvirate was not as simple as all that for the Schnozzola. "Wait a minute, Toots," he said. "I got to think of the others."

"Well, think of me too," she said.

"I will! I will! Give me a chance."

He called his partners together, to ask what they thought of the proposal. "Times is tough," he said, "but I won't leave my pals."

"Jim," said Clayton, "we want you to be the success you deserve. The other things don't matter."

"Success?" Jimmy asked. "Well, I think success is not to worry too much, to do the best you can, stick to your friends, and pray they'll stick to you. The rest is in God's hands."

"I'll do whatever you want, Jimmy," said Jackson.

Clayton was thinking hard. "I believe in God too," he said, "but for the moment let's go over and ask Sime Silverman what he recommends we ought to do."

The wise little publisher of *Variety* had seen many changes on Broadway in his time, and now the Avenue was changing again in appearance and mood. Sime told the three men that the prosperous night-club era not only had reached its close but never would come back in the same carefree way as in the twenties. "The cover charge is on the way out," he said. "And so are the times we have known. Only the Casino in Central Park has stayed out of the red, and that was Jimmy Walker's own pet place. I know how close and loyal you three mugs are, and I love you for your loyalty, but for that very reason you should let Jimmy go ahead and not stand in the way of his picture career."

"I won't make a move without my partners," said Jimmy.

"Well," said Sime, "you'd better take care of your partners in some other way."

"Jim," said Clayton, "Sime is right. Go ahead. I'll come out there if you want me to. There's no doubt in my mind you're going to be a success. I always told you you have a different style; you have a creative mind. And you're going to be big. If you do want me to go out there with you, I'll hang up my dancing shoes and look after your interests."

"Without you doin' the business," said Durante, "I don't want to go out there. And you'll get a third of everythin' I make as long as we live."

Clayton put his arms about Durante. "That's good enough for me."

"How about you, Eddie?" asked Jim.

"Well," said Jackson, "I like to sing, you know. It's in my blood. But I'll go out there and look things over. When do we leave?"

Durante said they would go soon. "They got a picture for me, Mr. Thalberg says, called *Get-Rich-Quick Wallingford*. Our pal Charlie MacArthur is writin' it. But if anything happens out there, if I feel disqualified with makin' pictures, we'll just put the trio together and go right back where we was."

"God bless you, boys," said Sime Silverman. "I'll be in your corner all the way."

Jimmy and Eddie were to go to California at once. Lou was to stay on in New York to collect six thousand dollars owed them by the Silver Slipper and attend to some other personal matters.

When Durante mentioned going to California by ship via the Panama Canal, Jackson said, "Jimmy, will you do me a favor?"

"Do you a favor? Anythin' you want."

"You know I'm nervous. I'll never make it by boat. I'm too nervous for the boat, Jimmy."

The next afternoon Jackson, a Dodger fan, went to Ebbets Field to see a double-header. Brooklyn dropped both games, a circumstance that made Eddie quite blue. While he was at the ball park Jimmy called up Mrs. Jackson to tell her that he had suddenly decided to leave that night for California. The party would go to Florida by train, take a boat from there to Havana, and then board the S.S. *California* for the voyage through the Canal.

Eddie knew nothing about this until he arrived home at about six o'clock. He telephoned Jimmy. "What's this I hear about going from Havana by boat?"

"Oh, it ain't nothin'," said the Schnozzola. "Nothin'. Like you're goin' on a lake. It's July now anyway. Summertime. Look, there's a little thing I want to tell you about. Lou got knocked out again, and he's flat. So pick up about thirty-five hundred dollars, will you?"

"Why do you want that much?"

"Well, there's about seven of us goin', and I ain't got a quarter. I'll meet you at the Astor, and everything will be all right. But get the money."

Eddie met Jimmy and paid for the tickets. Durante had but a small grip, as if he were going to Newark.

"For the love of Mike, Jimmy!" said Jackson. "Ain't you got a trunk? You're going to California!"

"I'll buy a trunk in Havana."

Jeanne Durante decided to stay in New York for a time to rent the Flushing house. She planned to drive cross-country to California in August.

Jeanne's father, Mr. Olson, however, went on the boat trip, and so did Jim's sister. Mrs. Romano had been inconsolable over the death of her son, and Jimmy persuaded her to go on this voyage with her surviving sons, Julie and Bob. These relatives, Jack Harvey, and Eddie Jackson comprised the Durante party bound for California.

In the dining saloon the first night out of Havana the party was given menus printed in French. Eddie looked at Jim, "What'll it be?"

The Schnozzola called to the steward, "We have seven in our party. Let's have seven steaks and French-fried potatoes and everybody coffee and apple pie."

Jackson said, "But, Jimmy, the rest of the party don't want steak."

"What's the difference?" asked Jimmy. "Who can read this kind of menu? We have gotta learn the ropes. So let's have steak till we get an interrupter."

When the ship had passed through the Canal and put in at San Diego Jimmy said to Jackson, "I hear from our stewart that horses are runnin' at Caliente. Let's go over there. Lou ain't here to stop us."

"He won't like it if we lose."

"Never mind that. He won't know. Let me hold the money for a while, Eddie. How much you got?"

"Oh, I don't know. About eighteen hundred dollars, I guess."

"Let me hold it, because you'll get in wrong someplace. You're too innocent."

"I won't get in wrong," said Eddie.

"Aw, yes yah will," said Durante. "You're an innocent guy, and I'm not. Let me hold it."

At Caliente, Jimmy not only lost on the horses but also got into a crap game and dropped the rest of the roll. "Ain'tcha got some more money?" he asked Eddie.

"About four dollars."

"Well, lemme have it. We've lost it all. We've lost it all."

"What do you mean *we* lost it all? *You* lost it all!"

"Well, suppose we'd won, I'd given yah half, wouldn't I?"

"I don't say you would or wouldn't. But I know, Jim, we didn't make anything up about splitting or anything. You owe me eighteen hundred and something. That's all I know."

"Well, don't worry about it," said Jim. "We got cab fare."

From San Diego, Jim sent a wire, collect, to Clayton, asking for a thousand dollars. Clayton wired back, "Will send it to you at Los Angeles."

Durante sent some more wires, and Clayton finally replied, "What's the matter with you? Gambling again?"

The Schnozzola became so frightened that he did not send another wire. Aboard ship a few hours later he was improvising a song, "Our pockets are empty. Good-bye, Caliente!"

After the Schnozzola and Eddie had left New York, Clayton walked over to the office where one of the bosses of the Silver Slipper did business, as did the Princess's lover. Lou asked the receptionist if Big George, a lieutenant of the boss, was in, and she said, "He's expected soon."

Clayton had not spoken to the Broadway Othello since the name-calling incident at the Silver Slipper. But the man heard Lou's voice and sent out for him to come in to see him.

Lou said in a loud tone, "There's no point of me going in there to see him. I just came up to get two checks cashed, because I've been shortening up a bit, and Big George told me to come up to the office to collect our last two weeks' salary."

Big George showed up and invited Clayton to his office, the same room used by the Princess's lover. Clayton did not look at Othello or speak to him, but sat down beside Big George's desk, his back to the other partner.

"Jimmy has gone out to California to make pictures," he explained to Big George, "and if possible I'd like to have the money for those two checks; that is, if you are sitting easy."

"That's all right, Lou." Big George brought a roll of currency from his pocket.

Clayton thanked George and rose to leave. "Wait a minute," said Othello, "I want to talk to you." He followed Clayton to the office doorway. "What's the matter with you?"

Clayton wheeled. "Evidently you misunderstood me the night you called me those vile names. Evidently you thought I was kidding or something. I told you you'd never have an opportunity to call me that again. Now let's not have any words about it. I did not come up here to see you. My deal was with George, and he's paid me."

The man repeated, "What's the matter with you?"

"I told you before there's nothing the matter with me," said Clayton. "I know you come from Tenth Avenue, and I know the kind of people who've been associating with you. I've been around myself a good many years, and I've seen a lot of things happen. I've seen a lot of people go up, and I've seen a lot of people come back down. I've always prided myself on having a lot of people who are friends in show business and out of show business, and these people respect me for what I am, because I always try to act the part of a gentleman. I know how to keep my mouth shut, and many times I've closed my eyes not to see a lot of things that were happening. If I wasn't involved, and my friends weren't involved, that was fairdinkum. But when you called me a rat, that's what I still resent. And one of these days you'll wish that you had the friendship of me, the same guy you called a rat."

"Wait a minute now," said the man. "You got through with your speech. Let me say something."

"You can say anything you want," said Lou, "but anything you are going to say to me is not going to interest me."

"Well, I don't know whether it's going to interest you. In fact, I don't care. But what I am going to say is this: when I called you a rat I didn't mean it the way you took it. Because I didn't mean to offend you. I was just burned up about my girl."

Clayton turned and went out of the office. The man ran after him. "I'm not going to take this from you. You're not going to get out of the office that way."

Clayton said, "Did I have to come up here and go through all this to get this money? What's your next move?"

"I want you to put out your hand and shake with me, and then I'll know you accepted my apology."

Lou put out his hand. "Long as you said you did not mean it, your apology is granted."

Some years after this the Princess's friend chanced to be vacationing in Culver City near the M-G-M Studios. The police picked him up and found a pistol in his possession—a serious matter in view of the man's police record. Clayton persuaded a police official to release the fellow, return his pistol, and let him leave town.

While Jimmy was waiting to go into his first picture for Metro-Goldwyn-Mayer, he rented an ocean-front bungalow at Venice for his relatives. He stayed there enjoying the sun and the beach until Jeanne motored in from New York. The now happy Durantes had a short vacation at Clear Lake—where tourists sometimes mistook the Schnozzola for a gas station attendant and tipped him—then went to live at 926 North Marino Street in Pasadena, near the Blenmans. Jeanne rented a small apartment nearby for her father, of whom she was most fond. The Durantes kept it a secret from the Blenmans that Mr. Olson was their neighbor. They did not wish to risk embarrassing anyone concerned.

There was a curious ending to this secret, and of it Durante says, "Jeanne's dad liked to nip a little bit, and that was one reason why my missus wanted him to come out to California, so she could keep an eye on him. He was such a nice old guy too.

"The Blenmans lived around the corner from a carbarn that was on Oak Street or Fair Oak or Oak somethin'. Jeanne's dad used to sit on a bench by the carbarn to see the passers-by and talk to anybody who would sit on the bench. Now Mr. Blenman used to go out for walks, and when he got tired he'd sit on this same bench. One night he came into the house and said, 'Gee, but I met a fine gentleman. We're pals already. After dinner I go down and sit on the bench near the carbarn, and it seems this old fellow does the same thing every night. What a helluva nice man he is! He says he has a beautiful fine daughter livin' out here.'

"For some time we never connected this up with Jeanne's dad until one day after dinner Jeanne happened to go out with Mr.

Blenman and was introduced to what turned out to be her own dad."

The men were somewhat astonished at this turn of affairs; they remained friends, but on a more formal basis than before. Mr. Olson never called at the house where his former wife resided. He had old-fashioned ideas about such things—and so had the lady.

And now the call came from the studio for Durante to report at the Culver City motion-picture lot.

"God bless you, Tootis," Jeanne said as he drove off with noisy cries and much honking of the horn.

XV

The Nose Out West

THE SCHNOZZOLA's first Hollywood picture, *Get-Rich-Quick Wallingford*, brought him immediate popularity. The Cyrano of the Cellars had put his nose to a golden grindstone. His producers all but kissed him.

The chief drawback of the enjoyment of Hollywood fame, however, is that it comes all at once and then departs at the same rate of speed. After the celluloid dream is done, the ex-star awakens in a world of toothless tigers, shabby dancing bears, and groggy gypsies of Hasbeen Land. In the hangover stillness that follows box-office defeat, the ones who had faith in yesterday's puffs in the fan magazines belatedly learn that movie stardom is an impression made upon a looking-glass. It is all very sad and mystifying and as final as the tomb.

Jimmy Durante soon would know how suddenly failure follows success in Hollywood. But here we see a man different in character and spirit from most marchers in the parade of heroes who become zeros overnight. The unpretentious fellow never believed he was great to begin with, and managed by means of his simple acceptance of both joy and sorrow to stay spiritually solvent and unafraid.

Playwright Charles MacArthur had written a robust script founded upon George Wood Chester's Wallingford story. Actor William Haines, attempting what is called a comeback, played the lead, and Sam Wood directed it. Both the picture and Durante received favorable reviews, and few actors became more popular on the Culver City lot than the Great Nostril.

His large dressing room was divided into two compartments by a portiere. In one enclosure Jimmy lay down to rest between shots, and in the other Clayton received or sent telephone messages, many of them to bookmakers.

Louis B. Mayer, executive head of the studio, and Dr. A. P. Giannini of the Bank of America were frequent visitors in the

Durante dressing room, and upon entering it would rub Jimmy's nose for luck.

Unable to remember almost anyone's name or title, the Schnozzola greeted all callers with a big hello. He had been given to understand that Mayer was the studio cashier. L. B. had said at their first meeting that he paid out all the checks. Whenever Jimmy saw Mayer he would call out, "I'll be in to see you on payday. Always glad to see the cashier."

Durante disliked going to parties, but during his first weeks in Hollywood was persuaded to attend social evenings at the mansions of M-G-M executives. Lou Clayton would do a dance or two, with Jimmy at the piano, and Eddie Jackson would coonshout the old songs. Durante's hosts had one objection to him as a guest: he made kindling wood of their grand pianos.

The acclaim that Durante received for *Wallingford* placed him in great demand on the M-G-M lot; but no stories of any consequence were available. Producers of pictures that needed uplift called upon him to do mere comedy bits instead of worthwhile roles. His personality, his gifts as a clown, brightened these otherwise dull photoplays, but such stop-gap casting caused a slump in his popularity.

In four pictures that first year he applied the pulmotor to weak scenes. Sometimes he would merely walk on, make characteristic movements of his head, roll his little eyes, and say, "Hot-cha, hotcha!" and then exit.

This expression, which Jimmy had originated in the night clubs, delighted the picture-makers, but Durante grew tired of saying little else while performing for the screen. He eventually refused to say "hot-cha" ever again.

In 1931, 1932, and on into 1933 a succession of mediocre pictures, some of them expensively mounted, alarmed Durante's mentor. Where would it all end? Lou asked. Jim had followed the *Wallingford* picture with a washout, *The Cuban Love Song*, in which Lawrence Tibbett and Lupe Velez appeared. The Schnozzola played the part of a clown. Then came another dilly, released in January of 1932, *The Passionate Plumber*. It starred Buster Keaton and Polly Moran, and Durante again played a clown.

The Durante contract at M-G-M provided for six-month options. Clayton endeavored to persuade the bosses to let Jim go on the radio, for the Schnozz had several attractive offers in that direction.

But the studios were fighting radio, as they later would resist television. With hundreds of millions of dollars invested, the film magnates never willingly embrace competitors in other fields of entertainment. A shotgun is necessarily present at each wedding of the movies to a new idea.

Early in 1933 Durante received an offer to appear in the Brown and Henderson musical comedy *Strike Me Pink*, which was backed by Waxey Gordon, bootleg syndicate head, collector of first editions, graduate of Sing Sing, and would-be emulator of Florenz Ziegfeld.

Durante was cool to the idea, for Jeanne objected to their leaving California; moreover, he wanted no part of Waxey Gordon or his mob. Nor did Clayton, for that matter, but Benevolent Charlie, a friend of the old days, could not be ignored, and Charlie had asked Clayton to do him a great favor and persuade Durante to appear.

Since coming to California, Jimmy had received letters and wires from the mugs who adored him. He never had been, and never would be, a party to the rackets. None of the underworld men or women had ever entered his home. But when Benevolent Charlie told Lou that Waxey Gordon had invested more than a hundred and fifty thousand dollars in *Strike Me Pink*, and that it looked as if the show would fail without immediate recasting, Durante left the decision to Clayton.

Jimmy had just finished a picture in Honolulu, *Hell's Below*. Benevolent Charlie urged him to fly East to see a tryout of *Strike Me Pink*. But Durante would not board an airplane except in a great emergency, so he and Clayton took a train for New York.

In the club car aboard the Santa Fe Chief, Durante greeted its occupants with his customary big hello. Everyone seemed to take to him immensely, although one unsmiling fellow put down his ginger-ale glass to glare at the Schnozzola.

Two gentlemen sitting across the aisle from Jimmy were discussing big-game hunting in Africa. One said that he actually had found the graveyard for elephants, then added, "These great beasts sometimes travel as much as two thousand miles to die there."

Durante cut in, "It's the trip that kills them."

The game hunters left off speaking, and the unsmiling fellow who had been staring at Jimmy came over to sit beside him.

"You know something?" this man said matter-of-factly, "I've always detested you, Durante."

The Schnozzola shriveled, for nothing hurts him so much as to hear that someone dislikes him.

"Do yah know me?" asked Durante almost timidly.

"I never set eyes on you except in the movies."

"Then what did I do to yah? I never say any lines that have a double entry."

"Durante," the man said, "I always speak my mind. I run my business that way, right from the shoulder."

"Gee whiz!" Jimmy groaned. "Can I reprieve myself in some way with yah?"

"And," the man went on to say, "when I'm wrong I'm always the first to admit it. Like the time I voted for Hoover."

Durante got up from his chair with a sad, "Excuse me," but the man said with an air of authority, "Sit down, Durante!" Jimmy meekly obeyed him.

"Now listen," the man said. "I sincerely like you, Jimmy Durante."

The Schnozzola couldn't believe his ears. "Yah *do*?"

"Yes. I've hated you all along, but I've been watching you here, and listening to you, and I was all wrong about you. You are a wonderful man."

"Gee!" Durante said. "I'm so glad."

Clayton had come into the car, and Jimmy turned to him happily. "Lou! Lou! This man here says he likes me!"

Clayton glanced at the man. "So what?"

The first day after their arrival in New York Jimmy and Lou motored to Philadelphia to see a performance of *Strike Me Pink*. They left after the first act.

The next day Clayton conferred with Benevolent Charlie. "The show stinks to the skies. Further and more, you know how I stand with Waxey Gordon. And I wish you wouldn't ask me to do this favor."

"Well," said Benevolent Charlie, "I *have* to ask you."

"All right then. I can never refuse anything you ask. So tell that party, that friend of yours who suddenly has become such a big impresario on Broadway, to fly out to California and meet us there. We first have to convince the studio to allow us to do this show."

Gordon duly arrived out West. He promised Clayton that the three partners would be reunited in his show. The next step was to pry Durante loose from the studio. Waxey and Lou went to see

Eddie Mannix, an M-G-M executive who knew all the angles. Mannix said that he had to take up the matter with Irving Thalberg.

As Mannix left the office Gordon asked Clayton, "Who is this certain party Thalberg?"

"The biggest man in Hollywood," replied Clayton.

"Is he that big?"

"He's bigger than any of us."

"Bigger than Durante?"

"Bigger than anybody."

"Then to hell with Durante!" Gordon shouted in all seriousness. "Let's put Thalberg in the show!"

The trio arrived in New York on Lincoln's Birthday. Gordon announced without any warning that Durante must rehearse without his two pals. "We don't want Clayton or Jackson in this show because it's high class. There ain't no sawdust on the floor."

"But you'll pay my partners, won't you?" asked Durante.

"Pay 'em? Not me!" Gordon snorted.

"Then," said Durante, "I'll pay them. Each gets a third of what I get."

Clayton, a man of his word, who expected others to be like him in this respect, was enraged. But Gordon pointed out that the contract called only for Durante's services.

Clayton took Jackson aside. "Eddie, we are doing this for Benevolent Charlie, but they're not going to throw Jimmy Durante on the spears. On opening night you sit on the right side of the house, and I'll sit on the left, down front, both of us in our dinner clothes. And the first time Jim hits a snag, the hell with the book! You and me will fly onto that stage and turn things upside down."

During the tryout week in Newark, Durante pointed out to the writers of the show that he needed a strong finish for one of the skits, a six-day bicycle-race sequence. The night of the New York premiere on March 5 the writers had not yet come through. So at the close of the skit he let the audience know the fix he was in and proceeded to put a finish to it himself: he hurled his bicycle into the orchestra pit. At the next performance the musicians refused to take their places until Durante promised, in writing, not to throw anything at them.

Jimmy did not need the assistance of his watchful partners. He ripped and tore right through the show, and *Strike Me Pink* became a hit. The musical itself was not a great one, and it might be of interest to note that none of the Durante musical plays, except one, had real size. The exception was *Jumbo*. But in everything, good or not so good, Durante enlivened the scenes and drew in the customers.

In *Strike Me Pink* Jimmy did a number with Lupe Velez that called for some hip-bumping. One night Durante placed a monkey-wrench in his pocket, and after the fiery little actress hipped into it she reached into Durante's pocket, seized the wrench, and ran Jimmy off the stage, down the steps, up one aisle, and back again. She wrestled with him, and he threw her into the orchestra pit.

Of the tragedy that years later found Lupe Velez a suicide, Durante says, "This great little girl was a female Pagliacci. She seemed so happy, so full of life, that you didn't think she ever had a care in the world. Did you ever see her at the fights? Hittin' the canvas of the ring apron and callin' out to the fighter she liked? But they used to tell me at the time of *Strike Me Pink* that she used to go to the bar at Frankie and Johnny's place and sit there all alone. I never asked her what the trouble was, for around me she seemed happy. And then out in Hollywood she got blue about some fellow, I read or heard, and poor kid! Well, who can see into another person's soul?"

The Schnozzola received three thousand dollars a week in *Strike Me Pink* and split that money three ways with his partners. He had been promised twenty-five per cent of all business in excess of thirty thousand dollars. Although the musical had opened on the night of the portentous Bank Holiday in March, it did a box-office business of from thirty-four to thirty-six thousand dollars each week.

One day in May Lou said to Durante, "Jim, I notice they're not paying your percentage share each week."

"Percentage share?" said Jim. "They don't give me a quarter outside of my salary."

Clayton called upon Waxey, who said, "Lou, you must have misunderstood us. We said that only after we got our original money out, then Jimmy would get a percentage over thirty thousand dollars."

Clayton got in touch with the M-G-M executives and asked them to recall Durante to Hollywood at once. Thereupon Gordon made loser's music. "How could you do this to me? Can't you see we got a big hit? And now you're taking a powder!"

"You got your money," Clayton replied. "And we've done our best for Benevolent Charlie. You don't count. You lied to us and cold-cocked us. From a guy who peddled alcohol and bootleg booze, you were going to be a big impresario. You were going to take hold of Broadway."

Strike Me Pink lasted thirteen weeks. With the time spent on rehearsals, Durante had overstayed by several weeks the three-month period of his leave from the studio. On the last night the cast and crew nailed down all the props. When Jimmy sought to lift pieces of furniture he could not. Durante took the audience into his confidence, and everyone enjoyed the fun. By the last curtain the cast had torn off all Jimmy's clothes except his shorts and his socks.

Durante returned to Hollywood to do an especially weak picture with Buster Keaton, *What No Beer,* and then another limp one, *Baron Munchhausen,* with Jack Pearl.

At about this time the Schnozzola received a threatening letter demanding twenty-five thousand dollars, or else. Clayton interrupted his golf games at the Hillcrest Club to do some sleuthing. He finally smoked out the source of the threat, a young hoodlum who admitted having written the letter. Clayton gave him a beating designed to make the extortionist allergic to pen and ink for the rest of his life.

After the Pearl picture Jimmy was farmed out to Twentieth Century-Fox Studios for *George White's "Scandals,"* and to United Artists for *Palooka.* He returned to his home lot to perform before the cameras with Laurel and Hardy in *The Hollywood Party.*

In *Palooka* the song "Inka Dinka Do" was born. It came in as a chorus after a verse that recommended that you say it with flowers or say it with sweets, but never say it with ink, and trailed off into "Inka Dinka Do." Harry Donnelly had much to do with the shaping of this song.

Shrewd as he was, Clayton had some things to learn about the fine print in Hollywood documents. Durante's contract did not specify how many pictures a year he was to make. Producers on the lookout for comedy sequences could utilize the Durante personality at will. This was a shortsighted policy of course; but in Hollywood talent is seldom conserved.

It got so that Clayton could stand it no longer. He made a trip East. Jimmy's name was in lights on the Capitol Theatre, and across the street it was displayed for another production, and two blocks up the Avenue it was again twinkling on the marquee. Whenever the Schnozzola had a part in a picture, however small the role, New York theater managers put his name in lights.

Back in Hollywood, Clayton consulted one of the executives. "What are you throwing this man in every picture for? Let him get his teeth into some pictures. Give him a part to play. He'll play it."

Perhaps an actor of different temperament from Durante's would have kicked over the traces, sulked, left the studio, or invited a suspension. But not Jim. He would do anything asked of him.

"Just wait," Clayton told Jimmy, "till the time presents itself, and we'll get money and get rid of these options, of which I knew nothing until now. We'll get something big to put it in your lap. In a way I'm glad you don't have an exorbitant opinion about yourself, and that you aren't domineering. You have never asked for anything that isn't yours, but you are great, and we will prove it if we have to."

"Aw, forget it, Lou," said Jim. "We're all right."

Eddie Jackson, at this time in 1933, was becoming restless. He had made a few trips back to New York to see his wife, who had expressed her unhappiness over her husband's long absences from home. He confided in Jim that he would like to return to vaude-ville and asked the Schnozzola for a leave of absence. "Jimmy, all I've done is to go to some parties here and sing."

"Go ahead," said Durante, "if it will make you happy. I'm always here."

Durante felt sad to see Eddie leave. The Three Musketeers had been together for so long. They were to come together again, years afterward, but there would be few occasions of contact, even by mail, during the years when Eddie tried to form a vaudeville combination to take the place of the old trio of Clayton, Jackson, and Durante.

XVI

Actors Are People

OTHER THAN *Wallingford*, there had been but one bright spot in Jim's early Hollywood career. In 1932 he was lent to Paramount for a part in *The Phantom President*. His success in that picture might be called accidental. It came about when George M. Cohan, a good friend of the trio, did his first, and last, work in front of California cameras.

During one of Clayton's trips East he happened to meet Cohan at Dinty Moore's Restaurant. Cohan had something of a problem at the moment, having broken a false tooth at the matinee performance that day. He had to be onstage within the next two hours, and the missing tooth would, as he put it, "crucify him." Clayton happened to know a very good dentist and had him leave his home after office hours to supply a temporary tooth for Mr. Cohan's bridge.

The next day George M. thanked Lou for "having saved his life," and added, "Now I'm going to do something for you." He went on to say that he had agreed to go to California at the close of his play to do *The Phantom President*. "It's a political satire. A medicine man who looks like a candidate who wants to be President but has no political charm, according to this story. I'm to be a traveling medicine man who looks like the candidate. As long as Jimmy Durante is being lent to Paramount for this picture, I want to see that a good pal gets a break. I'm not so hot about going to California, because I just don't know how things are done out there. I hear bad reports, but it's a lot of money, and I'll be glad to be with Durante, and I'm going to see that his part is good. You tell me they've been ruining him out there, so let's see what we can do."

Cohan arrived in Hollywood the latter part of June of 1932. The company began shooting on July 18 and finished work early in September. During that time George M. Cohan, the idol of Broadway, suffered the miseries. This beloved man, one of America's foremost actors, received what is known as the brush-off and learned at first hand that certain cinema Pooh-Bahs kept their wits in a deep freeze.

Some years later a studio made Cohan's life story, *Yankee Doodle Dandy*, with James Cagney playing the part of Cohan, and thus acknowledged the greatness of the man. But in 1932, no, or nix, as the boys say.

Cohan motored to the Paramount gate the first day and sought to drive his car inside the lot. The gateman asked for his pass.

"My name is George M. Cohan," the actor replied politely. "I'm doing a picture here."

"You can't drive in," the doorman said.

Cohan wondered if he were in deepest Africa. The doorman never had heard of Mr. Cohan; nor, when George M. finally reported for work, did the bosses seem to care who he was or what he had done on the stage.

The picture had been in progress for about a week when Cohan said to Durante in Clayton's presence, "Jimmy, I love you. If it was anybody else in this picture but you, I'd throw up the job. But I want you to walk away with this picture. This racket out here isn't my business. I don't know why they wanted me to come out here in the first place, or why I ever was dumb enough to come. But I want you to walk away with this picture, Jim, because I love the ground you walk on."

"Aw gee, George!" the Schnozzola said, "you got me all flustered up. I don't know how to suppress it in words."

Cohan turned to Clayton. "I've played all through the country, singing my own songs, dancing, or appearing as a star in productions. The public of most cities seemed to like me, and I've done pretty well up to now, but out here I'm dirt, and all the things I can throw to Jimmy in this picture I will. I'll give him not only the bones but the meat."

Another well-known actor, Ed Wynn, suffered an unnerving experience in the Hollywood Land of Nod. Wynn's radio success as commander of the fire laddies had led to an M-G-M contract to make the *Fire Chief*. Wynn was to receive a hundred and fifty thousand dollars for the picture.

On Durante's return to Hollywood after the close of *Strike Me Pink* he was called to the office of an M-G-M executive. Ed Wynn was there. The executive said to Durante, "You know Mr. Wynn?"

"Sure," said Jimmy. "I've always been a great admirer of his."

"The reason I got Jimmy up here, Ed," the executive announced, "is that I'm thinking of putting Durante in a picture with you."

Wynn, who had been sitting down, leaped up and slapped his hand on the table. "No! No! This is not going to be a Jimmy Durante picture!"

"Well," said Durante, "you needn't worry, Ed. I'll only be a featured player."

"Not in any picture I'm going to be in!" exclaimed Wynn.

The executive argued back and forth with Wynn, saying that it was for the good of the production, that Ed had not made a picture as yet, that he needed other names to help him. Wynn declared that if it was a bad picture all the names in the world wouldn't help it.

At this the executive said to Durante, "Thanks for coming up, Jimmy. I'll be calling you."

One day the Schnozzola was walking past Wynn's dressing room. Ed called out, "Ain't you afraid of getting fired?"

"For what?"

Wynn seemed very sad. "For speaking to me. Everybody around here thinks I got leprosy."

"Why? There must be a reason. It's like the guy who goes to the chair, and the other guy says, 'What did you do?' And he says, 'Nothin'.' So the other guy says, 'You must've done somethin'.' What is it, Ed?"

"Oh, the big guns got mad because I walked into a meeting the other day and said, 'I got more money than the whole lot of you put together, and I can buy and sell you.' I guess I must have talked out of turn."

The Fire Chief was not a successful picture.

"I don't know the true facts of the Ed Wynn story," Durante says, "only what I heard. But it is out of turn for an actor to go in and tell the executives where they get off. Some great actors are not recognized out here or properly respected, like George M. Cohan, but there is another side to the matter, and we gotta be fair-minded. I mean about lots of newcomers. I really think the movies sperl a person when they come out here. I really think they do. They give so much attention to an actor. They give you attention when you're only sittin' down. They come over with a chair when you're shootin' a picture, and you have a special make-up

man, and a personal property man, and you go back to your dressin'
room, lay down, and there's a fellow watchin' out for you.

"If you can't take that sort of thing, you gotta be sperled. And
some of the unexperienced fellows and girls take it like it's comin'
to them. They never had that attention before in the theater. We
just don't get it there. We're only actors. We don't get it when
we go and play a vaudeville date. Sometimes we're put in the cellar
for a dressin' room. And the only one who comes around is a guy
who yells 'Five minutes!' And if there's any make-up you've gotta
go and put that make-up on yourself. But in the movies, if you
go to your dressin' room, in case you're workin' on an outside
lot, they got a car to take you there and back. They wake you
up in the mornin'. They've got doctors and everything. Even
flowers.

"Believe me, they give you a million dollars' worth of publicity.
And if you're not careful, you get to believe that publicity, the
things they write about you. Well, you gotta get sperled. If you
can't take it, it's just too bad. And that's why the saying is, 'Goin'
Hollywood.' "

This adulation, remarks Durante, not only can stop overnight
but even in an hour, and then the spoiled actor is, in his words,
"out on a raft."

"I think," continues the wise Schnozzola, "the reason that a studio
takes so much guff from an actor or an actress is because they've
got so much money tied up in this person. They've spent millions.
They build a man up from nothin'. And finally when they get you
someplace, where you figure, 'Gee, look! Lookit! I'm worth more
money than everybody!' the actor wants to go in and get the say
on the story. Then he wants the say on the director. He wants to
have the say who's to be alongside him in the castin'. And believe
me, I don't know today how studios keep goin'. The aggravation
that goes on at them! That's why I say I want to have a word of
praise for Mr. L. B. Mayer, one of the finest men in the world. He's
like a daddy to every one of them. The minute you go up, and you
got any trouble on the lot, and there's nobody else can handle it,
you know Mr. Mayer's a very busy man, but he will send for you
and he will talk to you, and when you leave that office, believe me,
if you're a boy or girl, you oughtta feel ashamed of yourself that
you were doing all that stuff. I hear he's resignin', and I'm sorry to
hear it."

In 1933, just before *Strike Me Pink* closed, Jimmy's policeman brother Albert fell ill, and was operated on for an intestinal obstruction. Durante was with the big fellow when he died.

"The death of Al left a big hole in my life," Durante says. "He was so strong, and it didn't seem right. I had taken my dad to California and left him there to get the sun while I was in the East. We never told him for a long time of Al's death, and maybe it was wrong. For Pop would say, 'I wonder why Al doesn't write to me?' Finally, when we did let him know, he said, 'You oughtta have told me. He was my son, and I would have gone to him.' How is anybody to know what is best? Tell 'em or not tell 'em? Sometimes I think a lie is the longest distance between two pernts."

In 1932 Jimmy and Jeanne moved to an apartment on Detroit Street in Los Angeles so that Durante might be nearer to his studio. In 1934 they rented an apartment on Olympic Boulevard, and later bought a home at No. 5778 on the same broad thoroughfare.

One day when Mrs. Durante was at a beauty parlor, having her hair waved, she met a young Negro woman of much intelligence and genuine goodness of heart. Maggie Arnold was the granddaughter of a Texas minister and had moved with her parents and her sister Hazel to California.

Jeanne Durante invited Maggie to work for her. The girl was employed elsewhere but offered to send her sister Hazel to the Olympic home. Not long after this Hazel had to stay away from work while having a baby, so Maggie went to the Durantes, became their loyal friend, and cared for Mrs. Durante during her many sieges of illness. Maggie later bought a home of her own, but she works every day except Sunday for the Schnozzola, keeps his house in order, packs his things when he is to leave town.

"Maggie is like my own flesh and blood," Durante will say. "And I'd sooner lose my right arm."

Bartolomeo Durante also looked upon Maggie as a friend. Each morning during his stay in California the old man would give Maggie a dime and a flower he had picked from the garden. It was Maggie who kept a close eye on the genial old fellow when he set out to barber someone whom he had persuaded to be his free customer.

Jeanne's brother Earl, always sickly as a result of his having been gassed in World War I, had a place at Sierra Madre, California. He frequently was a house guest of the Durantes.

Jeanne worried about her brother's ill health. She felt that he would soon die. She got to thinking about death, perhaps too fixedly, and purchased a burial plot at a cemetery in Arcadia, near Pasadena. The plot had places for four graves.

The furniture at the Olympic Boulevard house was plain, notwithstanding Jim's income of more than eighty thousand a year. Jeanne had brought a few personal things from New York, among them an old music box that Jim's father had given his son.

Once in the thirties, and before Maggie had come to work for them, Jimmy and Jeanne decided to take their holiday in Palm Springs instead of at Clear Lake. Before going away, the Schnozzola installed iron bars on the windows of their home. They owned few valuables, it is true, but there had been several house-breakings reported in the neighborhood, and Jeanne once again found herself shuddering at night while Jim was away at benefits or at studio executives' parties.

During that Palm Springs vacation Jeanne said, "Tootis, I want to settle down here sometime." She had been looking at an acre or so of vacant property across the road from the Mirador Hotel, where they were staying. "If you want to buy it, Toots," Jimmy said, "then go ahead and do it."

One evening the owner of the hotel said to Durante, "Jimmy, Professor Albert Einstein is down here with his wife. He plays the violin, and he wants to know would you come on down and accompany him on the piano?"

"Sure thing," the Schnozzola said. "But who's the Professor? A concert player?"

"Are you kidding? Just come on down."

Mr. Durante was introduced to the scientist in the lobby. Dr. Einstein did not speak much English, and Mrs. Einstein did the translating for him. As she talked to Jimmy her husband nodded his head and appeared to be very happy over the prospect of playing the fiddle with the Schnozz as his accompanist.

Jimmy sat down at the piano, and the scientist tuned, then chinned the violin.

"The piece we played," Durante recalls, "was in E minor, a very hard key for me. And you know it's one of those things where you play a few chords, and then he's got a run, and you play another couple of chords, and he keeps on runnin'. So he gives me the cue to start, and we start. After Einstein hits the run, I am supposed to come in with two chords. I come in late, and he turns around and gives me a look, and anyway he keeps on goin'. So the next time I strike a blue note he turns around, shakes his fuzzy hair, and gives me another look, but still keeps on goin'. Then about eight or ten bars later I am supposed to do a run after he does a run, and I make a big botch out of that. So he stops. He speaks to his wife. His wife turns to me and says firmly, 'Mr. Durante, Mr. Einstein has had enough! He's a little tired.' "

There was another musical incident some years later when Durante appeared with the Paul Whiteman radio show in New York. Durante did a number called, "Toscanini, Tchaikovsky, and Me." Before starting to play Jimmy would shout, "Can Toscanini play piano? No. Can Durante play piano? I'll show yah." And then Jimmy would play.

After the program Jimmy returned to the Hotel Astor. Entering the elevator, he saw Toscanini. The maestro looked at him severely. "Mr. Durante, I just heard your program; and I want to tell you something: I *do* play piano." Durante streaked out of the elevator and from that time on stayed out of Toscanini's sight.

The Durantes returned from their Palm Springs vacation to find that a burglar had ransacked their house. Though Jimmy had installed iron bars on all the windows, he had neglected to do so on the kitchen door, a flimsy barrier that had given way easily to the boots of the intruder. Some silverware and a few other things had been taken, among them the music box so highly prized by Jim. He advertised for the recovery of the box, offering a large reward and promising to ask no questions.

Several years afterward Durante received a letter from a convict: "Dear Jimmy, No doubt you will be surprised to hear from San Quentin Prison. I've been meaning to write to you for a long, long time to tell you where that there music box is located. Well, I turned it over to the sheriff's office substation, and I've written to tell 'em it was yours. I am so ashamed, Jimmy. I'll take no reward from you. I had no idea it was your house I broke into or I never would have did it. And the boys up here would never speak to me if they knew I'd stole something from their greatest pal."

After the music box had been returned the convict kept up a correspondence with Durante, and each year still sends Christmas cards drawn by himself.

Not long after the Schnozzola had arrived in California the newspapers carried stories of Legs Diamond's death. Although it was reported that the lead-heavy Mr. Diamond had been mortally shot upstate in New York, some persons still believe that he really died of overweight.

In connection with Legs' death, Jimmy received a letter from an ex-insurance man who wrote that he was down and out because his insurance firm had fired him for having written an accident and health policy for Mr. Diamond's wife Alice.

Alice had been winged soon after she sounded off that she knew who killed her husband. She was undergoing a course in target practice at the time she became the target.

Sometimes Jimmy and Lou went into a huddle with their old-time adviser and friend, Sime Silverman. Now sixty years old and stricken with tuberculosis, Sime spent much of his time in California. When in Los Angeles he stayed at the Ambassador Hotel.

Sime had become less and less active in the operation of the trade paper he had founded. Most of the work was left to editor Abel Green and other *Variety* staff members, whom he affectionately referred to as his "mugs."

In September of 1933 Silverman made a date for lunch with Durante, Clayton, casting director Ben Piazza, and Arthur Ungar, who had charge of the Hollywood edition of *Variety*. When Sime failed to appear on time at the Ambassador dining room Ungar called his chief's suite. There was no answer. Ungar and Piazza went upstairs to investigate. They found Sime on the bathroom floor, dying of a heart attack. At this Ungar himself suffered a heart seizure, and some years afterward succumbed to a coronary onset.

There was great sadness everywhere in the show world when Silverman died. No mourning borders appeared on the pages of *Variety*, for Sime disliked that sort of thing; but Abel Green, Jack Pulaski, and several other members of the staff wrote an obituary in memory of their great boss: "The Old Boy is gone. His monument isn't. *Variety* is Sime's monument."

Durante still keeps a silver-framed picture of Sime Silverman in his den. "Sime made us," Jim will say. "Discovered and made us."

Durante's picture career limped badly in the mid-thirties. Clayton complained to Mayer that Jimmy was not getting a fair break, and L. B. sent for Durante. "Jimmy, you know I can't look after every last detail in a studio of this great size. Now I suggest, as a public build-up, that you do personal appearances in our theaters."

Durante toured Baltimore, Brooklyn, Pittsburgh, and other cities during the latter part of 1934 and the early months of 1935. Packed houses greeted him everywhere. But while he was in Pittsburgh two experiences caused him much distress.

One afternoon Jimmy went among members of the audience to improvise jokes and comments. He paused in his mad gallop to kiss the head of a woman sitting in the fourth row, then returned to the stage, shouting, "Boy! I can't forget that gal!" The audience laughed and applauded.

The next day the kissed woman and her husband sued Durante for five thousand dollars, charging that he had humiliated her. She said, among other things, that the comedian had "overcome all my resistance." Her husband also felt humiliated.

While Clayton was "squaring this beef" at the lawyer's office, Durante sat like a disconsolate anteater in his suite high up in the William Penn Hotel. He kept moaning to his friends, "I'm as innocent as a little ram! There was no evil extent in my actions!"

Clayton returned to the hotel to find several pals waiting for him in the lobby. He informed them that the charge against Durante had been withdrawn. One friend asked, "Lou, how's chances of playing a gag on Durante?"

"You can do anything you want to with Durante," Clayton replied. "But just don't hurt him. What do you mean, you want to play a gag?"

It seemed that a fellow townsman, Luke Barnett, was the greatest practical joker in the world. Sometimes he would pose as a waiter at banquets, put his thumb in the soup while serving important persons, and otherwise annoy guests with rude comments on their lack of social graces. They cited the time that Babe Ruth had threatened to kill him for calling the home-run king an ignorant pig.

"We've booked no banquets," Clayton objected. "That's out."

"Well," said another fellow, "this Luke character sometimes poses as a revenue officer, and—"

"No. Jim's on the level with his taxes. He'd never fall for that." A third man had an idea. "Luke once in a while poses as a priest. It's one of his biggest numbers."

Clayton nodded. "Maybe you got something there. For a priest he'd go the limit. But see that nothing physical happens to Durante. No rough stuff, remember."

Clayton was introduced to Luke Barnett, rehearsed the prank, then retired to the Durante suite. There was a sitting room, with Lou's and Jimmy's respective bedrooms on either side of it.

The Schnozzola was clad in his bathrobe. "All the red corpsuckles is gone from my veins!" he moaned. "I'm just a hollow shelf!"

Lou tried to cheer him with the news that all charges had been dismissed, but Durante kept saying, "I know, Lou, but why does this here woman hate me? I never met her before."

Clayton went to his own room. In a short while a knock sounded at the outer door of the suite and Barnett, dressed in the black garb and Roman collar of a priest, entered. "I'd like to talk to Mr. Durante," said the pseudoclergyman with a thick Polish accent. "Is he in?"

"Just a minute, Father," Clayton said. "What's it all about?"

"If you don't mind"—and the caller pretended to be displeased—"I'll discuss my business with Mr. Durante."

"Not so fast!" Clayton said, knowing that Durante's door was open a little way and that Jimmy could overhear the conversation. "I happen to be Mr. Durante's partner and manager. If you want to see him, you'll have to explain just what it is you want to see him about."

"It's about a benefit. I'm Father Zbyszko of St. Vladimir's Church, and we owe a lot of money on our new parochial school."

"Well now," Clayton said, "Durante's pretty much fed up with all these benefits, and I don't—"

"Aw, gee! Hello, Father!" said Durante, coming into the room. "So glad to see yah! Here, gimme your hat. What can I do for yah?"

"You will maybe come out to our church basement and entertain the parishioners?" The false reverend gentleman looked fiercely at Lou. Then, as he seated himself on the sofa, he changed his tone and pointed a finger at the Schnozz. "Unless, of course, you are one of those lazy, stingy bums that never go to church and—"

"Aw, no, Father!" Jim protested. He displayed a crucifix ring on a finger of his left hand. "I never miss Sunday mass or neglect a day of obligation—unless I'm hide-bound for some place on a train."

The supposed priest frowned. "You interrupted me!"

"Gee, Father, I'm so sorry!"

"Quit swearing! And don't crush my hat. Have you no respect for the clergy?"

Jimmy carefully put aside the man's hat and said humbly, "Let me give you a check for five hundred dollars, Father."

"I'm no beggar, sir!" the caller informed him. "I'm only asking you to play a benefit for St. Vladimir's."

"Sure! Sure, Father!" Jim agreed. "Just you name the date. I'm eager to."

"That's better." The Father rose to leave. "Tomorrow night at eight o'clock then."

Clayton called Jim's attention to the fact that he must be onstage at the theater by eight, then turned to the sham priest. "Father, that's the time Mr. Durante must go on—" .

The visitor wheeled at the door. "You keep out of this!"

"Yes, Lou," Jim said, "we can work out somethin'."

"Now, besides all this," the man in black went on to say, "I also want to advertise on billboards and in the daily press that you'll perform at my church."

"That's complete out of the question," Lou said.

The visitor shouted at Clayton, "So you hate Catholics, eh?"

"No, no, Father, please!" Jim interceded. "Lou is for all creeds. He's just tryin' to explain we got an iron-bent contract with M-G-M. They're payin' me five thousand a week. And they have forbode me in writin' to let anyone advertise me at benefits."

The fake priest moved in on Durante. "Why, you big-nosed ham! What good are you to me if you won't let me advertise you? How in hell can I get anyone into the church benefit?"

Clayton interposed, "Father, it isn't nice of you to use that language."

"Please, Lou!" Jim pleaded.

But Clayton continued to address the visitor. "This man is more than willing to give you a donation. This man is willing to go over and entertain for you. But he simply cannot break his contract and let you advertise him, because the people that would come to the church benefit, those are the same people that you're gonna keep away from the theater."

"You damned bigot!" shouted the priest. "What the hell are you butting in for?"

While Durante was wondering at the uncloistered language of the visitor, Clayton and Barnett went into the routine they had rehearsed. Clayton aimed a blow at the visitor's jaw. The confused Durante failed to observe that the supposed clergyman held his left hand up to his chin and caught Clayton's right-hand blow on the palm of the hand. And down went the poor fellow, bellowing as though in great pain. Durante sprang toward them, crying out accusingly in his hoarse voice, "Lou! Lou! You've hit a priest!"

Barnett, who had some ripe berries in his mouth, bit on them. To the Schnozzola's great dismay, blood, or what seemed to be blood, oozed from the clerical lips. Durante turned pale. "Father! Father!" The victim writhed and "bled." Durante turned angrily on Lou. "How *could* you? A priest! I'm so ashamed!" He began to flail Lou's chest.

Clayton pinned Jim's arms to his sides and tried to explain that he'd "had enough of this insulting priest." Durante wrestled free, ran babbling into his bedroom, and locked the door behind him.

The priest immediately rose. He left the suite with a wink, one which suggested that the gag was not yet over, as indeed it was not.

Shortly there was a knock at the door.

"Who's there?" Clayton asked.

"The house detective."

Clayton opened the door. There were two detectives. Moreover, the priest stood between them.

"All right, gentlemen," Lou said loudly enough for Durante to hear, "as officers you may come in. But don't let this other gentleman in. Don't let the Father in here, because I do not like the language the Father uses."

"Now look here," the Father shouted, but at this Jim unlocked his door, came out, and said sternly, "Lou, go to your room! At onct! Please let me talk to the man. Let me talk to the Father."

Clayton retired to his room and shut the door, all but a crack.

One of the detectives said, "Sorry, Mr. Durante, but we've come to lock you up. A man that attacked an innocent woman patron yesterday, and now today slugs a priest is—"

"Just a minute, gentlemen," Jim interrupted. "You're makin' a mistake! It wasn't me. I didn't touch a hair of the Father. Ask the Father." He addressed that gentleman with a hoarse plea, "Father, did I do it? Was it *me* who put his hand on you? Wasn't it the *other* fellow?"

"*What* other fellow?" asked the prankster solemnly, then shouted, "No, you big-nosed bum! It was you. You hit me!" More "blood" began to ooze from his lips.

Jim leaped for the door of Clayton's room. Lou by now had closed and locked it. Durante hammered upon the panels. "Lou! Lou! It's me! Jimmy! Open up!"

As Lou opened the door the distraught Schnozzola said, "How do you like this? The Father says it was me who hit him, instead of you."

Clayton replied with simulated anger, "What are you telling the detectives it was *me* for? Did I tell them *you* hit him? What are you squealing on me for?"

Durante was in tears. "Do you want me to take the blame, Lou?"

"No, Jimmy, I don't want you to take the blame. But you don't have to say anything. You don't have to say it was you who hit him. It only goes to show you! I hit him, and he's blaming you."

By now Durante's eyes were leaking like faucets. He turned helplessly to his accuser. "Father! Father! How could you say it was me that struck you?"

At this the practical joker removed his clerical collar. Then he took off his black coat. "Jimmy, you're a great sport! The whole thing was just a gag."

Jim looked at Barnett and then at Clayton, who nodded. "It was a joke, Jim."

And now the irate Schnozzola shouted in all earnestness, "Knock his eye out, Lou! Murder him!"

XVII

A Nose Is a Nose Is a Nose

IN 1933 Durante received an offer of five thousand a week to appear on the radio each Sunday evening for the Chase and Sanborn Coffee hour. The M-G-M studio executives finally agreed to let the Schnozzola work on the side, to pick up one hundred and thirty thousand dollars in twenty-six weeks.

The Schnozzola's radio income might seem low in comparison to the salaries later paid Bob Hope, Jack Benny, and Red Skelton, reputedly as much as twenty thousand dollars or more a week. Their income taxes, fees for writers, musicians, supporting actors, guest stars, and various other expenses greatly reduce their net earnings.

Out of his five thousand dollars, Durante paid five writers, none of whom received less than three hundred dollars a week. Then, after Clayton had subtracted his third of the residue, and Uncle Sam had put a hand in Jimmy's pocket, less than a thousand dollars was left, which Jimmy put out here, there, and everywhere. He received thousands of requests for autographed pictures and paid for the prints and the mailing. He entertained friends and hangers-on at the best restaurants and tipped captains and waiters both-handedly. The Toms, Dicks, and Harrys used his hotel suite as a port of call, ran up long-distance telephone bills, and enjoyed room service.

James Durante paid his taxes cheerfully. "All I want or ever hope for," he has said, "is to not be a burden on anybody, and to keep working as long as God gives me my two legs to walk on, and to be able to do things for people I like."

In 1948, 1949, and 1950 the Schnozzola's gross income annually approached the half-million bracket. Of these gross earnings he managed, with Clayton's guidance, to put aside about fifty thousand dollars a year. In 1950, however, he saved nothing. In fact, he has had to draw upon his capital in 1951 to meet a tax deficit. His generosity, of course, accounts for much of his undeductable expenses. Whenever one of his friends falls ill or wishes to send a child to school or has a funeral in the family, Durante pays the bills.

In 1934 Jimmy took his yearly twelve weeks' leave from the studio to make personal appearances in New York. While at the Capitol Theatre he learned of Billy Rose's plans to stage an extravaganza of circus life. Rose well knew that the Schnozzola's talent of late had been strewn to the variable Hollywood winds. He commissioned MacArthur to urge Jim to play the comedy role of press agent in *Jumbo*. With the financial backing of multimillionaire Jock Whitney, and a lively book supplied by Hecht and MacArthur, Rose planned to put *Jumbo* in the old Hippodrome Theatre in mid-Manhattan. Songwriters Richard Rodgers and Larry Hart were to supply the lyrics and music, and Paul Whiteman and his band would play the tunes.

"It seems," Durante says, "that Hecht and MacArthur always showed up in time to save me from some dillemia; first with *Roadhouse Nights;* next when MacArthur gave me *Get-Rich-Quick Wallingford;* and now they concocked *Jumbo* for me. It is Hecht and MacArthur who give me lines in *Roadhouse Nights* that I am always fond of, like, 'It's the gallows!' and 'I'm just a tool for a beautiful dame!' And I told Charlie I would play *Jumbo*.

"As for this Billy Rose, he is dynamite. He tore out the insides of the old Hippodrome and made the stage like a circus ring, right in the middle of the place, with the people sitting all around, and a circular curtain to come down on the ring. I fell in love with the whole setup."

One day Clayton arrived at the Capitol Theatre during Durante's two-week personal-appearance engagement there, to collect money due the act. He then went to Jimmy's dressing room, where the Schnozz was waiting to go on for the first afternoon stage show. It was obvious to Clayton that Durante had something big on his mind.

"You must understand," Clayton once said, "that Jimmy Durante, with those little eyes of his, the way he looks at me, I can always tell when he's joking, and I can always tell when he's making with a lie. I never needed a search warrant to read his mind."

Clayton asked Jimmy what had gone wrong.

"I just got a call from California tellin' me my bank account is short! Can yah imagine? My bank account short?"

"How can it be short?" Lou inquired. "When we left, you had over eight thousand dollars in your checking account. All you've done during the duration of our tour is to pay out some bills and deposit checks from the theaters. And that would bring you into thirty-eight thousand or even more."

"Lou, all they told me is my checkin' account is short. And they say I have bought a shoe factory."

"Who is they?"

"The Bank of America," Jimmy replied. "Dr. Giannini in California."

Clayton got Dr. Giannini on the telephone immediately and was informed that a check for forty thousand dollars, apparently made out and signed by Jimmy, had been cashed at another bank and then cleared at the Giannini bank. The bank president added that it had been offered in part payment for a shoe factory.

Lou asked Dr. Giannini to hold the phone a minute. He turned to Durante. "Did you buy a shoe factory for forty thousand?"

"No," Jimmy said firmly. "I didn't even buy a pair of shoes." Jimmy thought a while, then added, "Oh, yes, I did buy a pair the other day and somebody asked me to autograph an old shoe. Jack Roth was buyin' some shoes hisself, and by mistake I picked up one of Jack's number elevens and autographed it—"

"It's a whole shoe factory and forty thousand dollars we're worrying about. Did you or did you not sign that check?"

"No. Positive."

Clayton informed Dr. Giannini that Durante and he would return to California soon and meantime to honor all of Jimmy's checks. Dr. Giannini promised that the Burns Detective Agency would begin an immediate investigation.

Upon their return to Los Angeles Clayton and Durante went at once to the main office of the Bank of America. Dr. Giannini and two Burns operatives awaited them.

Dr. Giannini explained that the bank cashier and the Burns men had examined all of Durante's recently canceled checks. They believed that the check for forty thousand was an expert forgery modeled upon a check for four hundred made out to Clayton. One of the detectives asked Clayton when and where he had cashed this check.

It bore the endorsement of Jeff Bernie, brother of orchestra leader Ben Bernie. Clayton knew that Jeff Bernie was innocent and wished to get in touch with him before involving him needlessly.

"Gentlemen," stalled Clayton, "I am very much worried, and for the life of me, right now I could not tell you who I gave the check to, as my mind will not function. The train trip has tired me out. But let me go on home and in the next twenty-four hours I will put on my thinking cap."

Clayton went to his apartment at the Chateau Marmont, turned on the radio, and chanced to hear Ben Bernie's band on the air. The program originated in Denver. Clayton put in a long-distance call and got Jeff on the phone.

"Jeff, I know you are perfectly innocent, because you would not be a party to anything like this. But before you are mixed up, I would like to ask you to straighten me out."

Bernie had cashed the check for Clayton one afternoon at the Santa Anita race track. Jeff had given the check to a fellow known to bookmakers as Teardrop Billy and had thought no more about it.

"That clears you complete," said Lou. "I'll go consult the Teardrop."

Clayton went to the Brown Derby Restaurant on Vine Street, where Billy used to dine. "Bill, I want to know what the score is. Jeff says he gave that check to you, and somebody had the unmitigated gall to make out a duplicate map. Don't look for any sympathy from me if you are participating in this. Because, if I find the hole card on any of you, whoever it is, I'm gonna see you don't get any the best of it."

"Lou, I remember very distinctly who I gave that bandage to, and believe me, I've nothing to do with this here phonus balonus. I give the map to Pieces Brody."

"Where's Pieces now keeping house?"

Billy named the Beverly Wilshire Hotel. Lou went there and cross-examined Pieces, who remembered cashing this check and several others to meet a turf expense. He convinced Lou that he had not been involved in the forgery.

"All right, Pieces, then I'll not put the finger on you, but you'll have to tell your story to the Burns people, because I'm not going to let Jim book this forty-thousand-dollar loser."

The Burns operatives traced the check to a bookie known as Lights Out Levy, who had given it to someone else, and so on. That check had agility.

The person or persons responsible for the forgery never were

found. Clayton believed the swindle was the work of an old confidence man known, among many other aliases, as "Dr. Kite." The
doctor was a scholarly man in appearance, with gold-rimmed nose-
glasses and an almost bald head, with the few remaining hairs trained
over the scalp like the strings of a bull fiddle.

His method was to place a legitimate check between sheets of
glass, with a strong light shining from below the glass to trans-
illuminate the paper. He then put a blank check, corresponding to
the one he intended to forge, on top of the glass and traced on it
the figures and signature. The Durante check for four hundred
dollars had been copied, but with two zeros added and the word
"thousand" instead of "hundred."

The confidence men—and investigation showed there had been
at least two—obviously had read the investment advertisements in
the newspapers and found a shoe factory listed for sale in Los
Angeles for seventy-five thousand dollars. On a certain Friday after
banking hours, they had called on the factory owner. They offered
to buy the factory, with a proviso that their four other partners
subsequently agree to the purchase. The man thought to be Dr.
Kite said that three partners were on their way from Boston. He
added that Mr. Durante was willing to put forty thousand into the
enterprise and brought out the check to verify the statement.

"Tell you what," the check-waver proposed. "Suppose you deposit this in your bank till we hear from the other members of
our board. And for every single day that passes by without our
final decision, including day after tomorrow which is Sunday, we
will give you one thousand dollars to be deducted from this check."

The proprietor had nothing to lose. He went to his bank and
deposited the forged check. It did not clear until Tuesday. That
day the confidence men returned to the factory with long faces.

"Our partners have decided not to buy," said one man. "So we
will have to write off a loss of three thousand dollars to you. You
will only have to return to us thirty-seven of our forty-thousand-
dollar check."

The owner withdrew thirty-seven thousand dollars and gave the
cash to the men, shook hands, and that was that. Durante, for once,
did not lose his shirt: an insurance company took care of the loss.

Since that time Durante's bank has made it a practice to call
whenever the Schnozz writes a check for more than a hundred dollars. "And," says Durante, "I always pay cash for my shoes."

At the close of his personal appearance tour of 1934 Durante had five months left before the termination of his contract. Clayton prevailed upon the studio to release the Schnozzola. Now, as a free agent, Durante planned to return to the stage in *Jumbo*.

Jeanne Durante complained about Jim's going East. "Tootis, we'd be lots happier if we had only a little ranch out here; even if we had to eat spinach three times a day."

"Come on East with me, Toots," he said. "After *Jumbo* we'll come right back to California for keeps."

The Durantes left Los Angeles by train. In New York they were given a fourth-floor suite, No. 472, at the Astor Hotel, a three-room apartment that Durante has occupied whenever he has been in Manhattan. The Wrigley chewing-gum sign was being built across the street from the hotel, and the noise bothered Jeanne. They moved to the Essex House on Central Park South. Then Jeanne decided to reopen their Flushing home.

On July 4, 1934, Jeanne and Jimmy visited Fanny Brice, then married to Billy Rose, at their summer place on Fire Island. Jeanne sat quietly in a corner of the living room where stage celebrities often gathered at night. That evening George Gershwin played the score of his new opera, *Porgy and Bess*, for the first time before an audience of professionals.

There were five postponements of *Jumbo*. Inasmuch as the rehearsals went on for several months, and the show technically did not come under the terms of an Actors Equity contract—it was classed as a circus—Clayton ran short of money.

"I tell you, Billy," he said one day, "if you don't give me an advance of ten thousand, you gotta get a new comedian."

"Don't be talking foolish. Jimmy'll not quit."

"Suppose then you try to find him tomorrow?"

When the Schnozzola came to town from Flushing next morning Lou said, "You've gotta do me a favor. Get in my car, for I gotta see a fellow who is very, very important, to close a deal, and I can't close it without you."

Durante was supposed to be at rehearsal at ten o'clock. They motored up to Westchester, to the Fennimore Golf Course at Mamaroneck, about an hour's drive from Times Square. Clayton took Jim to the locker room, talked to the pro, then to the assistant pro and to several club members.

Jimmy kept saying, "Lou, I've gotta get down to rehearsal!"

Lou kept Jimmy at the country club until twelve o'clock and then telephoned Rose. "Let me talk to Jimmy Durante, will you, Billy?"

"Lou," said the worried Rose, "he didn't show up for rehearsal today."

"I told you yesterday he wouldn't. But I can't imagine—"

"Lou, you know where Jimmy Durante is. Please don't do this to me!"

"Billy, don't tell me not to do this to you. I told you yesterday that we needed ten grand. We've been rehearsing for months, and the show might open and then blow up right in Jim's kisser."

Rose dug up the ten thousand, and rehearsals were resumed the next morning.

Jumbo opened on November 17, 1935, and became a smash hit. Staged by John Murray Anderson and directed by comedy wizard George Abbott, the spectacle had two acts and eleven scenes. At entrance time Paul Whiteman, by no means a featherweight, rode in on a big white horse. There was an elephant Big Rosie, alias Jumbo, and on Rosie's neck as she entered the ring sat Jimmy.

The plot concerned the bankrupt circus of a Mr. Considine and his big-top rival, a Mr. Mulligan. A Romeo and Juliet situation involving the Considine daughter and the Mulligan heir, the latter played by singer Donald Novis, complicated the feud between the circus proprietors. Because of Mr. Considine's passion for fire water, his menagerie and his circus went to pot. When income-tax fiends prepared to take over the Considine assets, his press agent, played by Durante, burned down his employer's residence to collect twelve thousand dollars' worth of fire insurance.

Charlie MacArthur had given Durante a line that Jimmy at first did not regard as a funny one. "I am trying to steal the elephant Jumbo," Jimmy has said, "and am walking along in this scene when the sheriff shouts, 'What are you doing with that elephant?' and I replies, 'What elephant?' To my surprise, this line got one of the biggest laughs in the show."

One night a Fire Department inspector warned Rose that too many customers were crowding the aisles of the Hippodrome. Billy discovered that scores of standees were somehow crashing the gate and undertook an investigation. The trail led to someone in the Durante dressing room.

Rose learned to his horror that drummer Roth—at Durante's re-

quest—was smuggling into the theater droves of taxicab drivers and
their families, hotel employees and children, who could not afford
tickets. When Rose caught Roth at the stage door in the act of
passing in some deadheads from the Luxor Turkish Baths—all good
friends of Jimmy's—the fiery impresario asked the Schnozzola for
an explanation.

With a great show of concern Durante gave Roth a lecture on
dishonesty and tried to cover his own guilt by shouting, "I insist
that you never do this terrible subterfuse again! Now go back to
your drums, Mr. Roth!"

Soon after *Jumbo* opened a Broadway beggar known as Cooney
the Boom, an ex-longshoreman, began to collect alms from Durante.
The Boom's story was that he no longer could tote bales on the
waterfront because salt-water fumes gave him asthma. He touched
Jimmy twice for fifty dollars a bite before the Schnozz reduced the
fee to five dollars a visit. The Boom thereupon devised a splendid
plan. He told some twenty or more pals at a Tenth Avenue dive
that he could steer them onto a sucker who was good for a fiver
to each man. But, he stipulated, he would let them in on the easy
mark only if they kicked back fifty per cent of the take.

The pals agreed to pay the Boom his commission. After each performance the moochers would form a line at the stage entrance.
Durante passed out fives, completely unaware that he was the victim of the Boom's syndicate.

Press agent Richard Maney has described Jimmy's dressing room
at the Hippodrome as "a composite of a bus terminal, the Automat,
and an Elks' lodge meeting. Many of Durante's callers are policemen without portfolio in search of a quick one, retired waiters,
cabaret performers, musicians, checkroom boys, and many others
who seek a haven or a fast buck."

Jumbo did capacity business until the Lenten season of 1936. At
that time Rose suggested a layoff, to be followed by a road appearance of the spectacle in Texas. Clayton persuaded Jimmy not to
go on the road, because it would involve a cut in salary.

When the show closed Jeanne said, "Jimmy, please let's go home.
I miss California and I miss Maggie." During the months the Durantes were in the East, Maggie had been going to school to become an expert hairdresser.

Jimmy said he'd like to go to Florida first, to enjoy the sun and
catch fish. Jeanne agreed reluctantly. They arrived in Miami dur-

ing Easter week and were met at the train by an old friend, Mert Wertheimer, who was operating a gambling casino, the Royal Palms.

"Jimmy," said Mert, "you've got to work a few nights for us at the Royal Palms."

Jeanne froze up, and Jimmy shook his head. "Now wait a minute. Under no conditions do I wanna go to work."

"He's not going to work," said Jeanne. "He's down here to vacation. My health is not so good, and we want to rest for the only week we'll be here."

Durante took Wertheimer aside. "Please don't aggravate her. I'm not gonna work, and anyway I got no act, no piano player, no music, and nothin' to go in there with."

"We're stuck for an act," said Mert. "We had a misunderstanding with Harry Richman, and he blew. Joe E. Lewis has filled in just fine, but he's got another engagement soon."

Clayton arrived in Miami next day and persuaded Durante to perform five nights at a thousand dollars a show. Without saying anything to Jeanne about this arrangement, the Schnozzola proceeded in his usual manner to tangle himself in knots. He wired pianist Donnelly to come to Miami and bring the music.

"What a dope I was!" Durante says of this episode, referring to it as "a sour antidote of my life." "I shoulda known they'd advertise me in the papers and that my missus would read it."

"You're not going to work!" Jeanne exclaimed. "You promised this would be a little vacation. And I'm not feeling well."

"All right, all right!" said the Schnozz. "But can't I just look in on Joe E. Lewis tonight?"

"If you'll not go on the floor."

Jimmy promised. He went to the Royal Palms, and as he stood outside, talking to some friends, a taxicab drove up with Jeanne in it. Durante looked about for a hiding place. The only sanctuary that he could see was an armored money-truck, waiting nearby to deliver bags of coins and sheaves of currency for the evening's business at the gambling tables.

The Schnozzola darted toward the money-truck, crying out to the guards, "Boys, protect me with your life!"

The guards recognized the Great Nostril and permitted him inside the vehicle. He hid there with an eye to a gun port while Jeanne searched the casino for him. When time came for Jim to do his act, he took a draw, as Clayton would say, and went on, but feared a scene when he saw Jeanne at a ringside table. Mrs. Durante endured this first night without argument but insisted that Jimmy not spend another evening as an entertainer on the floor.

"Aw, let me do these few nights, Toots," he pleaded.

"What are you trying to prove?" she asked. "How much punishment you can take?"

"I don't know just what I'm tryin' to prove, Toots. I should get my head exterminated, but these fellows are pals."

"People take advantage of your friendship, Jimmy. You'll never learn. So I'm putting my foot down."

Durante sneaked away the next night, once again taking refuge in the armored car until time to go on.

In recalling this "antidote" Durante says, "You know, when a person is sick, they're irritable, and instead of arguin' with them, if we only had the will power, we should never do it. But how many of us have got that will power, that when they say somethin' you don't try to say somethin' back? More so if you're married than you would to a friend. I don't know the difference, but when you're married, your wife says somethin' to you and it hurts you. One word leads to another, and there you are, two fine people in a mess of words that can't be unsaid in a hurry.

"Jeanne was one of the sweetest gals in the whole world when she wasn't sick, as anyone can tell you. She was so goodhearted and good-natured. And she says, 'All right, go on and do the other nights.' And I had to send for my sister Lily, Lord have mercy on her soul, to come down there, because I have to fill the engagement and be funny and throw hats and joke and sing in front of the people."

While the Durantes were packing up to return to California, Clayton booked Jim for personal appearances abroad. The Schnozz was to appear in Dublin, Liverpool, Glasgow, and Blackpool, then for two weeks at the Palladium in London. He was to receive a thousand pounds a week for his act, less transportation expenses and the salaries of pianist Harry Donnelly and drummer Jack Roth.

On their way west the Schnozz stopped over in Manhattan long enough to apply for a passport and have pictures taken to go with it. Lou had some difficulty in having Jim's passport approved. Durante had been brought into the world by a midwife, and no certificate of his birth could be found among the vital statistics files of the City of New York. Jimmy's sister suggested that St. James

Church, where Durante had been baptized, surely would have cer-
tified that event, and it had.

Durante once again neglected to take Jeanne into his confidence.
He couldn't stay in California longer than two weeks, if he was to
make steamship connections that would get him to Europe in time
for his foreign tour.

"When I reached home," says Jimmy, "I got to thinkin' to myself. I said, 'Gee, I'm crazy bookin' this.' Like Jeanne said, what
am I tryin' to prove? I know nothin' about Europe. Here we're
now home again, and Jeanne is dyin' to stay put. She's happy
again and feelin' a lot better, and here I've gone and booked that
foreign engagement. How am I gonna break the news to her? So
I am in a condition of metal confusion."

Durante finally blurted out that he was going abroad. "It means
a whole lot of pounds to us," he said.

"Why did you have to do this on the sly?" Jeanne asked. "Clayton?"

They had an argument. The ailing Jeanne kept asking why he
had taken this new engagement, and why hadn't he come home to
stay for a while. She said that they had been away from California
too long.

After much persuasion Jeanne agreed to accompany Jimmy. She
packed a trunk and other luggage, and the Durantes boarded the
Santa Fe Chief at the Los Angeles station. During the half-hour ride
from Los Angeles to Pasadena, Jeanne wept.

At the Pasadena station Jeanne suddenly ordered the porter to
put her hand luggage off the train. The trunk could go on to New
York, or Africa, for all she cared.

"Wait a minute, Jeanne, what are yah doin'?" Jimmy asked.

"Getting off."

"Don't do that!" Durante exclaimed. "Yah can't."

He got off the train to plead with her. Then he said, "Well, have
it your way, Toots. I'll only be away a month or six weeks, and
if you get worse, I'll come right back, irregardless."

Jimmy went on to New York alone. Jeanne telephoned him frequently, weeping and saying, "Come home! Come on home!"

Two days before sailing date Durante told Clayton he had decided not to go. Then the telephone rang, and Jeanne said, "Go
ahead, I want you to go now. I'll be all right."

"Are yah sure?"

"I'm sure, Tootis. Go ahead. Finish the job and then come home. I'll be waiting."

But next day Durante again informed Clayton that he would not go to Europe. Clayton tried to convince Jim that his appearances in foreign cities would greatly enhance the Durante reputation.

"No, Lou," Jimmy said. "I'm leavin' for California."

"All right then," Clayton said. "Give me your train ticket so's I can have the porter check your trunk."

Clayton sent Jimmy's trunk—which not only contained Durante's things but also several of Jeanne's dresses—to the French Line pier to be put aboard the *Normandie*, new queen of the French Line, which was on her first crossing from West to East.

XVIII

The Shanghaied Jester

Lou Clayton's seemingly ruthless policy of making decisions contrary to the wishes of Jimmy's wife should not be exclusively attributed to a desire for money. True, Clayton sought financial security for Durante; if left to his own oddities of purse, Jim would gallop over the hill to the poorhouse.

One must first consider Clayton's devotion to Durante, if any real understanding of this partnership is to be attained. Clayton believed with all his heart that his idol was a great artist. He regretted the fact that Jimmy never could be persuaded that he was a superior person, professionally or otherwise. Lou admired his friend for keeping his feet on the ground, but he thought that Jimmy should keep his head elsewhere.

The man with the king-size nose always worked hard at the trade of minstrelsy, but he probably labored even harder than he otherwise might have to achieve a measure of the importance that Clayton saw in him. Still, he winced whenever Lou described him as "a creative artist" or "the best comic."

Clayton had no qualms about shanghaiing the Schnozzola. Among other factors, he felt that a theatrical tour of the British Isles would serve to convince Jim of his own shining talents.

Clayton once said, "If your heart is in the right place and you are a nice man and you've studied the Ten Commandments—which take in everything—that's all a person needs in life. You don't have to worry about an education, or about good looks, beautiful features and nice blue eyes. Your affliction is not going to be a holdback to you. You're going to get along in life if you've got a great heart inside your body. All you have to know is the righteous way of life, and be generous, and you're going to get along. That was my theme and my thought about Jimmy Durante. His affliction of a big nose and a raw voice meant not a damn thing to me. Well, it's made Jimmy a millionaire.

"When I first met Jimmy Durante, to me his nose wasn't any

bigger than mine. And the more I look at him, the more I like to look at him. I know my eyesight is not bad; I can see pretty good. To me he's handsome; and I know he's handsome to a lot of people. Because he can walk into a dark room, and every bulb in that room can be burned out, and there's no matches, but believe me, you will feel that room light up when that face of his gets inside of it. That's my opinion of Jimmy Durante, and I've seen it happen time and time again.

"Jimmy's heart is in the right place, and that's what makes him understood by everybody. And when I wanted to take him abroad, I wanted the people over there to see him in the flesh, and know what a great man he was. And I wasn't going to let anything or anybody stop this, even if I had to trick him into getting on the boat."

Clayton lured the Schnozzola aboard the *Normandie* on sailing night by persuading him to attend a bon voyage party for some departing theatrical people. Martin Beck, the vaudeville magnate, was aboard, as were Max Gordon, Broadway producer, and Ben Goetz, London representative of M-G-M Studios. Besides, said Lou, he wanted to talk to producer Gordon about a musical based upon *Cyrano de Bergerac*.

At Clayton's request Goetz had a piano placed in his suite. Jimmy and Lou arrived at about ten o'clock at night. The party was going strong. The ship would sail at high tide at eleven-thirty.

Jimmy sat down at the piano to play and sing. Clayton helped out with dances. The Schnozz became so preoccupied with his singing and clowning that he did not observe several guests leaving the suite. Nor did he hear the first warnings of "All ashore that's going ashore." When tugs nosed in and began to whistle, and the big ship's whistle blasted a reply, Jimmy shouted, "Ha! Ha! Somebody's competin' with me!"

Clayton and Goetz exchanged winks. Jimmy was singing, "Hello, everybody! Folks, we like you here. Hello, everybody! Folks, we're here to bring you good cheer."

Suddenly Jim stopped playing. "Lou, the boat's shakin'! Can't you feel the viperations?" He sprang up from the piano and ran to a porthole. The lights of the pier were receding. "Help!" he howled, "we're on the brainy deep!"

"Don't worry about it," Lou said. "We'll get off at One Hundred and Twenty-fifth Street."

"Why, you bum!" Durante screamed. "One Hundred and Twenty-fift' Street! What do you think this is? The night boat to Albany?"

"Well," said Clayton, "we'll get off at Portsmouth, or wherever it is we get off," and he escorted his amazed pal to their suite on A-deck.

Lou told the Schnozzola his reasons for the kidnaping. He then outlined the route of their tour, the towns they would play, and said they must rehearse painstakingly so as not to use certain slang expressions that were all right for American audiences but meant something quite different in England.

"Lou," asked the Schnozz, "how do you know that the people in Dublin, Ireland, will understand me? Do they talk English over there?"

"They talk English better than you and me put together."

Jimmy cabled Jeanne, then proceeded to have a good time aboard. He entertained, presided at the auctions of the ship's pool, and everyone seemed to like him immensely.

Durante had no trouble in clearing his baggage through the English Customs, though one inspector seemed a bit intrigued by Jeanne's dresses.

"I'm not effeminoot," Durante said. "And even if I was, I'm so ugly nobody'd believe it."

When Durante and his party got off the boat train at Waterloo Station a frowsy fellow asked Jimmy for two shillings for some tea. Jimmy asked Lou how much two shillings was. Clayton said that it was about fifty cents in American money.

Durante turned to the fellow. "Why, you can get *coffee* for five cents!"

The fellow looked accusingly at Jimmy. "You tend to your business, and don't butt into mine!"

Jimmy and his troupe remained for three days in London before going to Ireland. Clayton arranged a press conference at which Durante was astonished to learn that he was well known to the English columnists.

The *Daily Express* reported that Durante had a nose like a snow plow, a cigar like that bit of the carpet you put the rocking chair over, clothes that should belong to somebody else, a bald head with a few inquiring wisps, and that his one absorbing passion was vaudeville.

It was a May morning of 1936, cold and blowy, when the Durante troupe went aboard an inter-island boat at Liverpool to cross the Irish Sea. In each cabin a large tin vessel stood near the berths.

"Do they expect you to get sick on this trip?" asked Durante.

"No," said Clayton, "that's just in case."

Half an hour from port it seemed as though the boat were standing on end. "It's like a straw they tossed out on this ocean. And they don't even give yah a chance to kneel down and pray," the Schnozzola groaned. "Oh, Lou, please save me!"

"Jim, this is one time you'll have to do the best you can without me. I'm trying to save myself. I'm in the same shape you're in."

The Schnozzola regarded Dublin as "very pictorious." They were to play the Theatre Royal on Hawkins Street and had lodgings at the Gresham Hotel. Theater manager McGrath heard Jimmy rehearsing his song, "Again You Turna," and said, "Jimmy, do you want to do that number with girls?"

"Great!" said Jim.

Durante recalls this incident with a smile. "We got ten little Irish colleens. None of them knew how to dance. I'm tryin' to do 'Again You Turna' until one gal got a little dizzy, you know. She had to get off the stage, but it made a big hit with the crowd because everybody knew these little colleens and were so tickled for them to be on the stage. But on account of the one little kid gettin' dizzy, we canceled that. I was very happy in Dublin. I went over a hundred times better than I expected, and they liked me. They really liked me."

After the first show Durante saw a large group of children outside the theater. They set up a chorus, "We want Schnozzle! We want Schnozzle!" Jimmy arranged and paid for a special matinee at which eighteen hundred children were admitted free. After each day's performance children on bicycles or on foot would follow Durante's taxicab to his hotel.

As the troupe boarded the boat for the return voyage to Liverpool, hundreds of people gathered on the pier to sing "Come back to Erin." Durante choked up, and Lou lent him his handkerchief.

The Nose played a successful week in Liverpool and then went to "Glasscow." Sir Harry Lauder, the great Scotch comedian, sat in the third row at the Schnozzola's first performance. Jimmy made a speech in which he said that he used to save up his barbershop money to see Harry Lauder perform in New York. The audience applauded; Sir Harry Lauder went up on the stage and stood beside Durante. He said that he was glad to see his own people receive the American artist in Glasgow, as they had received Sir Harry in America.

The next day Sir Harry invited Jimmy to lunch at his mansion. "Everything that you see here in this building," he told Jimmy, "was bought with money I earned in America." Sir Harry dressed Jimmy in kilts, gave him a crooked stick, and tried to teach him the Highland Fling to the accompaniment of a phonograph record. But the Schnozzola's fling was a Charleston.

As in Dublin, the children of Glasgow became Durante fans. A half-dozen or so of them one day climbed upon the running board of the taxicab in which Jim was a passenger. Before the matinee next afternoon the theater doorman said, "Jimmy, a cab driver wants to see you."

"What's he want? Send him in."

The cab driver came in. "Mr. Durante, I know it's not your fault, but those childer yesterday broke the side window."

"Go ahead and have it fixed," Jimmy said. "I'll pay for it."

The cab driver returned next afternoon with a bill for ten shillings. Durante paid it, but the cabby did not go.

"What's the matter?" asked Jimmy. "Wasn't the ten shillings all right?"

"Yes, but you know, Mr. Durante, while they were fixing the glass, I lost a half-day."

"How much will that be?" asked Jim.

"Well," said the Scotsman, "a few pence will be all right."

Jimmy did not know what pence were, so he gave him a banknote.

During the tour Jack Roth borrowed drums at each theater the troupe played. At the close of the Glasgow engagement Roth was gathering up the sheet music when the house drummer announced, "I have a claim."

"Yes?"

"You must pay me for the use of my drums."

"No kidding!" said Roth. "I didn't injure them."

"I know, lad, but there was some wearing away of the skins."

"That's ridiculous!" said Durante's drummer.

"You don't want any trouble?"

"Hell, no! Come on and tell it to Mr. Durante."

In the dressing room the Schnozz listened with amazement to the house drummer's complaint: "Mr. Roth used my drums for one full week, and you must pay me for their use."

Durante became very concerned. Drummers at other theaters had been delighted to let Roth use their equipment. It also meant that they could go off duty for an hour or so.

"Just wait a minute!" Durante said. "That's never happened to me, and I'm not gonna pay it."

"Then," the drummer said, "I will summon the union representatives to take action wherever you play in Britain!"

The Schnozz shouted, "All right! Don't pull a gun on me." He had an idea that it would cost many pounds to settle the claim. "Just how much will it be?"

After a bit of hemming and hawing the drummer said, "I must have five shillings. No less."

Durante was amazed that the argument had gone on for so long for such a small amount. He sat down, wheezing, "All right! All right! Give him the blood money, Jack."

Before leaving Scotland Clayton and Durante played a round of golf on the famed St. Andrews course.

"I have never seen so many places where the ball could get lost," Durante says. "They really got flowers, and they have one big green with two holes on it. It's most confusin'. And you go one way, and the other fellow's comin' another way, and in between you're separated by beautiful flowers. Well, I didn't do the course in par. Half the time the ball is in the flowers. If you took a walk, you are exploring. I guess I did myself in par. Over there, I busted out laughin' to see them goin' around the course with big umbrellas like the kind we used to have on wagons. All of a sudden it's nice weather, and all of a sudden it's rainin'. The sun is shinin', but it's rainin'."

After the game Lou received a telephone call from Harry Foster, London representative of the William Morris theatrical agency. Jimmy listened on an extension in his room. Foster was saying that a Denham studio wanted Mr. Durante to appear in a picture, *Land without Music*.

"Richard Tauber, the opera singer, is in the cast," Foster explained. "Mr. Forde will direct it. The studio is prepared to give Mr. Durante four thousand pounds, or roughly the equivalent of twenty thousand dollars in American money for four weeks' work."

"They must think Durante is only a bricklayer!" said Clayton. "I want forty thousand dollars, and I don't want it roughly, but in American money."

Durante hung up and ran into Clayton's room. "Knock it off, Lou!" he whispered hoarsely. "Please knock it off!"

Clayton paid him no heed. "Maybe," he continued into the phone, "if I can sit down and talk to these people in person they will consent to our price."

Foster explained that English magnates did not do business that way. They had but one price and would neither raise nor lower it.

Durante, unable to influence Clayton, returned to his room to listen in again. "I will be in London tomorrow morning," Lou was saying, "and will go to the Savoy Hotel to register; then I will go out to Denham to see these people. I'll not let them or anyone else, even the King, knock Jimmy Durante off a pedestal!"

"What's a pedasill?" Durante blurted out on the extension.

Foster was plainly amazed at this interruption. "Who was that?"

"It's nothing," Clayton said. "Something's the matter with our connection," and he hung up.

Durante charged back into Lou's room. "I don't know what your pedasill is—"

"It's a thing they put statues of heroes and big politicians on in the park."

"I don't want nobody to put me on a pedasill." And Jimmy gave Lou a tongue lashing. "Are you crazy? Dickerin' over a pedasill? We are over here gettin' a thousand pounds, or whatever you call it, a week. If you'd knock off this offer, we'd get that twenty grand and save transportation expense comin' over again. What are we gonna do back in America? Let's knock it off."

"Not for any bargain-basement price!"

"Bargain basement! Twenty thousand dollars, Lou! It's a European picture; they never show it in America, so it can't hurt me."

"Jim," said Clayton, "you can always get twenty thousand. Let's see if I can't get forty. You know my slogan in life is, 'If I can't get five I'll take two, and if I can't get two, I'll take one.' According to your rate, the way you go along, we do things for nothing. Because with you it's, 'Let's knock it off.' "

Jimmy had no answer to this. He left the room, got his hat, and sulked out of the hotel. Clayton caught the next train to London.

There, Foster again advised Clayton that he would be stepping out of line to dicker for the raise in pay.

"Mr. Foster, do me a favor please. When I go out to Denham, I don't want any help from you. I don't want you to prompt me, and I don't want you to say anything."

Foster drove Lou to Denham. Clayton listened to the story outline, then said, "I'll tell you, gentlemen, the story is all right. It has to have a little bolstering up, especially because Jimmy Durante can't say all those words. You'll have to take out some of the articulations. But the most important thing is the money part."

He then went on to say that he wanted ten thousand dollars a week, or forty thousand for four weeks. There was a calendar on the desk, and Clayton pointed to it. "If there are any retakes to be made, Sunday is just the same as Monday to us, and we have to sail on the *Normandie* on a Tuesday after the four weeks are done, because a gentleman by the name of Vinton Freedley has been calling me and cabling me across the water in regards to a show by Russell Crouse and Howard Lindsey, called *Red, Hot and Blue!* Jimmy Durante, Ethel Merman, and a fellow named Bob Hope are in this, and we gotta be there. And there's also a radio program I wanted to knock off."

If Jimmy Durante were to miss the ship, the picture company would have to pay him a full week's salary, ten thousand dollars, even though he spent but one day on retakes.

Clayton called Jimmy, who was in Blackpool with the troupe. "I got the contract in my pocket."

"Good, Lou! Good! Twenty grand is not to be sneezed at, even with a nose like mine."

"I got forty. If we stay over, we get another ten. Now I'm going up to Glen Eagles during the duration while you have a week off in London. They've got two golf courses up there, the King's course and the Queen's course, and I want to play them. I'll see you when you open at the Palladium."

"Gee, Lou!" Jim said. "Don't ever pay no attention to me when I say 'Knock it off,' but just keep on lookin' for more bargains."

Durante made a great hit at the Palladium. He stomped, shouted, sang, threw hats, clowned, and waved his nose like a defiant flag. It was recalled by one critic that, a century and a half before, the French actor Dugazon, a scientific master of facial expression, had demonstrated that his nose was capable of no fewer than twenty-four distinct movements. Dugazon had declared that one could be sad with his nose, contemptuous with his nose, rude, and even dignified. Jimmy nasally demonstrated all those things at the Palladium.

At the conclusion of the motion-picture assignment Jimmy wanted to make a "Crook's tour" of the Continent and suggested that Lou and the rest of the troupe return on the *Normandie* and let him have a holiday all by himself. Provided with travelers' checks, Jimmy set off for Paris. He forgot to cable Jeanne that he was going to stay on and that he had plans for a New York show.

Clayton sailed to New York to confer with Freedley on the contract for *Red, Hot and Blue!*. The agent for the now-celebrated Ethel Merman insisted that his client's name be billed over the Schnozzle's. Clayton refused to permit this. A compromise was reached—the names were to be alternated on the playbills from day to day.

Two weeks went by with no word from Jim, and Lou became perturbed. He cabled Paris to find out what forwarding address Durante had left at the George V Hotel. The hotel could not say where the guest had gone. Cable inquiries to Monte Carlo and Rome brought no further information. The Schnozzola had disappeared.

Clayton enlisted the aid of police headquarters in various countries, Scotland Yard and the Sûreté in Paris. He also got in touch with friends in London, Paris, and Rome, but no one knew Durante's whereabouts.

Clayton, dining at Dinty Moore's, chanced to mention his worries to a veteran waiter.

"Oh," said the waiter, "I heard from Jimmy only two days ago."

"The hell you did!" Clayton exclaimed. "No offense intended, but I think if he had time to get in touch with you, he might at least get in touch with his partner. Where is he?"

The waiter produced a postcard. "It's from the Isle of Capri, and it says, 'A big hello to you from me who is explorin' the Blue Ghetto.'"

Clayton cabled the Naples authorities to locate Durante at once.

Of his "Crook's tour" Jimmy recalls, "I was all messed up, as usual. My passport was only for the British Isles, and who am I to know about gettin' what they call 'veezees'? I got no veezees. I barely got A, B, and Cses. I get on a boat and go to France, where I have no entry. So I have to go see the United States console, and

I wait around four hours, and he gets me a permit to stay a few days only in France. Then I go to the George V Hotel and get ready to see Paris, the Follies Bergère. What animation! I sure liked that town. All the monuments and tombs that are full of ancient hysteria.

"Now I want to go over to Monte Carlo to see how they gamble. I cashed in all my travelers' checks, and I got more than five thousand dollars in cash on the hip. Well, at Monte Carlo I can't understand a thing they say except 'Monsoor,' so after I go for maybe three hundred on the wheel I say, 'This is not for me. I don't want to be one of them fellows who turns blue and commits suicide.'

"So I want to go to San Remo on the Italian river area. And I go there. And I meet a fellow who runs the hotel who has a frock coat, you know, like an undertaker. I give him a letter from my Paris hotel to his hotel, tellin' who I am, and I put all my money in a box he has ready for my dough, and I take it with me upstairs. They got nets over the beds. Nets! Gee! I never slept in a bed like a butterfly in a net before. I look at the net while I got fixed up to go out for a ride, and in all my excitement to get my key handed in, I forget the money-box in my room. So I go out and get in a carriage. I am ridin'. Giddap! Giddap! I am suddenly thinkin' I left all my money in a box on the table in my room, so I drive back and open the box and start to count the money, and I'm seven hundred short. But I don't put in a squawk. No, sir! I'm so tickled they didn't pinch it all.

"Now I want to go back to Monte Carlo and to France, but I get to the border and I got no veezee to get back. They won't let me in, so I talk to some guys and pass them a little dough. So I go back to London, and when I get off the boat they won't let me into England neither. They say I got only one entry; I can only go in once. So the man says, 'Back to the line.' Everybody's gettin' off the boat, and I'm left alone. And there's a fellow takin' tickets, and, oh gee! he's a mean guy. The first mean guy I met. He wouldn't even look up at you, and wouldn't talk. If I'd known the words I would of sung 'Rude Britonia.' I go to the head Custom Inspector, and he is so nice, and he says, 'Mr. Durante, anytime you leave a country, make sure your passport has a veezee.' "

Durante went back to Italy, to visit Salerno, the birthplace of his parents. There he came upon his self-exiled brother-in-law, Genaro Romano.

"When you comin' home?" he asked Romano.

That gentleman said nothing until Jimmy gave him several thousand lire. Romano said, "*Grazie,*" tipped his hat, and walked off to make an investment. Nonetheless, during World War II, the Schnozzola financed Romano's return to America. Thereafter his brother-in-law enjoyed Jim's bounty in California until he died.

Jimmy spent but one day in Rome. When asked how he had expected to see what he called "the External City" in that brief time, he replied, "Are you kiddin'? By five o'clock in the afternoon I didn't know what to do with myself."

At Naples Jim boarded the *Conte di Savoia* for home. The former Queen of Spain was on this ship, and when the Schnozzola was introduced to Her Majesty she graciously exchanged salutations with him and discussed historical matters.

The Schnozzola sent Jeanne Durante a cable: "Dearest Toots, I came over here to make personal appearances, but I wound up making a personal disappearance."

XIX

Back from Elbow

WHEN THE *Conte di Savoia* docked that late summer day of 1936, banners were flying and a crowd was waiting to greet Victoria Eugenia, former Queen of Spain, and her daughter the Infanta Beatrice. Suddenly a hoarse whoop was heard, and Jimmy Durante, shouting and tossing his hat in the air, came dancing down the gangplank, at the foot of which Clayton stood as though to waylay him. The crowd set up a great cheer.

"Lou," Durante cried happily as they embraced, "I feel just like Napoleon did."

"Yeah?" Clayton studied his friend for a moment. "You a friend of Napoleon?"

"No," said the Schnozz, "he's dead and gone."

"Sorry to hear it," Lou said ironically.

"I met the Queen of Spain on this boat, and she tells me all about Napoleon's life and how tickled to death he is when he gets back from Elbow."

"Aha!" exclaimed Clayton. "You're going for queens, eh? Well, just forget these crowned heads, because you're going right now to the Alvin Theatre to rehearse."

Jeanne Durante arrived from California and the Schnozzola asked her not to reopen their Flushing house. It would be more convenient for him, while rehearsing, to live at the Astor.

From their corner sitting room the Durantes could see and hear Broadway. At night the neon signs and electric bulbs turned Times Square into a crater of fire; but somehow the old-time gaiety had gone from the Great White Way. Even the three years of legalized drink that followed the repeal of Prohibition in 1933 had not given Dutch courage to Broadway strollers beset—as were so many other citizens—by unemployment woes.

Jeanne's health was bad, but she seemed relatively content now that she had rejoined her Jimmy. She saw a few old friends such as the Werners on occasion, but most of the time she sat in her hotel suite, sewing.

"I only wish," Durante told Jeanne, "that an actor's life was different, and that a fellow didn't have to knock around like a loose nut in a boiler."

The show opened in the early fall, received good reviews, and did fair business. Early in 1937 the original cast went to Chicago. The scenery and the "props" were late in arriving, so the Windy City opening was postponed. This was followed by mishaps, illnesses among members of the troupe, and by various other aggravations. The show stayed six weeks in Chicago.

A handwriting expert, Muriel Stafford, analyzed the Schnozzola's penmanship and wrote of it in her Chicago newspaper column: "He is creative, imaginative, literary, cultured, and versatile. The signature has the dash of a man who thinks faster than he can write."

"Is she knockin' me?" Jimmy inquired.

After the show closed in Chicago, Durante played the Chez Paree night club. Jeanne Durante went on to California, and Clayton moved into the Congress Hotel to stay with the Schnozzola.

Showman Billy Rose, now operating the Casa Manana in New York, invited Durante to play four weeks at his new night spot, so back to New York went Clayton and Durante. On board the Twentieth Century Durante ran into Eddie Cantor. The old friends discussed routines for Jimmy's act at the Casa Manana.

"Jimmy," Cantor said, "I used to walk around the floor in a regular suit and say, 'You know, Florenz Ziegfeld wants me to wear a tuxedo, but I don't like 'em.' And Florenz says to me, 'Why you haven't even got a tuxedo.' So I'd call out, 'Bring out my dinner coat,' and I'd walk around the ringside and show the audience the buttonholes, the silk lapels, the material of the coat, and let 'em feel it. The routine was pretty good but not quite my meat. But for you it would be tops."

The vaudeville team of Long and Kaye appeared on the bill in which Durante tried out the tuxedo bit. Jimmy asked Kaye if he would help out by "mingling with the people" and showing them the coat. The then obscure Danny Kaye amazed Jim with his performance as a stooge. He seemed to be on crazy wings as he flew from table to table, babbling in Russian and exhibiting the tuxedo. "Kaye even then," says Jim, "was a house afire."

At the close of the engagement Durante forgot to stake Kaye for having helped him. After Danny Kaye had become a motion-picture star, he playfully dunned the Schnozzola for his tip.

Some years afterward, when Durante and Eddie Jackson once again performed together in a vaudeville act, the Schnozzola decided to revive the tuxedo routine. Several tough young men were among the audience that afternoon at the Metropolitan Theatre in Brooklyn as Eddie went out to "mingle with the people." One of the toughies seized the tuxedo from the startled Jackson's hands.

"Give it back," said Eddie.

"Try and get it!" was the challenge.

The tough fellows proceeded to rip the tuxedo to bits. Durante decided never again to do that routine.

The Schnozzola and Clayton entrained for the West in the late spring of 1937. They stayed over in Chicago for Durante to do a Sunday broadcast.

At the hotel after the program Clayton received a visitor known among gentlemen of chance as Hole Card Harvey. Harvey brought from his pocket a tissue-paper parcel containing some thirty thousand dollars' worth of diamond rings and other pieces of jewelry. "They belong to my wife," explained Harvey. "But I got to raise twenty-five hundred before morning. How about it?"

"I've always held you in the highest esteem," Lou replied, "and there's no sense in you giving me any security."

"Well," replied Hole Card Harvey, "you'd be doing me a big favor, Lou, if you'd freeze this jewelry; because I'm a cinch to get knocked out and then go hock it someplace. I'm playing cards and I'm playing the horses, and if you'll keep the wife's square-cuts, I won't be in a position to send 'em down a bookie's sewer."

Clayton placed the gems in one of his several secret pockets. "I see your point, pal."

Later that night Clayton had some wine and caviar with an old acquaintance, Long Tack Ziggy. Clayton seldom drank to excess, but tonight he sipped a toast too many to the furtherance of Ziggy's romance with a damsel at the table.

"I'm gettin' exactly nowhere with this señorita," Ziggy confided, half in jest.

The several glasses of Tiffany water had made Lou sympathetic. He got out the tissue-paper parcel, held it beneath the table, and selected a ring. "Let the nice lady wear this for a few hours. It will bring you luck."

Clayton awakened later that day with cobwebs in his usually unforgetful head. Not until he and Jimmy were on their way to the station did he remember the ring. At the train gate he gave Jimmy the railway tickets and went to call Long Tack. When he returned to the train platform Jimmy was peering worriedly from the rear window of the observation car.

The train began to move. Clayton tripped, on purpose, fell down on the platform, brushed himself off, then pointed overhead to indicate that he would fly to meet Durante in Los Angeles. The Schnozz put his hand to his head, a familiar gesture of his, as if to say, "Do I have to ride this train alone?"

Clayton retrieved the ring and early next morning boarded a plane for Albuquerque, New Mexico. He arrived there that afternoon and went shopping. Lou bought two women's hats with feathers on them and an Indian blanket. He removed the sweatband from his own hat and pinned the feathers to it. He put on this headdress, wrapped the blanket around him, and joined a group of depot Indians who sold trinkets to tourists.

Clayton had found out where Jimmy's car was likely to stand after the train pulled in and made ready to pose there as a Zuñi merchant. When the Schnozzola got off the train for a bit of exercise Lou went into a violent dance. He permitted Jimmy to see but one-quarter of his profile.

Durante applauded. "Great work, Chief! Mighty fine hoofin'!"

The dancer put his hands to his own throat, as Jimmy would do it, presented his profile, then said, "Hot-cha! Hot-cha!"

Durante grew hysterical as he recognized Clayton. "Lou! How long yah been here?"

"Jim, I been here long enough to turn native."

"Well," said Durante, "you're gettin' on the train with me."

"No, I'm gonna take the plane in."

"Oh, no, you're not gonna do that to me. I had the toughest time ridin' on this train all alone." He then went on to say, "I've been writin' some songs but can't get the right feelin' into 'em."

Jimmy's files still hold some of these roughly sketched song ideas. One of them reads: "You have a dollar. I have a dollar. We swap. Now you have my dollar and I have your dollar. We are not better off. You have an idea. I have an idea. We swap. Now you have two ideas, and I have two ideas. Both are richer. When you gave, you have. What I got, you did not lose. That's cooperation."

Another dealt with love. "On the downtown side of an uptown street is the home of the girl I'd like to meet. But I'm on the uptown, and she's on the downtown, on the downtown side of an uptown street. . . . Oh, to be uptown when I'm downtown! Never on the right side for us to meet. Oh, it's hell to be on the downtown side of an uptown street, when the gal you want to meet is on the uptown side of a downtown street!"

On the way from Albuquerque to Los Angeles, Lou said, "Jimmy, I ran into a fellow who caught Eddie Jackson's act."

Durante brightened. "Aw, gee! How is he?"

"I think he's all right financially. But I'm not satisfied with what I hear he's doing."

"How do you mean?"

"It's like this," Clayton explained. "He's entertaining on the floor in a minor league Brooklyn café. The report has it he's got a couple of partners, and they've given him a piece of the place, and got him telling a lot of off-color jokes on the floor."

"That's bad," Jimmy said. "We'll wire him to cut it out. Remind me."

"Putting Eddie in a café without us," Clayton said, "is like putting a boat in the water without somebody to run it. Eddie's not a handshaker, not a mixer, and no good at business. If he don't go busted with a place doing no business, he will go busted with those entertainers bringing in guests to eat and drink the profits."

"I miss our old trio," Durante mused.

"He'll be back someday, Jim."

"Well, Eddie knows where to reach me always."

"Yes," Clayton said, "and our old pact holds good as long as we got breath left in us."

"Yeah," said Jimmy thoughtfully, "we always got our pack."

"We were stand-up men for each other," Clayton once said. "We could go to each other with all our troubles, regardless of day or night. We never had to ask the other if he needed a transfusion of blood. We could drain the other fellow's blood till nothing would be left in his body. And we never betrayed a trust, or let each other down, never. Clayton, Jackson, and Durante took nothing away from each other. Because if you have it, that's all right with me, and when I have it, I know it's all right with you. And one looks out for the other, and we see that neither of the three will ever want a roof over their head. And that was our pact, and it was our make-up. And we loved the world, but if the world got too tough, then we loved each other against the world or the devil himself."

XX

Stormy Weather

JIMMY DURANTE returned to Los Angeles in 1937 to find that Hollywood, the town with the shortest of memories, had almost forgotten him. So he and Jeanne went in their automobile to Clear Lake to try to regain a measure of health and happiness.

On the way Jeanne said, "Let's buy a dog."

"All right," said Durante, "but let's get it on the way back."

"No," she insisted. "I want one now."

At a pet shop in Bakersfield, Jeanne chose a female cocker spaniel. She named the puppy "Muggins" and held it close to her as she would a child.

Later on during the journey northward the Durantes stopped over at a place celebrated for its split pea soup. They returned to their coupé to find that Muggins had made a mess of things.

"Couldn't we have bought that dog comin' back? Just lookit!" shouted the Schnozzola. "He's played haddock with our clothes!"

At Clear Lake, Jeanne's spirits improved somewhat, but not her health. She had become quite thin.

Upon their return to Los Angeles the Durantes consulted Dr. Louis Bilon, their close friend and family physician. Dr. Bilon endeavored to build up Jeanne's resistance.

The years from 1938 to 1943 were to be lean ones, touched with heartache, for the Schnozzola. A man of lesser stamina might well have been defeated.

The motion-picture makers no longer had Durante in mind. Hollywood is a celluloid gut that must be nourished endlessly, an all-devouring gut that greedily takes in and speedily rids itself of talents fed to it from enchanted salvers. A victim of this gluttony enjoys a drugged moment of wealth, huzzas, and statuettes, Cadillacs and other vain substitutes for the soul's ease, but once the jaws of the man-eater close upon him, his lot becomes that of any other morsel swallowed at last night's supper show.

There were times when casting directors and agents, among them

Jim's old friend Lou Irwin, telephoned the Durante home with prospects of employment; but the ill Jeanne frequently neglected to give these messages to her husband. And now the radio sponsors failed to renew the Schnozzola's contract.

The Durante money began to fade away, but Jeanne did not want to sell her real estate holdings; nor did Jimmy ask her to do so.

To add to the Schnozzola's worries, Lou Clayton was severely injured in an auto accident in 1938. The driver of a jalopy ran into Lou's car on Sunset Boulevard in Hollywood. Clayton plunged through the windshield. His throat was cut from ear to ear, and his nose smashed. Lou spent some months of that year, and weeks at a time during the following three years, in various hospitals both in Hollywood and New York. In all, he underwent twenty-one corrective operations, skin grafts, and plastic procedures on his nose and throat.

As soon as Clayton was able to speak again he said to his friend, "All you need now, Jim, is for the house to fall in on you."

Notwithstanding his hospitalization, Clayton arranged for Jim to appear with Ethel Merman in *Stars in Your Eyes*. The book was by J. P. McEvoy, the lyrics by Dorothy Field, the music by Arthur Schwartz. Joshua Logan staged this Dwight Deere Wiman production, which opened January 13, 1939, in New Haven. The show moved to Boston and then to New York, where it stayed at the Majestic Theatre for sixteen weeks.

Stars in Your Eyes was well received by the critics, one of whom said that "looking at Durante is like watching all three rings of a circus at once." Another critic said that the Schnozzola had "more profile" than all the Barrymores.

During Lou's first months in the hospital Durante's long-time friend Jimmy Kelly, Greenwich Village café owner and politician, bought a race horse named Westbrook. Kelly made Jimmy his partner in the one-horse stable and retained the services of trainer J. A. Coburn. Kelly paid one thousand dollars out of his own pocket for Westbrook and bought feed for the hayburner.

Jimmy informed Clayton that Westbrook was running at Jamaica Race Track, New York, with Jockey W. Fagan in the irons. "Lou, the trainer says this horse is sharp and ready to go."

When Clayton learned that the odds were fifteen to one, he said, "I'd like to pay part of this big hospital bill; so I'll have you place a hundred bucks for me on Westbrook's nose."

When Westbrook won Lou asked, "Jimmy, did you get that bet down?"

Jim fidgeted. "I didn't really believe he was gonna win, Lou, so I just didn't place a bet."

Clayton was furious. "Go on home!"

Three weeks later Westbrook again went to the post. Since the Schnozzola's steed had won its first race out, the odds had fallen to eight to one.

"What about your stable today? Any whispers?"

"I don't know," said Jim. "He might be ready."

"Well, put a hundred bucks on him for me."

"You sure you oughtta, Lou?"

"I really wish you would."

"Okay then," said Jim. "And I'll bet myself."

Westbrook again won. Clayton expected Jim to bring him eight hundred dollars. He asked the horse owner, "Well, did you place the bet?"

"Yes, I did."

"How much did you collect?"

"We won sixteen dollars."

"You dope!" Clayton closed his eyes.

"Lou! Lou!" Jimmy shouted. "Don't go into a comma on me. Gee!"

"I simply can't stand looking at you," Clayton said, his eyes still closed. "And I hope that pig with the elegant name drops dead!"

Jim tried to explain his two-dollar wagers, but Clayton groaned, "Please go! You're making an atheist out of me."

"A what?"

"Never mind. Just leave quietly."

A few days later Durante told Clayton, "Well, we're shippin' Westbrook to Suffolk Downs."

"I don't give a damn where you send that pig to. I only hope he gets a heart attack. I never want to hear his fancy name again."

At Suffolk Downs Westbrook broke a leg and was destroyed.

"Lou!" Jimmy cried out as he waved a telegram under Clayton's bandaged nose. "You put a curse on the poor horse!"

"I sure did!" Clayton agreed. "And let's change the subject."

Jimmy did not know at the time that Westbrook had been claimed for fourteen hundred dollars previous to this race. The two Jimmies, Durante and Kelly, were not out of pocket. In fact, the unlucky claimant had to pay the track a fee of fifteen dollars to cart Westbrook's remains from the back stretch.

Clayton's throat wounds eventually healed. The one on his nose, however, did not respond readily to treatment, and he feared he had cancer, a disease referred to by Broadwayites as "Big Casino." His old friend, Dr. Benjamin Gilbert, assured him that the place on his nose would heal.

Clayton brought suit against one of his doctors, a plastic surgeon, and asked for sixty thousand dollars' damages. He lost the case.

When Lou's nose did heal, a scar remained just below the bridge. He still could not shake the belief that one day he would become a victim of cancer. When his friend Damon Runyon died of that disease, and Rex Beach committed suicide rather than endure its slow agony, Clayton said, "A strong man simply can't take a draw with Big Casino. The odds are too long."

The medical and legal expenses incurred by Clayton as an aftermath of the automobile accident reached the astounding total of seventy-seven thousand dollars. Inasmuch as Durante's income had dwindled, Lou now found himself out of "scratch." He decided to forego all dice and card games and retire from big play.

Jeanne Durante had been unable to go with Jimmy to New York for the *Stars in Your Eyes* engagement. She did, however, go with him to New York in 1940, when he played in *Keep Off the Grass*, a short-lived musical. Jeanne, Maggie Arnold, and Muggins stayed five weeks in the East, then went home to California. Durante followed soon after.

The Schnozzola obtained loans on his life-insurance policies, and Jeanne Durante dipped into the fund put aside in the safe-deposit box. Faithful Maggie Arnold offered to stay on the job as housekeeper and Mrs. Durante's companion without pay, but Jimmy would not agree to that.

Clayton received several offers for night-club engagements for Jim, but the home-staying comedian vetoed all these proposals, and Jeanne approved the decisions.

Whenever Lou came up with a prospect Jeanne would say, "I'd rather have Jim than all the money in the world. We'll get by."

Jim stayed like an exile at the Olympic Boulevard home, puttering about the house or in the garden, but never complaining. The Schnozz missed the applause of the theater, not so much because of an actor's ego, but because the clapping of hands and the cheers were a noisy evidence that people liked him. He wanted to "mingle with the people" and to be liked, and to know that he was liked. Perhaps that has been his greatest ambition.

He gave so much of himself to so many persons, distributing himself in pieces, as it were, among so many, that he could not possibly give all of himself to any one person. Perhaps this wide distribution of self by popular actors accounts for much of their unhappiness in marriage. The wife or the husband of a public idol has the world for a rival.

Jeanne Durante wanted all of Jim. Strive as she sometimes did to be less possessive, she could not—particularly when ill or alone—surrender him to the admiration of others.

Clayton telephoned one day that Jim had been offered a two-weeks' night-club engagement as well as several weeks' booking at motion-picture theaters.

The Schnozzola again said, "No."

"What's the matter with you?" Clayton barked. "I need something for the pocket."

Durante advised him, "Partner, you'll have to get your tailor to make the pockets smaller."

At about this time an old friend of Jim's from night-club years, Louis Cohen, undertook to protect Durante from insolvency during one of Clayton's prolonged stays in New York.

Cohen at one time had supervised all real-estate transactions for Paramount Pictures, at a salary of two thousand a week. He had suffered reverses during the depression and now had charge of a real-estate office in Los Angeles.

Cohen persuaded Earl Carroll to book Jim at that showman's theater-restaurant in Hollywood for the New Year's week of 1941. On New Year's Eve Durante established a house record of eighteen thousand dollars for the opening night. Carroll held Durante over at a salary of twenty-five hundred a week, a five-hundred-dollar reduction from the Schnozzola's former rate of pay in the night clubs.

One evening Durante was sitting between acts at a table with actor John Barrymore, artist John Decker, and other friends. Barrymore was a frequent visitor at Carroll's, for he liked to step out of his loneliness, as he put it, and see someone other than his creditors.

Barrymore said to the Schnozzola, "You should play Hamlet."

"To hell with them small towns," Durante replied. "I'll take New York."

Jimmy did the dinner show, then went downtown to appear at a benefit performance for the Jockeys' Guild. Back at Earl Carroll's again for the supper show, Durante received a telegram from his nephew, Julie Romano. It said that Bartolomeo Durante, stricken with a heart attack, was in an oxygen tent at Midtown Hospital.

Durante's father had returned to the Ridgewood home after having trimmed the hair of the parish priest. The Romano family were in the basement laundry room. Lily was ironing. Julie and Bob were sitting nearby. The old man greeted his daughter and his grandsons, smiling as always, then suddenly collapsed. Lily caught him as he fell. The boys helped their grandfather upstairs, then called Dr. Wynne. He said that Bartolomeo had hardening of the arteries as well as a hopeless heart ailment.

As Lily and her sons were taking the old gentleman in the family car to the hospital, Bartolomeo smilingly asked, "Where we going?" And then he winked. "To visit friends?"

Although his father now was ninety-three years old, the devoted Schnozzola never had thought of the durable Bartolomeo as one likely to die soon. The old fellow had been ill but once before in his long life, a pneumonia attack many years before.

Durante disliked travel by air, but he said to Lou Cohen, "Get me a ticket. I've simply got to fly East for Pop."

This was wartime and it was not a simple matter to procure airplane passage for a civilian; but Cohen somehow managed to obtain a seat for his friend early the next morning.

The plane was grounded in Cheyenne, Wyoming. Durante managed to find a place on a train to Chicago. There, after some delay, he took another plane. Clayton met Jimmy at the airport and rode with him to the hospital, where Bartolomeo lay unconscious.

Jimmy thrust his head inside the oxygen tent. "Gee, Pop, hello!" The old man opened his eyes, smiled, and died.

Durante overheard one hospital attendant say to another, "All right, let's take him to the morgue."

To Jim's mind, "morgue" meant the Bellevue Hospital basement in which bodies of unidentified persons or of the unclaimed poor lay until removed in rough wooden boxes to unmarked graves in Potter's Field, on bleak Hart's Island up the East River.

Durante became frantic. When attendants sought to remove his father's body, Jimmy stood in their way, flailing at them, weeping, protesting, "Don't take my Pop to the morgue! I can pay. Tell 'em, Lou! Please, I'll pay yah! Aw, please!"

Clayton convinced Durante that the hospital morgue was but a room in which dead persons temporarily lay until claimed by regular undertakers.

Jimmy turned to his weeping sister. "Lily, there's just you and me left of the family. Thank God, you got your children! Pack up and come on out to the Coast. Jeanne won't mind. Let's try to look forwards."

There was a wake for Bartolomeo at the Ridgewood home. All day and into the night hundreds of persons to whom the kindly old man had given little presents each day during his twenty-one years in the neighborhood called to pay their respects.

"Pop left a lot of friends," Durante said to Clayton. "Who could be richer?"

Jimmy returned to Hollywood, but Clayton stayed on in New York. Lou Irwin and Lou Cohen persuaded Herbert Yates of Republic Studios to give the Schnozzola a part in a Gene Autry picture, *Melody Lane*. Jimmy could not ride a horse. He was lashed to the saddle each day, and the horse's head controlled by means of a thin wire.

"I'd never rode a horse," the Schnozzola says, "and the horse never had been rode. So we both started out on even terms. It was a catastrastroke!"

Clayton returned to Hollywood when a major studio wired him that the Schnozzola was being considered for a "fat" motion-picture role. But days went by and no definite word could be had from the picture magnates. After three weeks of mysterious silence Clayton made inquiries of a friend at the studio.

"They have decided," said this friend, "that Jimmy is too old for pictures."

"But he's only forty-eight!" Clayton protested. "My God! His talent don't age."

"I only know what they said at the second conference," the friend revealed. "It had been all set for Jim when we wired you. Then one of those whispers rose, and you know how it is out here—the slightest drop of cold water sends everybody into a chill. And from a little word the others begin to nod and agree, and then it's all off."

"Yes," Clayton said. "I know how it is. All right then. But we'll make 'em eat those whispers someday."

Early in 1942 Durante's professional plight reached the attention of L. B. Mayer, head of the M-G-M Studios. Mayer always had liked Jimmy, and the Schnozz had a high opinion of him. Mayer suggested that Durante play several weeks at Loew Theatres in Eastern cities.

"Take it," said Clayton. "Pick up Eddie Jackson and Jack Roth and get that dough."

"I don't know where Eddie now is," said Durante.

"I do. Harry Ritz ran into him in Akron a week ago. He's got a sawdust place there, and is not so hot."

After several false starts, and in a vain effort to find himself after he had left the trio, Eddie had become manager of the Wagon Wheel, an obscure café in Akron, Ohio. Several "name acts" that played the Palace Theatre in Akron also did free turns on occasion at Eddie's café. Ted Lewis, the Andrews Sisters, and Frank Sinatra appeared there out of friendship.

One week the Ritz Brothers played the Akron Palace. Harry Ritz asked Eddie, "Does the Schnozz know you're here?"

"No, I wouldn't bother Jimmy."

"That's false pride," said Harry Ritz. "We'll be back in California soon, and I'm going to make it my business to let your old pals know the score."

Jackson was reading the newspaper at his café when Durante telephoned from California. "Eddie, I didn't know what really happened to you. Do you need some money?"

Jackson did not tell his old friend that he had been divorced after twenty-four years of marriage, and that his money and peace of mind had been forfeited because of that misfortune. "Oh, I'm all right, Jimmy."

"Don't give me that! Harry Ritz told me all about you. That's why I'm callin'. I got eight weeks of vaudeville comin' up. Would you like to jern me?"

"My God!" cried Jackson. "Jimmy! Say that again!"

Jackson met the Schnozzola in Chicago. They sat up most of the night, "cutting up touches." "I'm not holdin' a million dollars," Durante said, "but I want you to spend what you make these weeks and have a real good time. It'll be like the old days."

"I'm the happiest man in the world, Jim. But I'm awful nervous."

"Applause will cure the noives, Eddie."

After some debate Jeanne had advised Jimmy to go on this vaude-ville tour of New York, Brooklyn, Hartford, Boston, Providence, and Pittsburgh. During his absence she again became quite ill. Dr. Bilon sent Mrs. Durante to Hollywood Presbyterian Hospital for observation.

She described her condition in a letter, written at the hospital on April 6, to Mrs. Lillian Werner and Jenice: "Received your Easter card today. Have been in and out of the hospital several times. Before Christmas suffered a hemorrhage. I lost the use of my right hand and arm from neuritis. I had it in a cast. Three weeks ago, early in the morning, when Jim was away, I had another hemor-rhage and now I have yellow jaundice, and am waiting to get it out of my blood stream.

"Mother is okay, but my brother Earl had a slight stroke in the left arm. He is all right now. My favorite Uncle Bill in Toledo, you know, he is the one who once visited me in New York, he had a stroke. He was in bed for several months and is up and around now with a cast. Jimmy has been in the East several weeks, and I expect to go home Tuesday. I am pretty weak."

After Durante's personal appearance tour Eddie said he would have to go back to Akron to straighten out his affairs. "Jim, I might open up a little cigar store there."

"Well, Eddie, if you wanna open a cigar store, that's up to you. Right now I ain't got no more work. But you can come out to California any time. I'm behind you."

Eddie stayed in Akron for about two months and then wrote Jim, asking what was doing in California. Jimmy replied that he was going to play some Army camps and might come on to New York if Jeanne got better.

"We'll all be together again," Jimmy wrote. "We never really was apart, you and me and Lou."

In the summer of 1942 Jimmy received word that his sister had suffered a severe dizzy spell. He telephoned his nephews to take their mother to the Astor Hotel, to spare her any household wor-ries, and boarded a train East. Jeanne stayed home with Maggie and Muggins.

No sooner had Durante arrived in New York than his sister had another dizzy spell, a worse one than the first. At the hospital a doctor said, "I don't think it's malignant, but we don't know."

"I watched the poor girl die," says Jim. "She was one of the sweetest persons that ever lived. I don't think she ever harmed a fly. Now we're at home there in Ridgewood for the wake, and I sit up all night, and while I'm waitin' there, I get the biggest shock of my life. Who walks in but my wife Jeanne? She had flown to New York, sick as she was. She looked like a ghost. And she gets awful sick the next day and has hemorrhages.

"Oh, I thought I'd never get her back to California alive. We got home on the train, with Jeanne very sick all the way, and I take her down to Palm Springs again, and wait for phone calls to get some work to pay the bills. I played some command performances for the Army, and that give me a little action at the canteens, but we really had to get money."

Jeanne's long periods of illness and mental depression made her quite irritable. One day late in November of 1942 Jimmy's patience became strained. He had words with Jeanne, then left the house without saying where he was going.

He sought out Clayton at the Hillcrest Country Club. "Get me a ticket to New York and a little money if you can find it. I'm gonna forget everythin' and cool off. And to hell with it!"

"Does Jeanne know?"

"I packed a grip on the sly, and I got it out there with the doorman."

"If that's the way you want it," Lou replied, "that's the way it's gonna be."

Durante got on the train to find almost everyone except the soldiers and sailors in a gay mood. Jimmy shut himself in his compartment but soon got restless and went to the dining car. He was unable to eat. Then he went to the club car, but he could not enter into the merry spirit of passengers on their way East on wartime business. The Schnozzola retired to his compartment, took off his clothes, and lay down; but he could not sleep.

In recollecting this incident Durante says, "I'm askin' myself, 'What the hell? She's sick there in the house. What am I doin'? What am I runnin' away from? What's the matter with me? Somethin' might happen.' "

Durante tried to put aside thoughts of Jeanne but could not. He had intended to have a good time, but now saw that self-accusa-

tions were to be his mental companions on the journey. "I'm sayin',
'It ain't her fault. I shouldn't have got mad! I shouldn't have argued
with her. And a man can't run away from anythin'.' "

Durante put on his clothes. The train stopped over for ten minutes at San Bernardino. "I get out, and I leave my hat in the car.
My valise is in there. And I go read the headlines at the newspaper
stand. I see where hundreds get killed in a night-club fire in Boston.
Well, the whole world is on fire. The war and everythin'. For
what? Then I see a telephone, and I go over to it. No, I won't call
up. The hell with it! I go back and forth to the telephone, wantin'
so bad to call, but never callin'. And I hear 'em yell out, 'All
aboard.' But I stand there with no hat, and I watch the train pull
out, and it's a funny feelin'. If I'd been a drinker, I'd of got drunk
as an outlet. But no, I had to run away on a train, and now the
train is runnin' away from me. And there's no escape, because a
man has got to face everythin', includin' hisself."

Durante hired an automobile to take him back to Los Angeles.
He arrived home during the early morning before dawn.

Jeanne awakened, and when Durante embraced her she said, "Gee,
Tootis, I'm so glad you got home before daybreak!"

Of this moment of reunion Jimmy says, "You could never pay
me in money how that stands out in my mind. In money you could
never pay me how she smiled. And I'm like a new man, and I'm
happy again. For all the weight of the world is off me, and I'm
lighted up again. I confess to Jeanne how I had started off to New
York, and she kissed me and said, 'You're kiddin'!' And I go to
the kitchen to make some tomato soup for both of us. And boy! I
am the one that can make it. You know? With real cream, and I
am happy."

A few days later Jeanne once again entered Hollywood Presbyterian Hospital for an abdominal operation performed by Dr. Bilon.
It was discovered that she had a malignancy. Never again would
she know even a semblance of good health.

"Oh, dear God!" Jimmy says, recalling this tragic circumstance.
"If I'd gone on to New York, it would have been even worse. For
in marriage, I don't know the lines but it's somethin' about for
bad or worse, and when we go through life we all got to carry a
cross of one kind or another. And right or wrong, how in hell
can a fellow leave a good wife? Because she becomes their right
arm. You're so used to each other. You think you're goin' out and

have a good time, like I've often thought. And you go out, and now what am I gonna do with myself? You don't know what the hell to do with yourself, so you call up this guy, and he's out. You call up this other guy, and he's out. And you wind up—you haven't done nothin', only enjoy four or five hours of misery—and you go home."

About this time Jimmy wrote to Jenice Werner: "Hello Niecie: Four weeks ago Jeanne was in the hospital. The doctors gave her up and told me there was no hope. So after being in there for a week she pleaded for me to take her home. So I did. And she had six blood transfusions. And believe it or not, the doctor couldn't believe she gets up a little bit, but still weak as can be. Only today they gave her that dextro-something. You know? Through the vein. Slow till the bottle is empty. I have dropped everything until I see her on her feet. She has two night nurses, and Maggie in the day-time."

Later that month Jeanne wrote to the Werners that she was now home and able to sit up at times to answer her mail. "It is all I can do," she wrote, "to get up to the bath now and have a hot tub. Am so very weak. Jimmy is so wonderful to me. Nearly went crazy, he so nearly lost me twice. We are happier than we have ever been. Still have Maggie and night nurse, and get no other help. Jimmy is doing our own gardening, and nice job too. He always was lucky cultivating plants, etc.

"I did quite a bit from my bedside. Ordered my few Christmas gifts, and Jimmy has helped me wrap them to mail. Changed my bedroom completely. Had chairs in the patio reupholstered in leather, plumbing fixed, and bought Jim a business desk for his den for Christmas. We have a large den off our bedroom, looking into the garden, which he has fixed up to perfection. He found out he can do many things and enjoy it."

Jeanne also bought Jimmy an electric organ. He tried to play it, but somehow—for him—"Umbriago" and "Inka Dinka Do" did not seem suited to cathedral tones.

XXI

Into the Dark Valley

NOTWITHSTANDING his great vitality and the strong, simple faith that allowed neither cynicism nor self-pity to enter his skull, Durante reached what he called "a lowest pernt." It was 1943, a time when war made some men prosperous, and the drafting or enlistment of young stars gave older actors an opportunity to lengthen or enhance their ordinarily brief careers in the theatrical noonday. Durante enjoyed neither an upsurge of wealth nor professional advantages.

He had an invalid wife from whom he dared not stay away for long at a time. The studios occasionally offered him small parts in inferior pictures. At any mention of his going to New York or Chicago for night-club engagements, Jeanne would weep. Again and again he canceled deals Clayton made for him.

Soon after New Year's of 1943 Clayton had a heart-to-heart talk with Jim. "Let's face it. You are slipping in the public mind. Soon it will mean curtains. You could easily see to it that Jeanne is taken care of by nurses during the duration while you go out and make some money. Jim, the Copacabana wants you, and New York wants you. You simply must do a couple of weeks in the East, because you have not been in a night club for years. The trio soon will be forgotten by everybody that hasn't got a long white beard."

One day early in February, as Clayton was putting on his golf shoes at the Hillcrest locker room, he received a long-distance call from a radio advertising agency. The New York sponsor of "The Camel Caravan" offered fifteen hundred dollars for Durante to do a "guest shot."

"Don't insult me!" said Clayton as of old. He hung up and went out to the green. He returned to the clubhouse at sundown to learn that New York again was calling.

"Durante will go to New York for two consecutive guest appearances, not one," Clayton told the agent. "Further and more, we want five thousand for these two appearances."

The conditions were accepted. Thereupon Clayton persuaded the manager of the Copa to book Durante for the two weeks he would be in New York, at three thousand dollars a week. This meant that Jimmy's two concurrent jobs would bring him eleven thousand dollars in all.

When Clayton informed the Schnozzola of these bookings, Durante seemed indifferent. He explained that Jeanne objected to his leaving her; that she was unable to travel East with him.

Later that day Jeanne asked, "Tootis, are you worrying a lot over that offer?"

"Well," said Jim, "I could pay some bills. But let's forget it."

"If you leave me this time, Jim, you will never see me alive again."

Durante looked at her in a shocked way. "Don't say that, Jeanne. Please don't say that! Because I'm not goin'."

After a little time she said, "Take it, Jimmy."

"Take what?"

"The two weeks in New York. I want you to go."

Clayton saw Durante off on the train. "After the first show, Jimmy, call me and let me know how it goes. If you bog down, I will fly East, put on my old shoes again, and go out on the floor and dance. I've wired Jackson in Akron to join up with you and Roth in New York."

Durante registered at the Hotel Astor three days before the opening date at the Copacabana. His first radio show as a guest for the Camel Cigarette sponsor was well received.

After the broadcast Jimmy called Jeanne. She said, "I liked the program, Jimmy. It was very good."

"Are you all right?"

"Yes, Mother is here with me, and Maggie, and I'm so glad."

Jimmy enjoyed his first night's sound sleep in some weeks. Early the next morning the phone rang beside his bed. Durante stirred resentfully. He had left word not to be awakened till one o'clock in the afternoon.

Mrs. Mary Blenman was on the telephone. She seemed very much confused but managed to say that her Jeanne was dead. She hung up before Jim could talk to Maggie.

For some moments Durante lay back in his bed with the receiver to his ear. He kept calling into the transmitter, "What? What? What?"

Now Maggie called, saying that Mrs. Blenman wanted to send her daughter's body to the Lamb Funeral Parlors in Pasadena. What were Durante's instructions? Maggie said that she had dressed Mrs. Durante's hair for the last time and would go to the funeral home to wait there until Durante arrived from the East. Jimmy told Maggie that she should "choose the best casket there is for Jeanne."

Durante telephoned Jack Roth and his cousin Frank Ross and the Werners to inform them of Jeanne's death. These friends arrived soon afterward to find Jimmy in a condition of frustration and despair.

Roth ordered breakfast for Jimmy, but it remained untouched. Ross tried to get a seat on a plane, but it was not until the next day that the sad and bewildered man was accommodated.

Durante says of that flight West, "I didn't mind the plane this time. Funny. Just dronin' along, yah know. Zoom! And zoom! And zoom! I thought it ironical that I had been at the bedside of everyone connected with me when they died, but now when Jeanne died I was not with her.

"I sat next to a man and he recognized me. And he said, 'Gee, Durante, I enjoy you an awful lot. You're a peach. I liked that joke when you was tellin' . . .' The man kept repeatin' some of the jokes I did, and I kept shuttin' my ears but just sayin', 'Thanks a million.' And he's sayin', and I can hear him dimly, 'Yeah, but you're a great comedian.' Well, not that I resented the man; but he got off at Detroit, and as nice as he was I am so glad to see him go. On this plane I can't sleep. My mind goes back to so many things, like, 'Why did I leave?' 'Did we need this money so bad I am goin' after.' Yes, we sure needed it, but we could of got along without it somehow. And when she says, 'I'm never gonna see you again, Jimmy,' well, I should have took that as an omen and stayed home. Everythin' she ever predicted for me came true. Even today. So what the hell! I don't know. Things goin' through your brain. Maybe if I was there it wouldn't have happened. But thank God she went to bed, and they said about four o'clock in the mornin' she passed away, after collapsin'. And you get to thinkin' and thinkin', not only about this, but about the little farm you never got for her, a place where you could have lived together on spinach, like she used to say. And you wonder why these things never happen. Always somethin' would come up. Well, while I'm thinkin' this, we get as far as Salt Lake City, and I get put off the plane. I can't go no farther, so now I'm laid over there, crazy."

It was seven o'clock in the morning when Durante was bumped off the plane in Salt Lake City to allow a sergeant to have his seat. At the commissary one of the attendants recognized the Schnozzola. He said that Jimmy should call up the general.

With his usual hesitancy to ask favors for himself, he told the general that he was Jimmy Durante but neglected to mention his wife's death as a reason for the journey.

The general must have presumed that Durante was just another of those pampered Hollywood persons who expected magic courtesies. "Look here," said the officer a bit gruffly, "you know we have a war on, don't you?"

To this Jimmy replied, "I know. God, yes, I know!"

"Well," the general said, "we can't put a sergeant off just to let an actor on."

"I know that, General. I wouldn't expect you to do that. I just wondered if there was a chance."

"No, nothing can be done in the matter."

Jimmy was a bit angry at first, and then said to himself, "He's right. There's a war goin' on. What the hell! They need every space available."

That afternoon someone explained things to the general. He gave Jimmy a priority for a seat, and Durante went on to Los Angeles. Clayton met him at the airport. They rode directly to the Lamb funeral home in Pasadena. Maggie and Muggins were waiting there.

Jimmy and Lou knelt beside the casket. Durante kept saying the rosary over and over. Long after midnight Clayton urged Jim to go home. He refused and stayed for three days and nights at the mortuary.

On the third day Clayton compelled Durante to eat a sandwich he had brought. "Look, Jim, you must eat something, and besides, you should go ahead with Jeanne's burial. It's crazy to postpone it any longer."

The morning of the funeral Jimmy and Clayton were alone in the room where Jeanne's body lay.

"When this is over," said Clayton, "we've got to get you another house. You'll go crazy in the old place."

"I been thinkin'," Jimmy said. "I've only got you left now, Lou. And if you leave me, I can't tell what I might do to myself."

Clayton said severely, "Jim, I'll leave you someday. I'm six years older than you, and the day will come when I leave you for keeps, and make up your mind to that. But meanwhile you're going right back to New York and get to work."

Maggie arrived with a clean white shirt for Durante and a black tie. He had not taken off his clothes since his arrival.

As Clayton tied the tie for his friend, Jimmy asked him, "Lou, do you think the radio people and the Copa still want me?"

"The bookings still go," Clayton replied. "They have merely been postponed."

"Oh," said Jim, "New York has forgot me."

"Look," Clayton said, "you are to join Jackson in New York. I'll be sitting at the telephone in my apartment or at Hillcrest. You call me after the first show."

Jeanne's funeral was held February 17, 1943. Mrs. Blenman, Durante, Lou Cohen, Clayton, and Maggie accompanied the body to the Mountain View Cemetery in Arcadia. Jeanne's father, Mr. Olson, who had died in 1941, was buried there, and also her brother Earl, who had passed away shortly before.

After the burial Clayton went home with Durante. Jimmy behaved in a dazed fashion. He went from room to room, stood in front of Jeanne's pictures for minutes at a time, opened clothes closets to look at her things, and would not go to bed to rest.

Finally he said, "Look, Lou, I don't feel like workin' right away. Cancel the New York business. I'm in no condition."

"If that's the way you want it, Jim, that's the way it's gonna be. But suppose you go away to rest for a few days?"

Durante motored to Palm Springs, intending to stay there a week. His cousin Frank Ross went with him.

"You couldn't seem to escape the memories," Durante says. "The house across the street where Jeanne lived. So after a coupla days I said to Ross, 'Frank, we've gotta get outa here.' And so I come back home and Clayton said, 'You better go to New York right now.' "

"You know, it's a funny thing. You see every place you've been with somebody you love; you go down to Palm Springs, those places, you wander back in thoughts to the Lake and how you stopped at the pea soup place, and where you bought the dog, and Arrowhead and Clear Lake, and all them other places. It's a habit. You don't even look for new places when you go around.

Just the places you liked when you used to go out to eat or stroll along, and you find yourself goin' back to them."

Jimmy unfailingly remembers the times with Jeanne and, more poignant still, the times he was away from her. He seldom discusses his and Jeanne's relationship during their twenty-two years together. But when Jim does speak out of the loneliness of his heart, he overemphasizes the many things he left undone, and listens perhaps unreasonably to the echoes of self-blame.

In retrospect he cherishes the glad days, of course, seizing upon each bright hour they spent at Clear Lake, remembering her smiles, her songs. But mostly he recalls her tears, her loneliness, how circumstance stood as a high and thorny hedge between them because he lived by night and she by day. Only their mutual devotion could have sustained them through the years.

The public knew nothing of Jimmy Durante's burdens. Laughing strangers care little about the private woes of their clowns. Who has looked upon the other side of the moon?

Jackson met Durante in New York. The Big Town had not forgotten them. On opening night the Copacabana was packed. After the first show Jimmy telephoned Clayton. "They're hangin' on the walls, Lou."

At the end of the Schnozzola's two weeks at the Copa, the manager offered him a five-hundred-dollar-a-week raise to stay over. Durante hesitated, and when Lou pressed him to work on, Jimmy said, "Let's put it this way, I'll stay as long as I feel like it."

Durante remained at the Copa for fourteen weeks. He says of this return to the night-club floor, "I'm thinkin' all the time, 'Gee! Wouldn't it have been nice if she'd been here to see the crowds in the café?' I don't know if she'd like it. But it's a big openin' and you're on the verge of a big thing and you say, Aw gee! it would have been nice. Like your dad. Wouldn't it have been nice if your dad was here? Or your mother?

"I mean them things come to you when you're succeedin'. It's funny what happens when you're in trouble and you're an actor. The minute that band plays and you get out on the floor, you seem to forget everythin'. Everythin' else goes from your mind, thinkin' of your jokes. Your mind is flashin' ahead to what's goin' to come after this, and the only time anythin' ever distracts from you, if you look to the first row in a theater or the first row in a café, and you see a guy with a puss on him, and he's lookin' at you like he hates your guts, and you haven't never done nothin' to the guy; and you think of it, that annoys you. But I never done nothin' to the man, and you look over there and don't keep lookin' at him. You're up in the air. And the band plays. And you forget even your griefs for a moment, like a shot of dope. It's the only way I can explain it—you forget everythin' until you come off. Then when you come off, you flop down."

XXII

Again on the Pedasill

DRUMMER JACK ROTH rolled his sticks against the skins. The horn players lipped the opening bars of "Inka Dinka Do." Jimmy Durante prowled into the spotlight with his old battle cry, "Lemme hear that band!" Eddie Jackson strutted in. The clappers clapped.

The Schnozzola and his partner were on at the midnight show, the final performance of their fourteen record-breaking weeks at New York's Copacabana Club. Suddenly, to the astonishment of all, a figure came whirling out of the ringside shadows and slid with dervish speed across the floor.

Unannounced, Clayton had come to town, put on his dancing shoes, and for tonight's last show rejoined his partners—their first time together as entertainers in twelve years.

Old-timers stood beside their tables to applaud. Some of them wept, for the Three Musketeers of Broadway seemed to have turned back to a forgotten calendar and from its faded pages evoked the gypsy heydays of the twenties. The nostalgic audience demanded all the old routines until past three o'clock in the morning. The merry men sang, danced, cavorted, ad libbed, and stormed about like demented senators filibustering in the psychopathic ward.

Clayton, Jackson, and Durante. . . . Would a war-beggared world have the belly ever to laugh again?

The great clown had just turned fifty. The Schnozzola's fourteen weeks at the Copacabana demonstrated that the public still idolized him, and the celluloid Caesars of Hollywood forgot their recent thumbs-down verdict. Durante had reaffirmed his comedian's art three thousand miles away from the sun-kissed announcers of his professional demise.

Clayton immediately negotiated a five-year contract with M-G-M. The Schnozzola was to make two pictures a year at seventy-five thousand dollars each. Afterward the studio canceled this contract. In its stead the producers gave Jimmy another five-year-document which called for him to appear in but one picture a year at a hundred and fifty thousand. There were no options. If the studio had no picture ready or suitable for Durante, he could make one picture a year for any other major studio of his choice. He was permitted to do radio shows, appear in theaters, or perform in night clubs.

In the late spring of 1943 an advertising agency designated Garry Moore, a young master of ceremonies from Chicago, to assist comedians Abbott and Costello on the summer replacement program for Camel cigarettes. Shortly thereafter, Lou Costello fell ill with rheumatic fever. The Camel people had to find a substitute program immediately. Inasmuch as Moore was a youngster, comparatively unknown to the radio public, the agency selected Durante to give balance to the show. Durante signed a five-year contract, at five thousand a week for forty weeks each year, to appear on the Camel cigarette program.

Durante and Moore clicked from the beginning. The young, literate, educated, fast-talking Moore, and veteran Jimmy, the frustrated fumbler of words and syntax, became a popular combination. Among his several talents, Moore was an accomplished radio writer. He had a surefire understanding of the Schnozzola's type of comedy and also admired him as a man.

Durante and Moore stayed together as a radio team until late in 1947, and their program won several awards. Eventually Moore decided to quit, because he wished to keep his own identity as a comic. It was a very honest separation, and Durante looks back upon their association as the happiest of all his radio years.

A personable young executive, Phil Cohan, had charge of the "Camel Caravan." He became Durante's producer, both for radio and television. According to Cohan, the seemingly haphazard Jim is a perfectionist in his radio and television work. In contrast to the improvisation of the night clubs, the Schnozzola goes to his room with a script to "woodshed it" for hours.

"You gotta treat a scrip' like a wife," Durante says, "and go to bed with it."

Before radio or television time Jimmy will sit with Cohan and his staff until the last moment, revising jokes and lines. As for Durante's genius at scrambling words, his producer says that he actually does not try to mispronounce them.

One of the Schnozzola's writers, Jackie Barnett, agrees with Cohan: "His mispronunciation of the English language is natural to him. For example, I had the word 'nostalgic' in one of the scripts. I knew it was a big word for Jimmy and wanted him to say it as 'neuralgic.' I was sure it would bring a laugh, so I wrote 'neuralgic' in the script. But when he came to it, he pronounced it 'nostalgic.' He doesn't purposely mispronounce a word. He says that if he did so it would look as if he were trying to be funny. He wants the real words set down in a script, because he knows that he can manhandle them on sight, as he did 'catastrastroke' and 'corpsuckles.' "

Garry Moore has also analyzed the Schnozzola's left-handed delivery: "Jimmy Durante knows at all times what he is talking about. It would be very easy for him to learn that 'catastrophe' is not 'catastrastroke'; but it first came to his eye that way; and he doesn't bother to change it, because everyone knows what he is talking about. So why change it and spoil a laugh? He takes the easy way out, and lets bad enough alone."

If you were to sit with Jimmy and indulge in serious conversation, he might use words that would lead you to think his brain was in a meat-grinder—unless you happened to be well acquainted with Durante and his ways. If familiar with his jabberwocky lapses, you would know that when he says, "I feel perfectly abdominal today," he means "abominable." Sometimes, however, he astonishes everyone by using a long word in the right place and enunciating it with professorial authority.

Barnett, one of the brightest members of the Durante group, is a songwriter as well as an author of gay routines. As an entertainer in night clubs, Jackie used to close his act with an imitation of Durante, his hero even before he had met the man.

Barnett teamed up as a writer with Eddie Davis, author of *Hold on to Your Hats*. The fact that Davis could not spell correctly or write sound English endeared him at once to Durante.

Davis originally had been a cab driver. He became a fabulous character along Broadway and in Hollywood. Bald, middle-aged, and always tanned from hours as a sun-worshiper, Eddie has astounding vitality, notwithstanding his chronic asthma.

Davis took his bride-to-be to their wedding in his own taxicab. He drove in the front seat in a full-dress suit, and his fiancée sat in the back seat in her bridal gown. Eddie didn't have enough money to pay for the wedding, so he asked his friends to give him their presents in advance of the ceremony.

Davis's wife had a wonderful influence on him. He covered up his seeming illiteracy by being noisy and wild, but she would quiet him. All he wanted in life was to make her happy and to get luxuries for her.

Davis used to walk onstage uninvited during benefit shows, take off his cabby hat, and interrupt the proceedings. One time he strolled onto the stage when Will Rogers had just made his exit. Announcer Ted Husing was filling in during the scene-change interval. Davis butted in, and the audience loved the anonymous buffoon.

Will Rogers was waiting for Eddie outside. "You did a wonderful job, son. I'm going over to another benefit. Would you like to appear there with me?"

"Certainly." Eddie put on his cabby hat.

"What's that?" asked Rogers.

"Well," said Davis, "I just followed you. Now you follow me. Get into my cab. I'll take you to the benefit, but you've got to pay the fare."

Davis got his big start as a gag writer by trailing Eddie Cantor around New York in the taxicab. No matter where Cantor went, it seemed that any cab he summoned would have Davis at the wheel. Instead of watching traffic, Davis would look back at Cantor and fire jokes at him. The accident-shy comedian finally asked, "How much do you make a week?"

"Oh, I'd say an average of eighteen dollars."

"Look," said Cantor, "I'm going to give you twenty dollars a week *not* to drive this cab any more. Just sit home and write jokes."

Within the year Cantor was paying Davis twelve hundred and fifty dollars a week. Davis stayed with his discoverer for five years. He also wrote pictures, including *Road to Morocco*, helped with the screen adaptation of *George White's "Scandals"*—in which Durante appeared—and did books for several stage musicals. At the time Davis teamed up with Barnett he had had a bad streak because of illness. That was before he wrote *Follow the Girls* and made a fortune.

Barnett was sitting in his and Davis's office in the Paramount Building one night when Jimmy Durante telephoned. "Come on right over to my hotel. I'm goin' on the 'Camel Caravan' tomorrow night. The scrip' looks weak, and maybe you can t'row in a couple jokes."

Barnett and Davis picked up the Durante script at the mail desk of the Astor. Over dinner they rewrote it, then went upstairs to the Schnozzola's suite. They knocked on the door.

Durante called out, "Gimme a big entrance, Eddie!"

Davis took off his pants and, clad in his long underwear, walked into a roomful of people. Barnett's introduction to the Schnozzola in person was an imitation of his hero. Jimmy, convulsed with laughter, rolled on the floor. "What a crazy thing! First this fellow Davis comes in without his pants, and then he brings in a kid that imitates me!"

Jackie worked for Durante until the Army claimed him. After the war he rejoined the Schnozzola's troupe. He says that writing for the Schnozzola presents certain mental hazards. "The man's magnetism rubs off on you to an extent that you forget all material things. Because, when that man goes out on the stage or on the night-club floor, or to the radio mike, and says the things that you have written, he's so thrilling that you are honored. You love him, and you would work for nothing just to be near this man. As a result a writer is apt to lose his own identity and begin to live the life of Durante. He has to respond to telephone calls at any hour to go over to his house to confer on stories or songs or gags."

In regard to his own habit of throwing big words up for grabs, the Schnozzola has this to say: "When you try to mispronounce a word, or the boys write it in all balled up, you don't get real laughs, because people seem to know. And you can't deliberately say the big wardrobe names the writers mix up for you, or by double-talkin' to people. But if they know you didn't do it deliberate, then it gets a laugh."

The Schnozzola feels that his writers are sometimes unreasonably insistent about having him say things that he thinks are entirely wrong for his style of entertainment. "Sometimes writers give me ulcers, and they keep tryin' to put in those double-entry jokes, although they know I am dead set against anything blue. Why they do it I simply don't know. And writers sometimes get jealous and pick on each other when they shouldn't. It's the scrip' that counts. You'll get a team of writers, and one will be great, and the other won't be any good. I don't know why that is. And I don't think they put their best attention on the very first scrip', but wait till it's gone over and over, and then bear down on the final scrip'. And I never will know why one writer who is doin' all right by hisself and gettin' plenty of dough will try without any good reason to get the other fellow in Dutch with me. Because, when anyone tries to get some other fellow in bad with me, it only gets the other fellow in solid with me. I like to see 'em fight and argue and keep on their toes, but all done in the open, and not behind anybody's back. It ain't crickets."

Durante makes a point of having every actor who has a part, however small, on his program in attendance at his story conferences. He believes that a performer should know the whole scheme of the script even if that man has but one word to say over the air. Unlike many stars, Durante never treats a bit player as a lesser animal.

"I don't like the cask system," says Mr. Malaprop. "Maybe we ain't all born equal, but it's a cinch we all die equal."

One of the reasons Jimmy does not go to Hollywood parties often is that when hosts invite him they do not always ask his aides to come. "My pals are good people or they wouldn't be with my combination," he says. "They are not college swells, I know, but they ain't loud drunks either, and they don't try to get rheumatic with the hostess, or swear out loud, or tell dirty jokes. So I only go to buffets like Joe Pasternak's or Lawrence Melcure's parties [Mr. Lauritz Melchoir], because my people are welcome there."

Of this thoughtfulness on the Schnozzola's part, columnist Earl Wilson once said, "Unless I'm vastly mistaken, Jimmy's one of the nicest men alive."

One of the guest stars on Jim's radio program was screen actress Greer Garson. When the Schnozzola and his troupe arrived at Miss Garson's house for a conference, Jimmy warned them, "Fellows, let's all be polite, because Miss Garson is a very high-class lady star."

Miss Garson came downstairs to find Jimmy sitting absentmindedly with his hat on. Reading the script, she commented, "Well, Jimmy, what happens if these particular jokes die?"

He rose up from his chair and slapped his thighs. "Well, Miss Garson, if them jokes die, we'll all go down the terlet."

Suddenly he remembered his lecture on decorum, glared at his sniggering companions, and said, "Oh, pardon me, Miss Garson!"

On the "Information Please" program in the summer of 1946 moderator Clifton Fadiman referred to his guest of the evening as "Dr. Durante." Fadiman asked the Schnozzola, "If a man brings flies home to his pet, what kind of pet would that be?"

"A giraft," Jimmy replied.

The experts on this quiz show, John Kieran, Franklin P. Adams, Deems Taylor, and Dr. Durante were then asked, "Can you touch your scapula with your patella?"

The Schnozzola remarked, "I hope the program ain't gettin' off-color."

When asked in 1949 by columnists on the radio program "By-lines" how he felt when he heard a Durante imitation, the Schnozzola replied, "I feel pretty bad about it. The reason is they do the job better than I do. That is, all but the songs."

In discussing his many songs, the Schnozzola has confessed that he doesn't know exactly how to analyze them. "I think it's the drive that puts 'em over, and the no-rhyme, like sometimes when you're only talkin'. Anybody can tell which is my songs, like 'I was Walkin' down Broadway the Other Day,' or 'I'm Home the Other Day and I'm Sleepin'.' It's like, what do you call it? Narrationin' little stories. I try to get a little story in each song.

"Some of the songs I think are very pretty and would be a big hit if anybody else sang 'em. But nobody else seems to sing them after I get through. It's the truth. Let's take 'Umbriago.' Irving Caesar wrote it for me. Now Umbriago is a fine fellow. I love the character. I thought it would be a popular song, and I said to Irving, 'Don't make this song for Durante. Because I love the melody.' Well, I did the number, and tried to popularize it and make a big hit, and the only one to do it on the outside was the King's Men on Amos and Andy's program. And nobody else would do it, because everybody said they was imitatin' Durante.

"Now I think when I sing a song I roon it for anybody else. It's like the kiss of debt. Not that I do it so good to roon it, but believe me, we can hustle a song like 'Any State in the Forty-eight Is Great,' but I wouldn't care if the biggest publisher in the world had it, nobody would sing it after I did. And even Vaughn Monroe can't put one of my songs over. It's a funny thing, because I got an awful lot of songs, and some of them are good.

"Like when you come to the middle part of 'Inka Dinka Do,' it's a beautiful melody. I try to sing it right, but I do somethin' to it you just can't phantom out. And I got a song, 'Isn't It a Shame that Christmas Comes but Once a Year.' Now anyone can do that, I betcha a dollar. But when I do it, it's lucky if they even celebrate Christmas. And I got a song about Fathers' Day, a song you can only sing on Fathers' Day, but I murder it. The people like me to do the songs, but I feel sorry when a guy brings me a fine song, that maybe would score a hit, and sometimes I try to argue with them and say, 'Listen you only get a little bit outta me for this. Why don't you be smart and give it to somebody else, and make yourself a pot of money?' "

Many of Durante's songs, when recorded for phonograph platters, sell by the thousands, as did the one he sang with opera star Helen Traubel.

When Harry Donnelly, who had been Durante's pianist for all these years, decided to stay in New York, Jimmy employed Jules Buffano to serve as his musical foil. Buffano, author and composer of the popular song, "Thanks for the Buggy Ride," had been accompanist for that beloved Red-hot Mama of vaudeville, Miss Sophie Tucker. He now appears with Durante, Jackson, and Roth in Jim's night-club shows and on his television programs.

Upon Durante's return to the major studios an effort was made at first to give him suitable parts. He played the role of Banjo in Warner Brothers' screen version of the George S. Kaufman and Moss Hart play *The Man Who Came to Dinner*. Monty Woolley, the stage portrayer of this lampoon of Alexander Woollcott, also appeared in the screen version, with Billie Burke, Bette Davis, and Ann Sheridan. Durante's part was the one generally assumed to have been inspired by Harpo Marx.

All went well with Jimmy for a time. Each Sunday morning he drove to Arcadia to kneel beside Jeanne's grave and the graves of her father and brother. He wished Jeanne were with him now to share his success.

"Cemeteries always make me feel that nothin' much is important in the way of money or fame," he has said. "And I know that Jeanne has only taken the train ahead."

He once again stood on a "pedasill," but he missed Jeanne.

Many listeners to the Durante radio programs and viewers of his television performances have wondered about his oft-repeated closing line, "Good night, Mrs. Calabash, wherever you are." When he says that line his manner changes to one of great seriousness, and his voice takes on a tender, emotional depth. Who is Mrs. Calabash?

Assuredly there is some disguised significance here, for Durante will change the subject when questioned as to the identity of Mrs. Calabash. Nor will he permit his writers to involve this character in a slapstick routine.

At the close of Jim's second television show someone neglected to give him time to say the Mrs. Calabash farewell. He let it be known that the omission offended him. Without Mrs. Calabash, he said, there were to be no more Durante appearances on the television screen.

When asked to reveal the significance of the Calabash farewells, Jim replied, "That's my secret. I want it to rest where it is."

Durante's aversion to saying good-by or good night at any time is so well known among his friends as to make the Calabash farewell seem peculiarly interesting, and various explanations have been offered by Jimmy's friends. One of his writers thinks that the name itself was arrived at after hours of search by all concerned for an odd name for the Durante program. Other associates, among them Lou Clayton and Lou Cohen, have held that the name presented itself when Durante received a letter from the widowed mother of a small son. She had written that she liked Durante's program and that her son always referred to him as "Uncle Jimmy." The boy would say, "Mom, it's time to hear Uncle Jim, isn't it?"

Durante replied to this letter, saying that he would mention the lady's name on his next program. He kept this promise with a "Good night, Mrs. Calabash." Later on that year he added the words, "Wherever you are."

According to Lou Clayton, it is quite unlikely that anyone ever will know what really goes on in Jim's mind when he says his solemn good nights to Mrs. Calabash. "However," Lou added, "it might very well be that he is saying good night to the spirit of Jeanne, and covering up his sentiment with a kind of public privacy, if there's such a thing. That would be like him, to say it out loud, where everyone can hear it, but keep the secret of his feelings inside himself, like a prayer to somebody up in Heaven."

XXIII

The Club Schnozzola

Although Durante, at Clayton's oft-repeated urgings, promised to look for another house, he delayed moving out of the home where Jeanne Durante had died. He stayed on for two years at this scene of many reminders, as though clinging to an apparition. Jeanne's now widowed mother Mrs. Blenman came to live with Jimmy soon after the successive deaths of her two children.

Jeanne had built an aviary in the backyard for her hundred or more parakeets and lovebirds. Most of them by now had gone to bird heaven, but when friends suggested that Jimmy put a swimming pool on the site of the aviary he shook his head. He was slow to release a treasured yesterday.

In contrast to the lonely time when Jeanne had entertained but few persons other than relatives in her home, the Schnozzola's place began to take on the aspects of a man's club. Laughter and music resounded in the rooms of once-mirthless isolation. The sweet but jealous past was swallowed in the noisy present. The realistic Lou Clayton no longer had occasion to offend someone near to Jim who might, because of her wifely prejudice, delay or seek to abort the furtherance of his schemes to enlarge Durante's fame and fortune.

Friends trooped in and out each day from noon until after midnight. No one knocked or rang the doorbell. It was not a "madhouse," as has been said in various newspaper or magazine articles, for there was no boozy carousing here or in any other home where Durante resided. Much theatrical business was transacted in between the songs and the stories.

Lou Cohen sometimes spent the night at Jim's house. Jackson occupied a guest room until he persuaded Durante to lease an apartment elsewhere for Jack Roth and himself. Eddie and Jack liked to stay with the Schnozzola until their bedtime but sought to escape his unpredictable interruptions of their sleep. However, they could not always snooze in peace even in their own place, for Jimmy was one of the telephone company's busiest clients. Sometimes when an early morning idea occurred to him Durante would telephone various members of his troupe to return at once to the "clubhouse" to discuss what he called "disa and data."

Lou Clayton brought steaks to Muggins, the cocker spaniel, when meat was rationed and hard to come by. Mrs. Blenman frequently appropriated these cuts for herself and said prayers for Clayton's continued good health and luck at the butcher's.

The Schnozzola was fond of Muggins, but it must be conceded that the cocker spaniel merely tolerated him.

Durante loves animals and is puzzled whenever his well-meant shouts infuriate them. Rosie, the elephant of *Jumbo* days, eventually got to like Durante, but only after having tried to sit on him during rehearsal. A monkey in the musical production *Red, Hot and Blue!* bit him. A burro in Florenz Ziegfeld's *Show Girl* tried to kick him. Even a cow in a song tableau at the Earl Carroll café showed him her horns.

"I guess they think I'm a wild leper," he sighed.

Jim appeared one night at a benefit for the Lighthouse, an organization for the blind, one of Jeanne's pet charities. A Seeing-Eye dog, sitting beside its blind master, temporarily forgot its high-school education and almost drove the Schnozzola from the stage with furious snarls and barkings.

Durante's five-alarm voice causes man's best friends to grow violent whenever he rasps out, "Nice doggie," or, "Here, Prince, here!" A neighbor of Lou Cohen's, upon joining the Army, entrusted two Pekinese dogs, Hobby and Bobby, to Lou until he returned from overseas. The Schnozzola had a key to Cohen's front door. Whenever he burst in upon Cohen with his big hello the Pekes would yelp, run to the kitchen, and hide under the sink until Durante had left.

The Pekes eventually were reclaimed by their owner, and Cohen's daughter bought a toy bulldog. The Schnozzola did not know about this new pet until late one night as he let himself into the darkened house. The bulldog began to whimper, and Jimmy called out apprehensively, "Lou, do you hear a dog?"

The next day Durante again called upon the Cohens; but this time he whistled instead of speaking to the new dog. The animal picked up its ears, appraised Jimmy, then, as the Schnozzola settled back in an easy chair, leaped onto his lap, put a forepaw on either side of Durante's neck, and licked his chin.

The Schnozzola blushed at this unexpected show of affection. Afterwards Cohen's daughter got married and moved away, taking the dog with her. Durante was disconsolate.

At about this time a woman wrote to inform Jimmy that the old elephant Rosie had gone on a hunger strike. Rosie was living in retirement at a "lion farm" several miles from Hollywood. The writer felt sure that the animal would regain her appetite if Jimmy would only call upon Rosie to remind her of former triumphs on Broadway.

Together with Cohen, the Schnozzola motored out to the lion farm on "an error of mercy." Strolling in the rural zoo, Durante became so bewildered by roars from the lion yard as to forget temporarily the purpose of his visit.

He chanced to see a familar face, however, and said to the owner of it, "Aw gee, hello! How are yah?" He was speaking to Rosie's old-time trainer. "And, say, whatever became of what's-her-name the elephant?"

The man pointed to a nearby enclosure. "Rosie is right behind you, Jimmy."

The Schnozzola turned. Rosie's trunk was down, and she was swaying in a sad, slow kind of rumba. Durante whooped and ran inside the enclosure. "Rosie! Rosie! It's Nosey!"

As though responding to a cue, Rosie trumpeted and then lay down as she used to do in the act with Jimmy. He got down on the hay-strewn ground beside her, crying out, "Rosie ain't forgot me, Lou! Look! She stills loves me!"

It is said that Rosie resumed taking her vitamins and lived on for another year or so.

One noonday, as the Schnozzola sat in his breakfast room, enjoying his cornflakes and reading *Variety*, Muggins lay at his feet sound asleep. Jimmy choked on a cornflake, coughed, then half rose from his chair. Muggins awakened with a start. She sprang up and nipped her master's rear end.

Jimmy stood gaping at Muggins' show of ingratitude. The dog blinked, lowered its head, then waddled to a far corner of the room. Maggie came from the kitchen and Lou Cohen from the living room.

"I guess Muggins better go live with your sister," Jimmy said to Maggie.

In May of 1943 Mrs. Blenman wrote to the Werners: "So sweet of you to remember me on Mother's Day. Jeanne never failed me on that day. I miss her so much, and Earl too. Just can't pull myself together. Both children in one year is almost too much to take."

Jeanne had left her real-estate holdings to Mrs. Blenman. Jim heartily approved of this bequest, and for good measure set up a trust fund for his aging mother-in-law.

In a letter to the Werners dated January 5, 1945, Mrs. Blenman wrote in part: "Our Christmas was rather lonely. We always enjoy packing presents and sending cards. . . . I had such lovely letters from so many of Maud's [as she often referred to her daughter] friends, and my own, for it made me feel I was not alone. Jimmy has been so nice to me. He visits Maud's grave every Sunday, and has left word at the florist to have fresh flowers every week put on the grave. He told me he would never get married again."

Whether or not the Schnozzola will marry again often has been debated by his friends. Their opinions on this matter are divided.

During Durante's trip East in 1944 to play at the Copacabana, he met Margie Little, a pretty red-haired show girl. Margie had worked in an Atlantic City café, the Rumanian Village, the season before she met Jimmy at the Copa, where she appeared as a singer.

Columnists from time to time have reported Jim as engaged to Miss Little, but Durante always has denied these rumors.

In speaking of his association with Miss Little, Jim has said, "She was a very voracious girl—what's the word?—vivacious? Yeah, thanks! Full of life and really good company. Eddie and me used to meet Margie at Child's after the show and have laughs. We wasn't really goin' together then, but she used to kid me and say, 'When you goin' to get me an engagement ring?' And Eddie would cut in with, 'Well, Jim went to Cartier's today and put two dollars down on a gold hoop and the guy said it'll be ready next week.'

"One night I takes her home to her hotel on Sixty-sixth, and it's winter. And good night at the elevator. . . . Well, you know you try to kiss a girl, and she pushes you away. And I get sore. So I goes outside to call a cab, but the cab don't come, and so I walk around the block and am standin' again in front of the hotel. So all of a sudden I hear, boom! Right in front of me a big hairbrush lands; and Margie is leanin' out a window away up above me and laughin' down. And the next day I says to her never to speak to me again.

"Then she'd be in Child's, on one side of it and me on the other, and she'd come over and say, 'Well, what do you want?' And I'd say, 'Nothin'. I want nothin'. And who the hell sent for you anyway?' And she'd say, 'The waiter said you sent for me.' And so we made up, and she's been an awful lot of fun."

Miss Little later went to Hollywood; but Durante's producers would not allow Margie to appear in any of his pictures, because, as Jimmy put it, "Some girl you like will distrack!"

Miss Little became a student at a business school and forgot about a picture career. But she did not forget about Durante, nor he about her. They frequently have been seen together at the race track or at restaurants. They sometimes have had "words," but he and the fun-loving girl have been what Jimmy calls "congenital."

Durante's statement that he does not intend to remarry might turn out to be as fragile as the campaign promises of a politician. When a man of great vigor comes into his September days, he is more apt than not to feel a special loneliness that his men friends cannot dispel. Notwithstanding the other achievements of modern science, no satisfactory substitute has been found for a woman's presence in one's house.

The Schnozzola, to be sure, does not lead the kind of life that the world might call lonely. Everyone knows him, and almost everyone loves him. He seldom is by himself. Still, it is too true, as Walter Winchell once said, that a man can be surrounded by hundreds of friends and yet be starved for friendship.

One thinks back to certain popular artists of the stage, W. C. Fields, John Barrymore, and so many others of their profession, who, when away from applause, learned the pathos of silence. A middle-aged actor of keen sensibilities can be as lonely as a coin in a blind beggar's hat.

Whether or not Durante's romantic stirrings had anything to do with Mrs. Blenman's decision to move away, or whether the club-house atmosphere of his home caused her to seek a more private spot. Jim's mother-in-law expressed a desire to have a place of her own. On October 17, 1945, she wrote to the Werners: "Sometimes I wish I were with the kids up on the hill where they are buried. I am not living at Jimmy's. He bought me a new place in Pasadena, a lovely large house because I feel better off. Jimmy said

I would be welcome with him as long as I live, but I like my own home. I am seventy-five years young."

Mrs. Blenman's memory for recent events now began to decline and she showed other signs of mental distress. Durante yielded to the recommendation of doctors that she be placed for treatment in a private sanitarium. When the Werners wrote to her there, she penciled a rambling reply. "I can't remember who you are." She signed it "Mrs. Meline."

Mrs. Blenman failed to recognize Jimmy during his visits to the sanitarium. This made him so sad that he quit going to see her. He hired Bill Stecker, a former vaudeville performer, to call at the sanitarium twice each week to take Mrs. Blenman for automobile rides. Jim paid all his mother-in-law's bills for doctors and for her care at the rest home. He would not touch her trust fund or sell her real estate to defray these large expenses.

Mrs. Blenman died in 1950 while Durante was on a train en route to New York. He wired Stecker and Maggie to arrange for a funeral that would be "better than the best." Mrs. Blenman was buried in the fourth and last grave in the plot Jeanne had bought in the Arcadia cemetery.

XXIV

Mr. Jackson Goes Wooing

In 1945 Durante bought a new house at 511 North Beverly Drive, a one-story, eight-room house, painted battleship gray. Jimmy brought to it several keepsakes, among them the old music box and a small combination radio and record-player given him by Jeanne. The age and creaking condition of this last instrument annoyed Clayton, who complained that it was an antique. Durante paid out perhaps five times as much as its first cost to keep the player in repair.

There is nothing showy about the Schnozzola's pleasant new home. The street is lined with palms. There are roses in the front yard, and back of the house a swimming pool and a garage with an upstairs den and alcove, to which Jim retires when he wishes privacy. Many pictures of his celebrated friends and scenes from his motion pictures and musical shows hang on the walls of the garage apartment.

One sees calendars almost everywhere on the premises, with rings drawn about certain dates to signify the opening or closing days of race meets or big league baseball series.

The daily group that gathers here include radio producer Phil Cohan, Lou Cohen, Eddie Jackson, Jack Roth, Jules Buffano, and Jackie Barnett. Almost any day one may also see a congregation of ex-vaudevillians, athletes, clergymen, sports writers, radio and television executives, orchestra leader Roy Bargy, and Abe Lastfogel, sagacious executive of the William Morris theatrical agency. Many old friends of Jimmy's Broadway days appear on the scene from time to time, and the less prosperous ones frequently pass the hat.

The Schnozzola a few years ago decided to give his troupe "something to do." So he set up the Jimmy Durante Music Publishing Company in ground-floor quarters on Yucca Street, next door to the Hollywood office of *Variety*.

"The boys now have someplace to go to beside my home,"

Jimmy said. "They study the *Racin' Form* all day, and to date I think we've sold maybe one copy of 'The Lost Chord.'"

When a friend complimented Durante for "doing so many things for the boys," he replied, "I'm tired of hearing that. I'd rather have you say, look at the things the boys has done for me."

In June of 1946 Durante's motion picture *Two Sisters from Boston* had its premiere at the Capitol Theatre in New York. M-G-M took over a dance hall, formerly the Silver Slipper Café, where Clayton, Jackson, and Durante had performed in Prohibition days, to celebrate the occasion. The trio revived the Wood Number, sang "Jimmy, the Well-dressed Man," "Inka Dinka Do," and "Umbriago." The fun lasted all night.

During that time in New York Jimmy somehow acquired a masseur known as the Whale, who weighed almost three hundred pounds and had an enormous appetite. One night at the Copa, Durante told the Whale that Jackson had been drinking, that Eddie was great at ad libbing when a bit high, and that he wanted the Whale to make notes of Jackson's witty remarks on the night-club floor.

As Durante was undressing after the show he asked the Whale, "Did you set down them notes?"

The Whale replied that he had forgotten his pencil and paper.

"Too bad," Jimmy said. "For Jackson has a created mind when he gets a few powders in him. We'll try it again tomorrow night."

The next night Durante saw to it that the Whale had a pencil and paper, and ordered Jackson to swallow three double bourbons before going onto the floor. At the close of the performance, however, the Whale had entered nothing on his note-pad.

"I demand an exclamation," said Durante in a furious tone.

The Whale looked sad. "I got to admit that I don't know how to write."

"And you don't rub so good either," said Jim.

The Whale followed Jimmy to California. One evening, on returning home from a broadcast Durante found the Whale snoring hugely on a couch. His great weight made the couch sag.

"Use the floor after this!" Durante cried out. "You've made a canoe outta my couch!"

The Schnozzola persuaded Jackson and Roth to take the Whale to their apartment, where he at once made a "canoe" out of their settee, snored like a steam shovel all night, guzzled Roth's beer, and at two sittings devoured four pounds of sweet butter which the drummer had managed to put aside during a time of shortage. The Whale also broke Roth's couch during a siesta. "He's gotta go!" the drummer announced. "Anything he don't bust he eats."

Durante assigned Lou Clayton to deport the Whale. Clayton bought the huge fellow a ticket to New York, saying forthrightly, "Screw!"

In 1946 Eddie Jackson met a sweet-mannered widow, Jean Kantor, while double-dating with an old friend in Brooklyn. The attractive Mrs. Kantor designed women's hats for Best & Company.

Eddie soon fell in love with Jean but hesitated to confide in Jimmy that he wanted to marry her. He felt that Durante would recall to him the grievous hurt suffered when his first marriage collapsed after twenty-four years.

Jackson and Jean Kantor corresponded for several months, and Eddie could no longer withhold his secret from Durante. "Jimmy," he said at last, "I've got something to tell you, but please don't get mad."

"Eddie, just let me know what's on your mind, and if I can help you, you know I'll do it."

"Well then, Jim, you better sit down. I've met a little gal back home in Brooklyn, and she's no kid, but I'd like to marry her."

Durante leaped up from his chair. "What's that you say?"

"Gee, Jim, don't scream! I hoped you wouldn't want me to be lonesome."

"Lonesome!" shouted Durante, slapping his thighs. "Do you want to get trimmed again? Do you want to get hurt?"

"Please, Jim, gee. . . ."

Durante stalked angrily from the room, interrupting Jackson's cries. "Not another word outta you! It's a closed accident."

Against Durante's wishes, the lovesick Eddie went East to see his Jean. He returned to California to plead again with Jimmy, "Gee, I don't feel right! Believe me, I'm getting more nervous all the time. I love that gal."

Durante glowered. "Forget it! You're makin' a nervous wretch out of everybody."

When Eddie insisted upon getting married, Jimmy decided to plot against him. At a birthday party given for the wife of Durante's producer, Joseph Pasternak, the Schnozzola asked concert pianist and conductor José Iturbi and tenor Lauritz Melchior to help him dissuade Jackson. "I don't want my pal to hang by the rope," he explained.

When the Schnozzola sat down at the piano that night he pointedly neglected to call upon Jackson to sing with him. It was the first time he ever had treated Eddie in that shabby fashion. Jackson brooded in a corner as Jimmy played and sang. After his numbers the Schnozzola continued to ignore Jackson.

Several motion-picture personages wandered over to Eddie from time to time to say, "Sorry to hear you're going to get married." Or, "Too bad, Eddie." Melchior said that it would be a very risky thing for Eddie to take a new wife. Iturbi and Pasternak seconded the motion. Mayer called it "an almost fatal step."

On the way home Eddie said, "Jimmy, what in the world's the matter? Have I insulted everybody by a little thing like wanting to get married?"

"Little thing!" said Durante. Then he added sorrowfully, "Well, Eddie, go ahead and walk into this trap. But when you get tired of it, come back."

"Jimmy, I think I'll go into the hat business, because my girl has a millinery shop lined up."

"Well, hold on to your hats."

Eddie and his wife stayed in business in the East for only a few months. They called on Melchior one day backstage at the Metropolitan Opera House and were introduced to the great tenor's wife. The Melchiors promptly approved of Eddie's choice. Other friends, too, found Jean a most attractive person. They made it their business to tell Durante of Jackson's good fortune.

Durante invited the Jacksons to come West. Then, after he had met Jean, and saw how happy she and Eddie were, the Schnozzola bought them a cottage in which they have lived ever since.

Jackson wrote to his Brooklyn friends, boasting that he owned a "pearl-handled" mansion in Beverly Hills, and sent them photographs of Ginger Rogers' house.

Jimmy somehow found out about this. "What do you want to sound off like that for? Don't you know a good little home is better than a bad big one?"

X X V

A Narrow Screech

In December of 1947 Durante agreed to go on tour for the March of Dimes. He was to play one-night-stand benefits in seventeen cities, among them Chicago, St. Louis, and Kansas City, and then close early the next year at Warm Springs, Georgia. After that he would return to the Copacabana to discharge a promise made at the time of his latest appearance.

The hard-working clown had just recently completed two motion pictures: one with Frank Sinatra, *It Happened in Brooklyn*, and the other, *This Time for Keeps*, on location in Canada with swimming star Esther Williams. Besides these labors he had been appearing weekly on a radio show for the Rexall Drugstore chain. He also did numerous benefits for church organizations and charitable groups. Even a man of Durante's great stamina must become tired when pressed so relentlessly.

The railroad tickets for the March of Dimes tour, the hotel reservations, and arrangements for his broadcasts in various cities had been attended to by Clayton. A few days before Christmas, Lou said, "Jim, before you go on this long hard trip, I want you to have a thorough physical examination."

"Oh, I been up to Dr. Bilon last month," said the Schnozzola, "and he looked me over good."

"That was a month ago," said Clayton. "You're going to do this heavy work, and Lou Cohen and Maggie tell me you been having a little trouble with your insides. I want you to get X-rays and everything."

The Schnozzola and his friends celebrated a sunny Christmas Day beside the pool at his house, then next day Jim entered the hospital for a series of X-ray pictures and tests. He took with him several Western stories and a few other books, which he referred to as "non-friction," and sent out each morning for the scratch sheets to study the recent performances of race horses.

On the third day, as Durante was preparing to go home from the hospital, he dropped in at the X-ray laboratory to say good-by to the radiologist, Dr. Brown. The Schnozz playfully began to wrestle with the doctor. During the tussle Dr. Brown chanced to touch Jimmy on the lower right side of his belly. Durante winced, then doubled over.

"Why did you do that?" the doctor inquired.

"I dunno, Doc. But I got a kind of pain where you just touched me."

The doctor explored the sensitive place. Durante grunted. "Look here, Jim," said Dr. Brown, "we're going to take another picture of your lower intestine."

"Why the retakes?"

"We may have missed something."

After the plate had been developed and studied, Dr. Brown conferred with Dr. Bilon, who told Durante, "I think you'd better stay here another night."

"Something wrong?"

"There is a small growth on your lower intestine."

"But I got to rehearse with Roy Bargy's orchestra right after church tomorrow."

The doctors agreed to let Jimmy go to his rehearsal but advised him to return to the hospital afterward for further observation. He was told to have his Sunday night dinner as usual, then, at nine o'clock, to take castor oil, and to be at the hospital by ten.

After his rehearsal Durante went with Lou Cohen to the House of Murphy for corned beef and cabbage. Later the two friends walked to one of the nearby drugstores of the chain Durante represented each week on the radio, to get a dose of castor oil.

Aware of Jimmy's reticence in seeking even small favors, Cohen asked the clerk to mix some castor oil with orange juice. The clerk announced curtly that he had no time to practice medicine on the side. Jimmy overheard this and tugged at Cohen's coat.

The friends then went to a small drugstore at La Brea and Beverly Boulevard. The soda fountain had been closed, but the proprietor himself courteously offered to mix the oil and juice for Durante.

Jimmy telephoned Margie Little that he would see her next day, then returned to the hospital. Cohen went on home after promising to call with a car for Durante early next morning.

Cohen and Bill Stecker went to the hospital next day. Jimmy

was pacing the room. "Dr. Bilon says I got to be operated on. But I want to wait till the day after New Year's. Why spoil everybody's enjoyment of a holiday? Besides, who'll do my radio program when I'm flat on my back?"

"We'll get plenty of talent to stand in for you," Cohen said. "Don't worry."

"All right. Call up Lou Clayton at Hillcrest, and Eddie Jackson, and tell my nephews and Margie and Phil Cohan."

Clayton urged Jim to let a celebrated Chicago surgeon, who was on a holiday at Palm Springs, perform the operation.

"No," said Durante, "I want Dr. Bilon to do the job."

On New Year's Eve Durante's partners and his nephews, Bobby and Julie Romano, gathered in his hospital room. Mrs. Clayton, Mrs. Jackson, and Margie Little also were there. Jimmy gave Clayton a sealed envelope. "If I don't come out of this, Lou, here's some instructions."

"You'll come out of it, Jim. Now let's go downstairs a minute."

Outside the hospital Clayton said, "When I was a kid in St. Catherine's I learned to say the Hail Mary and Our Father. I got faith in God, no matter how I've lived or what I've seen. Let's both say the prayers with no roof over us to interfere."

After the prayers Jimmy asked, "Lou, where's your car parked?"

"Right across the street."

"Call upstairs and get Eddie Jackson and Lou Cohen to come down."

It was midnight as the friends got into Clayton's limousine. Jimmy turned on the radio. A medley of horns and gay shouts came over the air. Merrymakers at the St. Francis Hotel in San Francisco were welcoming in the year 1948.

"We never did miss a noisy New Year's," Durante said. "Remember, Lou, the time at the Durant Club when Jackson and me ran out on you?"

"It was the Dover Club," Clayton corrected him. Then he added, "And don't run out on me now, Big Nose!"

The others went on home and Lou Cohen stayed at the hospital to watch over Durante.

Next day the Schnozzola visited other patients, among them the father of Dorothy Lamour. He sang for various convalescents, talked to them, and also helped his nurse make selections for the races. She won three wagers.

That night Cohen sat in a chair in a room next to Jim's. He left the door open a crack in the event Jimmy should rouse from the sedative given him at bedtime.

At about half-past two in the morning Cohen heard Durante stirring and went into his room. Jim was sitting up. A dim light came from the adjoining room.

Cohen thought he saw tears in Jimmy's eyes. "What are you crying about?"

"Lou," said Durante, "I'm just layin' here prayin' to God. It's going to be a narrow screech, I know, and I got to wonderin' what would of happened to me all these years without you fellows. I'd like to live long enough to do a little good in this world to pay back what I owe."

XXVI

A Good-By Is Said

WHEN DURANTE roused from the "antiseptic" he saw Clayton and Jackson, his nephews, and Lou Cohen standing beside his bed.

"I didn't run out on you this time," he said smiling weakly. "I'm a very, very lucky guy."

Telegrams and letters came from all over America, and cablegrams from abroad. Several top-flight comedians offered to take over Durante's radio program at no cost to Jimmy, a demonstration of loyalty that moved him deeply. Red Skelton, Bob Hope, Al Jolson, and Frank Morgan appeared on the Schnozzola's weekly broadcast.

"There's great people in show business," said Jimmy. "They get knocked about so bad, and there's a knife out everywhere for 'em, especially in Hollywood, but believe me, this is a great world with great people in it, if you'll only open your eyes and look."

A long-time Durante friend, Frankie Harmon, owner of the Shangri-la Restaurant in Chicago, accompanied Jimmy and Lou Cohen to Palm Springs and stayed with the Schnozzola until he got well. The big-nosed fellow sat in the sun and counted his blessings.

When Durante returned home Lou Clayton gave him back the sealed envelope that had been entrusted to him on New Year's Eve. "And I hope it's a hundred years before you hand me another letter like this."

"But you didn't read it?"

"No, Jim. But I got an idea it took care of all of us."

"Maybe," Jim said as he tore up the envelope and its contents. "Maybe it did."

Durante returned to the studios and again there was a tendency on the part of producers to neglect his talents. As early as 1946 showman Billy Rose, always a fierce defender of the Schnozzola's art, had written an open letter to Jimmy's bosses: "I hope your geniuses don't cool him off. If they can refrain from getting too clever, the greatest of our clowns should be red fire until the angels come and get him. . . . When you cast him as a human being, rather than a jack-in-the-box specialty act, he set fire to the celluloid; but soon your hired hands were using him to prop up every crippled script on the lot. . . . So please tell your day laborers out there that when they mess up with Jimmy they're messing with the best-loved guy in show business. If they cool him off again, strong men will come down from the mountains and up from the valleys and turn your studio into a bowling alley."

Now in 1949 Clayton began once more to lay plans for the professional protection of his idol. Among other things, he had in mind the writing of a book on the life of his friend. Several authors had sought at various times to present the "inside" story of the Schnozzola's career, but Clayton enlisted a fellow, whom we shall refer to as the Monsignor, to do the job.

The sobriquet Monsignor had been accorded this gray-haired scrivener by ex-sports editor Mark Kelly, the ablest one of them all, in reference to the old chap's eleventh-hour efforts to atone for a life of strenuous unrestraint. The Monsignor, now slowed somewhat by his sixty years, was attempting to forget the world, the flesh, and Broadway.

"The Monsignor," said Jimmy, "has his good pernts, and if Lou wants him to do my story, then he's our boy."

The Monsignor proceeded to interview all manner of persons concerned with the Durante saga. He supervised numerous tape recordings over a period of six months, and had he not had this firsthand evidence available, it would have been impossible in this book to have quoted the Broadway graduates in their exact words.

The picture *The Great Rupert*, made for independent producer George Pal, brought Jim praise in 1950. The Schnozzola was to play the Copa, go on to Chicago for a Chez Paree engagement, and then return to California to do *The Milkman* for Universal Pictures. After these successive engagements the Schnozz and Clayton planned to sail for England to play the London Palladium. They looked forward to this as a holiday abroad.

In February 1950, during the Chez Paree engagement, Clayton

asked the Monsignor to meet him in Chicago. The Monsignor arrived on a very cold and windy day. Clayton was ill in bed at the Drake Hotel. They talked until early the next morning.

"I don't know," said Clayton, "but I have a hunch that my number is coming up soon. And I want to raise a monument to my pal Jimmy Durante. There's nobody as sweet as he is, or as great. In a bad world he's stayed good. He was lucky in taking the righteous road instead of the wrong road. The crazy age that produced us sent lots of other fellows to Sing Sing; but something inside of Jimmy Durante kept him good and honest and kind. And when you come near him it's like warming your hands at a fire. We were only small fry, but the success of Durante, who never graduated from grade school, only goes to show you the kind of country we're living in, how beautiful it is here, and what can become of a person who hasn't got an education or doesn't take beauty prizes, but has a lovely heart. I'd like to see this brought out in a book about my pal and as an example to others to keep trying when the going gets tough."

Restaurateur Toots Shor and his wife, a wonderful girl whom everyone calls "Baby," came up from their holiday in Hot Springs, Arkansas, to see Jimmy and his troupe. When the Shors called at Clayton's room, the doughty fellow got out of bed, leaped on and off chairs, talked and wrestled with the huge Toots. The visitors stayed until four o'clock in the morning.

Toots and Baby left for New York that afternoon, and the Monsignor took a plane for California. Two days later Durante called the Monsignor. "Lou is terrible sick. The doctors want to operate on his stomach."

Clayton refused to go under the knife in Chicago. He and Mrs. Clayton returned to Los Angeles by train. An ambulance met them at the station and took Lou to St. John's Hospital in Santa Monica.

Dr. Alfred Strauss of Chicago chanced to be on a holiday at Palm Springs. The celebrated surgeon went by airplane to Santa Monica to operate upon Clayton. Dr. William Alan MacDonald of St. John's, one of the most brilliant young surgeons on the West Coast, assisted Dr. Strauss.

Lou Clayton had a malignant ulcer of the stomach. The disease already had spread to the liver and was obstructing the flow of bile into the intestine. This meant that Clayton was doomed in any event. However, his life might be, and indeed was, prolonged, because the surgeons were able to bypass the obstruction to the flow of bile.

Durante telephoned the Monsignor. "Lou has got Big Casino, like he always feared. Nothing can save him."

The Durante household was indeed a sad one now. Clayton had been the real head of the family. He always had made the big decisions. Sometimes he had cast fear into members of the troupe, but he had always kept steady when others became unsure of themselves. He was, in a very real sense, the father, the patriarch.

Ida Clayton urged everyone to keep her husband in ignorance of his real condition. For the next five months he gradually wasted away, from a hundred and sixty pounds to less than a hundred. But even toward the last his eyes and his heart stayed alive.

Knowing that his friend would die soon, Jim found it more and more difficult to buoy Lou with optimistic words. "I've never lied to him before. That is, to lie about the big things. If he finds out now I'm lyin', it will be a tragedy to our friendship."

The Palladium engagement was canceled "until next year." Meanwhile Durante was working long hours at the Universal lot on *The Milkman* picture, making recordings of "Bill Bailey" with Jackson, and rehearsing for his weekly radio show.

Clayton left the hospital on Easter Day of 1950 to go to Jim's house. It was a somewhat warm day, and Clayton sat in a well-cushioned chair in Durante's back yard. He took off his shoes and stockings and placed his feet in the grass as if to draw strength from the earth.

Lou at times ignored the almost ceaseless ache in his belly as he dictated stories of the old days on Broadway. He would brighten for a little time, and when Jim came home would be happy.

Clayton's doctors advised Durante to allow his stricken friend to do anything he pleased. Weak as he was, Clayton drove his automobile from his Chateau Marmont apartment to Jim's almost every day.

Dr. Strauss left for Chicago after having placed Clayton in the hands of Dr. MacDonald and Dr. John C. Eagan, internist and chief of staff at St. John's. Durante sent a doctor to Boston to obtain a supply of the then rare drug, cortisone, to be administered to his friend.

Clayton sometimes dined out with Jimmy and other pals. His life-long habit of saying exactly what he thought never deserted him. One night a Hollywood fellow whom Lou thought a phony called out, "Why, Lou, you look just fine!"

"I look like hell," Clayton replied, "and you know it. You're as insincere as the headwaiter."

The Durante household was further saddened by the death of Muggins. The now fourteen-year-old dog had been living for some time with Maggie, who worked at Jim's only in the daytime. Durante buried Muggins in a dog cemetery in North Hollywood and put on a headstone the epitaph: "In loving memory of Muggins. From Jeanne Durante."

Notwithstanding his grave illness Clayton began to map out what he called a "real future" for Durante. That future, he decided, lay in television. One of the far-seeing men of Hollywood, agent Abe Lastfogel, felt as Clayton did, that television was made to order for the Schnozzola's warm, intimate kind of visual comedy.

Durante listened to these plans with a half-attentive ear. He had no intention of leaving California for the East, and certainly not without Clayton at his side. It was proposed that he make nine telecasts a year, one each month, and make them all in New York until the completion of the co-axial cable from Chicago to the West Coast. It then would be possible for Jimmy to make his telecasts in California.

"I won't fly back and forth between shows," he said. "So it means I got to leave my home, which I now am attached to, for eight or nine months runnin'. No, I'll wait till they get that co-actrical cable up to my front door."

Many conferences were held in Jim's back yard, with the Schnozzola, Clayton, Lastfogel, and executives of the broadcasting company participating.

"It is my hope that Durante will sign up for this," Clayton said. "It means an added annual income of two hundred thousand dollars for the next ten years. That would give him security. If he can't save something out of that for his old age, then to hell with him!"

Durante procrastinated. He would not sign the contract. Finally early in May he said to Clayton, "Lou, suppose you're not well enough to go East with me?"

Clayton studied Jim narrowly, as though to detect in Durante's question some doubt as to his eventual recovery. Then he said, "Since when did I ever let you down?"

"Never."

"All right then. Now let's hear Clem MacCarthy broadcast the Derby. I want to get my mind off your stubbornness."

As the weeks went by Clayton tried to conceal his sufferings, but his wife heard him praying at night that he be allowed to live to see Durante as a great television star. Once Ida found him weeping because of weakness. "Don't think I'm a crybaby, Ida. But I'm so slow getting well."

He could still smile when he was with Jim and his friends, as on a day when an interior decorator said, "Now, Mr. Durante, we should do over your dining room and put birds and flowers on the walls, and bring the outdoors indoors."

"When I want the outdoors," Jimmy replied, "I don't bring the outdoors indoors, but I go outdoors for the outdoors."

Lou would sit back against a heat-pad to ease his pain and look at the various familiar things in Durante's house, the pictures and trophies, and once he turned the pages of the guest book in which he had written, "To Jimmy Durante. With you I am a giant. Without you I am nothing."

Clayton visited Durante on the Universal set of *The Milkman* and had his last picture taken with his friend. When this photograph was delivered to the house Clayton wept openly.

Soon after this emotional display Clayton went outdoors, then, to the consternation of friends, dived into the swimming pool to retrieve four golf balls that had lain at the bottom for some days.

Early in June Clayton set up dates for Jimmy Durante to play at Wilbur Clarke's Desert Inn at Las Vegas and then at Mert Wertheimer's Riverside at Reno.

Jimmy was not sleeping well these nights. Usually he had no difficulty in dropping off to sleep, but now he lay awake, thinking of Lou's impending death. "It's like losin' Man-O'-War," he said. "And all we can do is let him do anything he wants. Like goin' to Las Vegas."

The Durante troupe went to Las Vegas late in June. Clayton seemed to brighten when he heard Durante's shouts from the gaming room. Jimmy, as usual, bet small amounts at the dice table, but whenever he won a few dollars he bellowed as though he had made a killing. The house really suffered, however, when Jim tossed the bones, for all play stopped at other tables or wheels or slot-machines while gamblers enjoyed his attempts to break the bank.

Clayton sometimes dragged Jim away from the gaming table. "You're ruining business for the owners."

On the second night at the Desert Inn, after Jimmy, Jackson, Roth, and Buffano had finished a most successful midnight show, Durante began losing at dice. He was three hundred dollars in arrears when the emaciated Clayton walked up to the scene where spectators had gathered six-deep to see and hear the dice-rolling Schnozzola.

Although he had not handled the dice for many years, Clayton "bought a stack" and warmed the cubes in his eloquent hands. As of old, he began rolling high and fast. Soon he was three thousand dollars on the wrong side of the bank. The veterans among the watchers exchanged glances, but Clayton did not alter his deadpan expression. He bought another thousand dollars in chips. Then, when it seemed that the fast-betting participant in so many big games of other years now was on his way to a sizable loss, Clayton made three numbers in a row.

"He's hot now," said an old gambler from the Broadway days. "Now watch him pyramid it into a chunk."

But instead of going on, Clayton cashed in his chips. He was but four hundred dollars ahead. He turned to Durante, gave him the three hundred the Schnozzola had dropped, and then handed the remaining hundred to the dealer to split up among his helpers.

Clayton, obviously pleased to get Jimmy off the hook, retired to bed. The impractical Mr. Durante, however, went to another gambling casino, where he not only lost the three hundred but sacrificed two hundred more.

After the Las Vegas engagement the troupe traveled by car to Reno. Soon it became necessary for Clayton to return to Los Angeles by airplane; Durante followed by car. Late in the night of August 26 Clayton telephoned Jimmy to come over to his apartment right away. Durante lay on the bed beside his friend until daylight, recalling old days and discussing plans for the future.

Lou, who had been heavily medicated, said that the floor was coming up to hit him. "But I'll get heavy and healthy again, Jim. Maybe I'll still be able to protect myself in the clinches."

"Yes," Durante said, "like the time when that crowd of tough guys jumped you, and you said, 'Fight fair, fellers—two at a time.'"

On Saturday morning of September 2 Durante called the Monsignor. "I ain't slept all night. Let's drive down to Del Mar and see the Derby. I want to get my mind off feeling so helpless over Lou for just a few hours."

On the way home, after having seen Great Circle win the big race, Durante said, "I feel kind of guilty leavin' Lou for the whole day."

Durante arrived at the Chateau Marmont at eleven that night. Clayton was in a strangely grim mood, swaying on his thin legs, yet purposefully standing up as though to dare someone to deal him a blow. He had hiccups and was quite yellow with jaundice.

"Come into the next room, Jim. There's something I got to say."

"Sure. Sure, Lou."

"Shut the door," said Clayton after they had entered his bedroom. "And damn these hiccups!"

Durante obeyed. "What's wrong?"

"Dr. MacDonald tells me what my chances are."

"Chances?"

"Don't play dumb with me, Jim! Dr. MacDonald says I might not snap out of this."

Durante fumbled for words. "Well, if he says 'might,' then he means that—"

"It's Big Casino. And I should have known it all along." Then he said, "I want you to go ahead and take that television contract."

"We'll settle that later. It's about you I'm concerned now, Lou."

"If only I'd not have these damned hiccups on top of everything else! The hiccups throw me."

It was with considerable difficulty that Clayton was persuaded to return to St. John's Hospital but once there his whole manner changed. He seemed resigned to death. He told the Reverend Father Herbert Rogers, chaplain of the hospital, "Well, I fought and I lost. I took a draw. I've had a very full life, Father, and I'm very grateful for it. There have been some tough times, but it really was fine."

"Well," said Father Rogers, "you know that this life isn't the last. There is another one."

"I'm sure of that, Father, very sure."

Although he seemed peaceful, and at last out of his great pain, his old-time bluntness sometimes asserted itself, as when a man who owed him a lot of money telephoned after long years of neglect to ask the nurse if he might do anything for Clayton.

The dying man insisted upon speaking to this caller. "I've gotten along without your help for thirty-one years. I don't know why I need it now."

Clayton sent for Eddie Jackson, Lou Cohen, Jules Buffano, and Jack Roth. When they came in from the anteroom Clayton said, "Take good care of the big-nosed fellow. If I ever hear of anyone hurting him, I'll come down from Heaven and kill him."

Durante stayed at the hospital whenever his work would permit him to do so. Although Clayton lay in a drugged sleep most of the time, he would rouse on occasion to smile at Jimmy. He even observed a cigar fragment on Durante's lip during one of these times, and never failed to remind the nurse to see that Jimmy was made comfortable in an easy chair.

His eyes stayed alive when the rest of him seemed dead. And, peculiarly, his feet stayed alive. Beneath the bed linen those once great dancing feet kept moving in a quick, almost ceaseless, steady rhythm, subsiding only when he was entirely under the influence of sedatives.

"Give me your hand," he said to Durante late in the night before he was to die.

The friends clasped hands. Lou said, "My Jimmy, my Jimmy." He never again opened his lips or his eyes.

Clayton died at nine o'clock the morning of Rosh Hashana, the Jewish New Year. He was placed in a crypt at Home of Peace Cemetery. George Jessel delivered the eulogy. Jimmy bought his friend a bronze casket, saying, "Lou always wanted the best," and on it placed a blanket of orchids, with the inscription on a satin ribbon, "To our pal Lou. From your partners."

The death of Clayton, as was expected, shook Durante. He stayed at home, speaking but seldom to anyone. Then, after some weeks of uncertainty and sorrow, he decided to go East to make the television shows.

"I'm only doin' it," he explained, "because Lou wanted it that way. As for me, I'd like to stay right here in California. For now without Lou it's like I lost both my arms and legs."

The triumph of Durante as a television star has been witnessed in millions of homes all over the land. He has fulfilled Clayton's hopes and dreams.

Durante still wants to return to his California house, to the gray house on the palm-lined street in Beverly Hills. But, as he has said, "I gotta bear by the tail, and a fellow can't walk out on his friends. Success is wonderful in one way, but in another it's a catastrostroke."

This great clown stays on with us, as great clowns always stay on in the hearts of men and women and children who seek in the refuge of merriment an hour of escape from the scowls of the long day. And in loving and admiring the clown, we cannot be expected to know that his art is most difficult to come by, or that his every success is challenged. The clown must make us laugh, although he himself may suffer pain, frustration, sadness, despair. To ask how he makes us laugh is almost as unanswerable as to inquire why we were born. Out of his seeming artlessness there shines a surviving sanity in a world gone daft. And against our modern will to destroy ourselves, and against our mad deeds that would undo the heritage that has made America so great, the sage laughter of the clown sounds high and wholesome, high and clean. It seems a glad summons to man's dimming hope, a call to hold fast.

And we feel something deep down, a stirring oneness with the loved little figure on the television screen, as he walks out of our living rooms and our hour of pleasure with his mystery-touched farewell—

"Good night, Mrs. Calabash, wherever you are."